DRESSMAKING IN DETAIL

Dressmaking in Detail

Ann Mactaggart

B. T. Batsford Ltd   London and Sydney

First published 1975
© Ann Mactaggart 1975

ISBN 0 7134 2701 9

Filmset by Keyspools Ltd, Golborne, Lancashire
Printed in Great Britain by
The Anchor Press, Tiptree, Essex
for the publishers
B. T. Batsford Ltd
4 Fitzhardinge Street London W1H 0AH
and 23 Cross Street Brookvale
NSW 2100 Australia

Contents

Introduction

Today, many women and girls are interested in dressmaking, but, unless they make a great many clothes, few are equally happy with all the techniques which rapidly changing fashions demand. All dressmakers strive for, and some achieve, a faultless garment; one which looks as if it has been created at the wave of a wand, and has not been laboured over. An amateurish looking garment lacks certainty, not only because of inaccurate seaming or too heavy pressing. More subtle points, which appear insignificant when the dressmaker is struggling with an unfamiliar process, are often the cause: openings which do not end quite level, collar points which are not exactly the same shape, or a pattern not perfectly matched. It is not that these points have been deliberately ignored – an 'it'll do as it is' attitude – but that it did not occur to the dressmaker to stop, look at the garment objectively, and criticize her work during the making. This book attempts to describe the technique of each process in such a way that the dressmaker is never at a loss, and can pay attention to the less obvious pitfalls. Its aim is to help a dressmaker not merely to do the process, but to do it well.

When using these instructions as a guide to an unfamiliar process, it is advisable to read the notes at the beginning of the section, as well as those which immediately precede the instructions. A clearer idea of the process will be gained if all the stages are followed through with the diagrams before beginning work. Many of the instructions have been tried out by people who have had difficulties with, or who have been afraid even to try, a certain process, and all have been surprised at the success of their results.

This book began its existence as a set of classroom worksheets, to be used not only for needlework theory lessons, but as a practical aid to amplify a primer when making up a garment. The notes and drawings together helped the students to grasp a process as a whole. Because they themselves could refer to the worksheets at any moment, much valuable time was saved, and the piecemeal element, which is an unavoidable part of explaining a process by word of mouth, was much reduced. Moreover the students developed their self reliance, and a skill, valuable in communications – that of turning the printed word into action.

1 Preparation

There is a natural human tendency to try to get results quickly, and dressmakers are no exception. In any craft, speed comes with experience and practice. Firstly there is the time gained by understanding what one is doing: being able to work confidently and continuously without pauses to check that one is on the right lines or to correct false starts. Secondly there is the time which can be gained from sheer manual dexterity, and finally there are the short cuts, where a process – usually pinning or basting – is omitted. Of these methods, the first two are responsible for most of the difference in the time taken by an inexperienced dressmaker and an experienced one to do the same work. But this unhurried speed can only be achieved as a result of hard work and by making many garments. The third method, that of short cuts, appears attractive to the inexperienced, but it takes experience to know just which tailor tack can be omitted, and where it will be safe to omit the basting, and it takes skill to use a sewing machine accurately without these aids. When all is said and done, very little time can be saved by short cuts even when they succeed, and a great deal may be lost when they go wrong.

Accuracy is important. There is a tendency to be very careful about the final stages in making a garment, but few people realize that each process relies on the one before it, and that therefore no process can ever be more accurate than the work which preceded it. It follows that cutting out, marking, basting and machine sewing must all be performed with equal care.

Choosing a fabric

Today, because of the bewildering range of fibres and weaves available, the amateur dressmaker cannot expect to be familiar with the characteristics of more than a few fabrics. Most bolts are now labelled with the fibre content of the fabrics, and are also marked 'washable' or 'dry clean'. Manufacturers sometimes issue care labels, to be given to the purchaser with the fabric when it is sold, and these should be sewn into the garment when it is finished.

When selecting a fabric, consider its basic fibre content. Remember that although synthetic fibres may launder easily, natural ones absorb perspiration, remain cool on a hot day, and retain the body heat efficiently in cold weather. Crumple a corner of the fabric, and hold it tightly for a few seconds; then look to see how well it recovers when released. Fabrics which crease easily often contain dressing to improve their appearance for sale. Unroll sufficient fabric from the bolt to be able to assess its bulk, texture and weight. Test the firmness of the weave by pulling a corner on the bias. If the fabric is sheer and slippery, it will require special techniques to sew it. If it is rough and likely to irritate the skin, it may require lining. If the fabric has a napped surface, or the design is large, or consists of stripes or checks, extra material will be needed. All these points should be considered in relation to the projected garment, because a wrong decision at this stage can result in many hours of wasted time and an unsatisfactory garment.

Some flaws in the weave or knit may only become apparent if the fabric is held up to the light, but while the material is being measured out, watch carefully to see whether the length includes any obvious flaws in the weave or printing. Sometimes these are marked with a thread sewn into the selvage. A good salesman will usually see them and offer to measure afresh or to allow extra length. If he misses a flaw never hesitate to point it out, because that fault may cause considerable difficulties when arranging the pattern pieces.

Although it is tempting to buy cheap fabric, to do so usually proves to be a false economy. Cheap fabric is often poor in quality, likely to require straightening, and also to contain undisclosed faults. A garment made with it will not retain its fresh appearance in the way that a similar garment made from good quality fabric will. Poor fabric has a way of degrading the work, and a feeling of not wanting to bother because 'it's only cheap material' creeps in. Good quality material, on the other hand, constitutes a challenge; one is extra careful because the material was expensive; but the way in which it handles and the ease with which an effect can be achieved, encourages the dressmaker to maintain her standards throughout the making of the garment.

After purchasing the fabric, buy the thread and other notions such as binding, zips or buttons. When matching the colour of thread and fabric, compare them in daylight if possible, as well as in artificial light. If the fabric colour is a difficult one to match, choose thread which is a shade duller or darker in tone because this will be less noticeable than a paler or brighter one. Patterned fabrics containing several colours can be matched either by choosing a thread that matches the predominating colour, or by selecting a toning neutral shade that will blend into the general colour scheme of the material.

After the material has been unfolded, any creases it may have acquired should be pressed out. The lengthwise crease which occurs in all fabrics which have been kept folded on a bolt should be tested to see whether it can be removed. If it proves difficult to press out, do not use this crease when positioning pattern pieces.

If one is unfortunate and finds a small flaw or mark on the RS (right side) of the fabric, make a tailor tack on the selvage level with the defect as a reminder of its position. If it should prove impossible to arrange the pattern pieces so that they avoid the flaw altogether, try to incorporate it in a dart or hem, or in an inconspicuous place – under an arm or collar for instance.

Straightening ends and grain
Before one can see whether the grain is true, (ie that the warp (lengthwise) and weft or filling (crosswise) threads are at right angles to each other), one must ensure that each end of the piece of material is formed by a single weft thread. If the fabric was torn off the bolt, it will already be in this state. If the fabric was cut off, snip the selvage 1 cm ($\frac{3}{8}$ in.) from the corner and pull on a weft

thread, snip the point at the far side where the material begins to pucker, and pull out the thread. Repeat the process at the other end. If the fabric has been cut very crookedly the thread may run out at the cut edge before reaching the far side. In that case pull a thread from the opposite selvage.

This method of straightening the ends may seem tedious, but it is accurate and works for most types of woven fabric. The ends of cotton and wool jersey fabrics can be straightened by carefully cutting along one of the rows of knitting as close to the end as possible. Those fabrics which have a permanent finish, or are bonded, cannot be straightened and must be used as they are.

When the ends have been straightened, fold the material in half matching the opposite selvages together along their entire length.

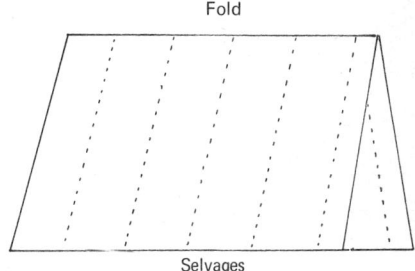

The weft ends will not line up after straightening if fabric is off grain

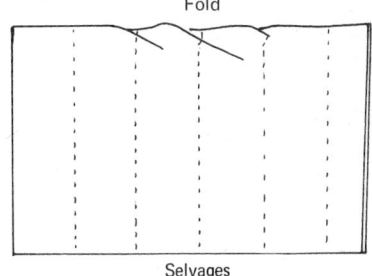

Bringing the weft ends together results in wrinkles forming over the fold

If the fabric lies smoothly it is on grain, but if slanting wrinkles form over the fold, the grain is not true and it must be straightened by pressing or by pulling in line with the shorter diagonal. To find which this is, open the fabric out flat and measure the distance between the diagonally opposite corners.

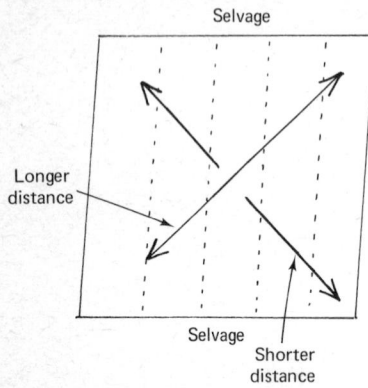

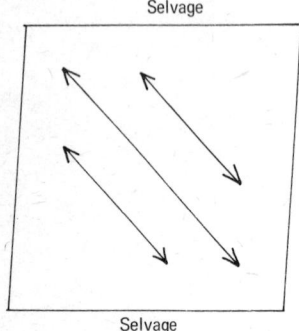

Pull or press the fabric in the direction of the arrows

Fabrics which present special problems include those with checks and stripes as well as those with large or directional designs. A dress made from any of these, or from a napped fabric, will need more material than one made from a plain fabric or one which has only a small all-over design. Included in a table to be found on the back of most pattern envelopes is a section giving an estimate of the amount required for these types of fabric, but very large designs may need even a little more. When using a fabric with a bold design, try to avoid letting its dominant feature disappear into a dart or occur close to an edge. Choose a pattern with few seams and make the strong parts of the fabric design complement the main features of the garment by the considered placing of the pattern pieces. Remember, however, that unless the material is identical on both sides it will not be possible to produce a symmetrical effect.

When placing pattern pieces on a napped fabric, such as velour, the pieces should be arranged so that the nap points down the finished garment. When working with velvet or corduroy the pile may point either up or down the garment, but the deepest colour will be obtained when it points upwards. Fabrics with a directional design should have all the pattern pieces arranged in one direction, and this must be settled by the content of the design.

When arranging pattern pieces on a striped or checked fabric, one can align the straight grain arrows using the design as a guide. Corresponding points on adjacent pattern pieces are indicated by balance marks, and these can be used to relate the design between neighbouring pieces. Thus when placing the sleeve pattern piece, arrange it so that its front and back dots come at the same places in the design as the dots in the armhole. This will ensure that any horizontal stripes match across. If the pattern includes a horizontal bust dart, match the design below this point because it is the section from the waist down which will be the most noticeable part of the side seam.

Before positioning pattern pieces on two thicknesses of fabric which has a balanced stripe or check, bring the corresponding parts of the design exactly together, and pin the layers at intervals all over the surface to keep them related.

When making up unbalanced checked or striped fabrics, look carefully after pinning on the pattern, but before cutting, to ensure that both right and left hand garment pieces will be formed. One must be especially careful when pieces have had to be placed head to tail on a single thickness of material.

Stripes may run parallel with the selvage, at right angles to it, or diagonally across the fabric. They may be balanced or unbalanced, and the fabric may be single or double sided. Except for diagonal stripes, which cannot be made up into a chevron pattern unless the design is balanced and the fabric is double sided, any kind of stripe can be made up to form chevrons whether the fabric is double sided or not. On single sided fabric, unbalanced lengthwise stripes may be made to balance if each pattern piece is not only turned over, but is also made to point in the opposite direction to that of its previous position. On these occasions it is advisable to work out on a measured width of floor or table exactly how much fabric will be needed. When working with unbalanced crosswise stripes, the pattern pieces must all be placed pointing in the same direction.

Checked designs present similar problems to stripes, but they must be matched vertically as well as horizontally. It is advisable to choose a simple basic dress pattern, as every seam and dart presents a matching problem. Small balanced checks on single and double sided fabrics are the easiest types to match.

Checks in which the lengthwise stripes are balanced and the crosswise stripes unbalanced, must have the pattern pieces arranged so that they all point in the same direction.

Checks in which the lengthwise stripes are unbalanced and the crosswise stripes are balanced must, if a symmetrical effect is desired, have their pattern pieces placed pointing in opposite directions. If the front or back pattern pieces are marked with the instruction 'place on a fold . . .', one must either make a seam at this point, or make a feature of the unbalanced effect of the fabric in the design of the garment.

When both lengthwise and crosswise stripes are unbalanced and the fabric is double sided, the design can still be balanced by cutting out each half of the garment separately, and arranging the pattern pieces so that they all point in the same direction. This last point must also be observed if the fabric is single sided, but in this case the lengthwise stripes cannot be balanced.

Taking measurements and making pattern adjustments
Most pattern manufacturers produce ranges of patterns, each range being designed for a particular age group or type of figure; for the best results, one should choose a pattern from the range which most nearly corresponds to ones own proportions. The size of pattern for a blouse, dress, coat or suit, should be chosen according to the bust measurement, and a skirt or trouser pattern according to the hip dimension. Ease is allowed on all patterns, both for movement and for other clothing – for a blouse under a suit jacket, for instance.

When taking measurements, the tape measure should be kept level and not pulled too tight. Measure over the foundation, and other undergarments that are normally worn. Measure around the fullest part of the bust, taking care not to let the tape dip at the back.

When measuring the waist, remember that it is smallest before breakfast, and that it will increase in size during the day. The hip measurement should be taken around the largest part of the body between the waist and the crotch. The back-neck-to-waist measurement cannot be taken accurately without assistance. Drop the head forward so that the large vertebra at the base of the neck projects more than the others. Hold the head up and measure from this point to the waist.

On most patterns there are printed lines at the most suitable places for lengthening or shortening, but if none are indicated, and adjustments need to be made, draw your own. Bodice adjustments are usually made between the underarm and the waist, and skirt adjustments below the hipline. These alterations are made at right angles to the vertical axis of the pattern pieces which will be parallel with the straight grain line or 'place-on-fold' line unless the garment is cut on the bias. To shorten the pattern, pin a parallel fold in the tissue, and remember that the pattern piece will be reduced by twice the width of the fold. To lengthen, cut along the line, and separate the pattern pieces by the amount needed. Pin both edges down on to another strip of tissue paper, taking care to keep the cut edges parallel. Remember that if one pattern piece is lengthened or shortened the neighbouring pieces must be altered at the same level, and by the same amount.

Avoid interfering with the outlines of darts, but if this is impossible they must be re-drawn. Watch for changes in the position of placement markings, which may result in pockets and buttonholes, for example, having to be re-sited.

When arranging the pattern pieces one normally follows the diagrams which will be found on the pattern instruction sheet. These show the way the pattern pieces should be placed on various widths and types of material. For easy reference the appropriate diagram can be circled. If the fabric presents special problems, eg is napped or has a one-way design, see page 10. If the centre fold has proved difficult to remove, avoid including this crease within the area of any pattern piece, and do not use it when placing pieces on a fold.

After the fabric has been straightened, place it on a hard surface and fold it as shown in the pattern instruction sheet. Line up the selvages exactly, and pin them together at 15 cm (6 in.) intervals. If the fabric is slippery it will help to pin across the ends as well. Occasionally one finds a fabric which cannot be laid quite flat because of tension in the selvage. In this case cut through the selvage at 5 cm to 10 cm (2 in. to 4 in.) intervals with diagonal snips.

Sort out the pattern pieces which will be needed, and check them to see whether any of them require lengthening or shortening. Iron any badly creased pattern pieces with a cool iron to flatten them, and place them on the material following the layout given in the diagram. If a pattern piece bears the instruction 'place-on-fold', make sure that it is the printed line which is placed exactly over the fold in the fabric. Do not cut away the outside margin of the paper pattern before placing the pattern on the material: it will fall away as the pattern and material are cut through together.

Arrange each piece of the pattern on the straight grain by measuring from each end of the straight grain arrow to the selvage, and adjusting the distances until they are exactly the same. Pin each pattern piece at the ends of the arrow, and gently smoothing it out, pin it at 10 cm (4 in.) intervals along the seam line, (the broken line 1·5 cm ($\frac{5}{8}$ in.) inside the cutting line). Pin across the seam line into each corner and use extra pins on curves. The pins must be inserted from the top surface without putting a hand underneath, because it is important not to disturb the relationship of the layers.

When cutting out, use shears with long, sharp blades and offset handles. Keep the lower blade and handle against the table all the time, and cut by pressing on the upper handle, not by squeezing the handles together. One should keep the scissors in line with the forearm and move around the table to follow the cut. Cut in the direction of the arrows where these are printed along the seam line.

Never cut along any line marked 'place-on-fold'. Cut outwards around the diamond shapes which are printed at intervals along the cutting line. These are balance marks, and they are brought together – matched – when making up the garment. If these marks were to be cut inwards, the notch would reduce the effective width of the seam allowance. If a balance mark is cut off by mistake, its position must be marked with a tailor tack. After the seams have been made, but before the raw edges are finished, the balance marks should be cut off. Fold up the pieces with the pattern still pinned to them.

There are several methods of transferring other pattern markings to the material, but whichever one is used the first essential is that it should be accurate. CF (centre front) and CB (centre back) lines, pleats, etc are always marked with uneven basting. It is important to mark centre lines even where there is no opening, so that during fitting it is easy to see whether the garment is hanging perfectly straight. Dots show the position of design features, and are used as register points which are brought together when making up the garment. Darts, fastenings, slashes, the ends of sections of ease or gather, the corners of pockets, etc, are all marked by dots. Although tailor's chalk and dressmaker's carbon have their uses, the most satisfactory method of marking dots is with tailor tacks. They can be used on any material, except sheet plastic, and are a quick and accurate way of marking points on both sides of two pieces of material.

After marking all the dots with tailor tacks, fold the pieces up and lay them on one side until they are needed. Unnecessary handling of the pieces at this stage may cause them to fray and to go out of shape. Some types of fabric fray readily because the weave is loose and the threads coarse, or because there is a marked difference between the size of the warp and weft threads. If fraying starts, and is allowed to continue during the construction of the garment, the entire seam allowance may disappear at corners and on curves. To prevent this, the raw edges of such fabrics should be finished, either by overcasting or with zigzag stitch, as soon as the pieces have been cut out and separated.

2 Hand sewing and stitches

Neat, even stitching can only be achieved if the hand movements involved in making each stitch are repeated exactly. To achieve this the same part of the finger tip must be used to drive the needle through the fabric for each stitch, and one should therefore always use a well fitting steel thimble to protect the finger.

The selection of the right kind and size of needle for the fabric and thread is important. Difficulty is likely to be experienced when trying to make small, neat stitches unless a thin thread and a fine needle are used. There are many sizes and types of needle; a 'No 8 sharp' is the most useful for general purpose sewing, but for fine fabrics a No 10 is preferable. A No 5 or 6 is usually used with twist for buttonholes.

When sewing, except when making tailor tacks, never use a piece of thread longer than 40 cm (15 in.), because a longer piece will wear before it is used up, and will form knots. Always begin sewing by making three or four tiny backstitches, and finish off each length of thread in the same way. It is often possible to conceal these stitches in a fold of the material so that the thread is apparently continuous. The tension is important: the stitches must be firm, but not pulled so tight that the fabric is puckered.

Knots are caused by a disturbance in the twist of the thread as it is pulled through the cloth. Too small a needle, which punches a hole of insufficient size for the thread to pass through comfortably, and too long a piece of thread will both contribute to the formation of knots.

Temporary stitches must be accurate and firm enough to hold the garment pieces in place during fitting, but they must be able to be removed easily once the permanent stitching has been put in, and for this reason, a knot should never be used to fasten on a thread.

The cotton used for basting has a rougher surface than mercerized cotton; it grips the fabric more effectively, and tailor tacks made with it are less likely to fall out during handling than those made with other threads. White thread is suitable for most purposes, but a pale colour will be easier to see on white fabric. On a dark coloured fabric, use a dark cotton of a different colour, because the hairs from a light coloured cotton may become entangled in the weave of the fabric and be difficult to remove. When assembling garments made from sheer fabric, it is an advantage to use silk for basting, because the fine, slippery thread is easier to remove without marking the material. Silk should also be used to baste finely woven wool fabrics when pressing must be done before the basting is removed, when preparing pleats for instance, because the silk will not mark the fabric.

The type of fibre in the sewing thread should, ideally correspond with that of the fabric. However, linen should be sewn with cotton, and wool with silk. A fabric composed of mixed fibres can be sewn with a thread made from any of its constituents.

Mercerized cotton is generally available in '40' — used for sewing medium and heavy-weight fabrics — and '50', which is used for fine fabrics. Twist, which is available in linen, silk and polyester, is a thick thread used for buttonholes, saddle-stitching and decorative top-stitching.

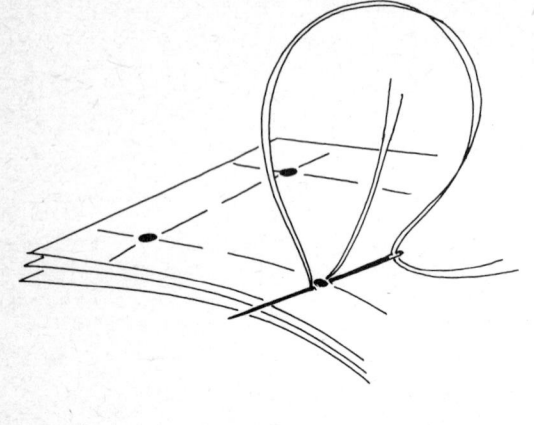

Tailor tacks are used to transfer the position of the dots marked on the pattern to the material.

Stage 1   Cut off approximately 1 m (3 ft 6 in.) of cotton. This will make four or five tailor tacks. Using it double, and without a knot at the end, make a small stitch, exactly on the mark, through the pattern and both layers of fabric. Pull the cotton through leaving an end about 5 cm (2 in.) long.

Stage 2   Make a second stitch on exactly the same spot forming a loop about 3 cm (1½ in.) long and cut the cotton, leaving an end of the same length as the first. The ends must be longer than the loop so that when the two layers of fabric are separated as far as the loop will allow, the ends will remain in the fabric.

Mark all the dots in this way. When the garment sections are required, take each pattern piece off by removing the pins and pulling the paper carefully from the loops. Separate the two layers of material to the full extent of the loops, and cut the threads between the layers leaving a tuft of threads in each layer.

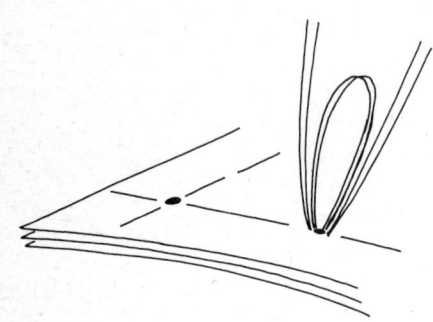

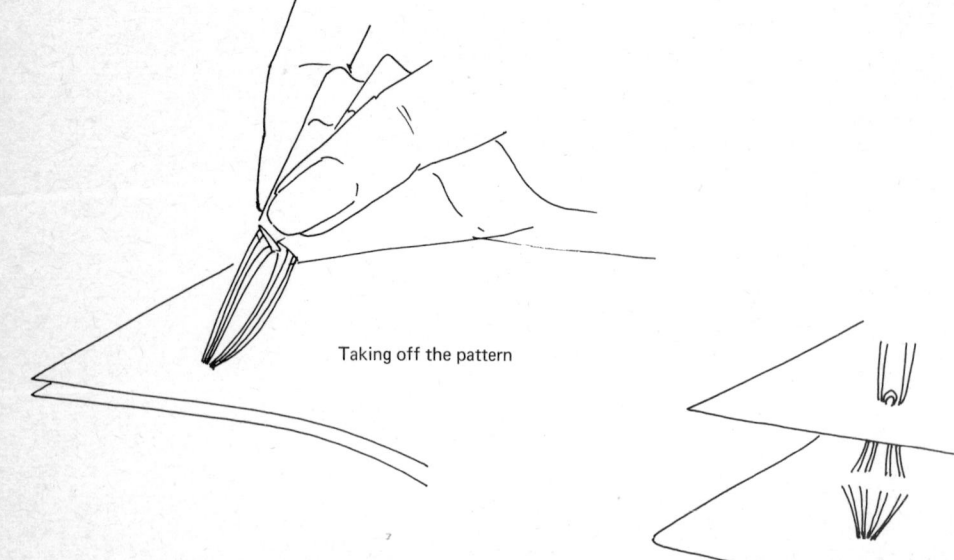

Taking off the pattern

When separating the layers of fabric, the threads are cut

Even basting is used to hold the pieces of a garment together during fitting and while stitching them permanently. When making the stitch, work with the material flat on a table, and pick up and leave equal amounts of fabric. Work away from the body, and sight along the line to be basted to keep the stitching straight. The length of stitch, which may be as short as 6 mm ($\frac{1}{4}$ in.) or as long as 1·5 cm ($\frac{5}{8}$ in.), will depend on how firm the basting needs to be. For example, the seams of a fitted bodice need to be more firmly basted than those of a full skirt, and in general short stitches will be required when working in fine or slippery fabric, as well as in heavy, springy ones, where a backstitch may need to be included at intervals.

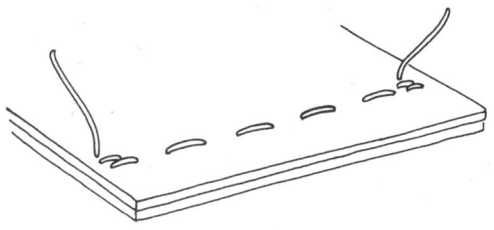

Uneven basting is a temporary stitch used to hold two or more layers of fabric together around their edges, in places where there is no strain. The length of the stitch on the upper surface of the fabric should be about twice that picked up by the needle. It too, should be made with the material flat on a table, and should be worked away from the body so that the line can be sighted along and the stitches kept straight. Its applications include inserting linings and mounting one fabric on another. It is also used when transferring lines from the pattern: the CF and CB lines, the hem level, and the lines of pleat folds, for example.

Diagonal basting is used to hold areas of fabric together. Typically it is used when attaching interlining and interfacing to a garment. Keep the work on a flat surface, and insert the needle at right angles to the line of stitches to form a sloping stitch on the upper surface.

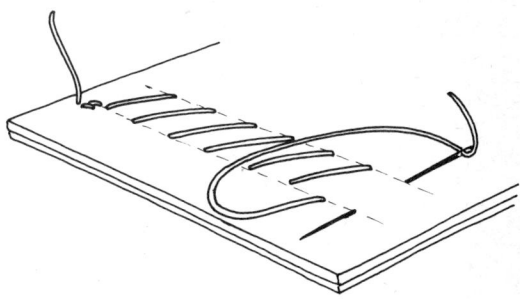

Slip basting is a firm, temporary stitch which is made from the RS, and is used to hold two pieces of fabric together when the design on the fabric has to be matched. The seam allowance of one piece is folded towards the WS, pressed, and the folded edge placed against the seam line of the other piece. The two pieces should be cross-pinned together from the RS. Lay the work out flat on a table, and catch only the extreme edge of the fold with the stitch so that the fabric can be folded RS together after basting, and the seam can be stitched from the WS in the usual way. The distance between the stitches may be as little as 6 mm ($\frac{1}{4}$ in.) or as much as 1 cm ($\frac{3}{8}$ in.), depending on the thickness of the fabric, and the position of the seam in the garment.

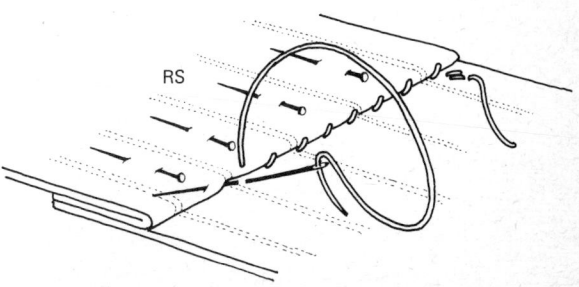

Running stitch was used formerly when sewing long seams which would receive little strain. It is now most frequently used when forming gathers, attaching binding, and for finishing the raw edges of seams. Begin with two or three concealed backstitches. Then weave the needle in and out of the fabric, picking up and leaving equal amounts of cloth. The number of stitches which can be collected on a needle will be determined by the thickness of the material and its flexibility. The stitches should be small: 1 to 2 mm ($\frac{1}{16}$ in.) for the maximum strength and a neat effect. Be careful that the material does not become eased on to the thread. If the stitching needs to be especially firm and resistant to slipping – when hand stay-stitching for instance – make a backstitch about every centimetre ($\frac{3}{8}$ in.).

Backstitch was formerly used to join bodice and armhole seams, where strength was required. Today it is still used for setting in sleeves if the material is particularly difficult to handle. It is also used to fasten thread ends, and for short sections of stitching when a sewing machine is not available. It is worked from right to left by a right-handed person and the reverse way if one is left-handed. The stitches should be kept small – 2 to 4 mm ($\frac{1}{16}$–$\frac{1}{8}$ in.) in length. The exact size depends on the thickness of the fabric. Pull the thread only just taut to avoid puckering the seam. When backstitching thin fabrics the stitches may be made with a single movement of the needle, but to obtain even stitching in thicker fabrics the needle should be passed down through the material and brought up again in two separate movements.

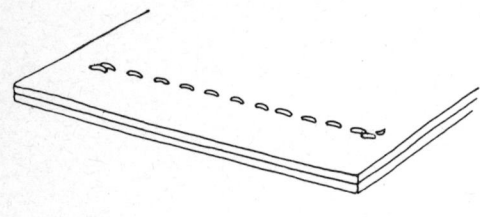

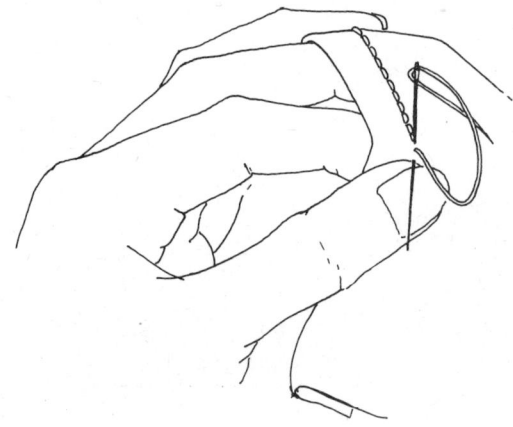

Oversewing or **whipstitch** is a strong stitch which is used for attaching tape loops, joining folded edges together, strengthening raw edges at the bottom of a slash, and for joining selvages when making a splice. The stitches may be touching, or separated by as much as 1 mm (less than $\frac{1}{16}$ in.). The stitch is worked from right to left by a right-handed person, and the reverse way if one is left-handed. The needle is inserted at right angles to the edge to form a sloping stitch.

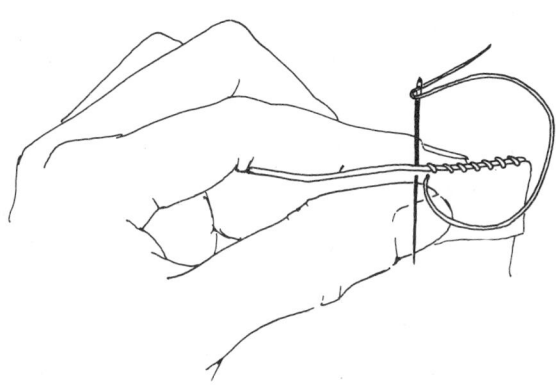

Overcasting is used for finishing raw edges, especially those of wool fabrics which fray easily and which require a soft flat finish. The thread must not be pulled tight or the edge of the fabric will be drawn up into a ridge. The needle is inserted at right angles to the edge to form a sloping stitch which may be worked in either direction. The stitches should be deep enough to secure the edge.

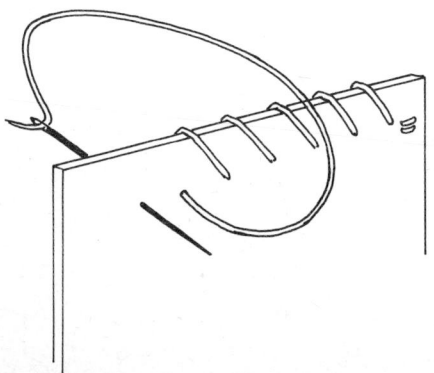

Overhand stitch is similar to oversewing. It is used for attaching lace and for fine gauging, but it can only be used on a folded edge or a selvage because of the very small amount of material taken up on the needle. It should be worked from right to left by a right-handed person, and the reverse way if one is left-handed. In this stitch the needle is inserted at an angle, so that the thread crosses the edge at right angles.

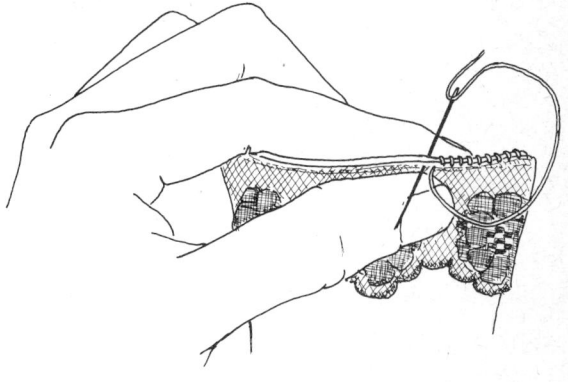

Herringbone stitch is used for securing hems in stretchy fabrics, and as a temporary stitch for holding pleats in place during making up. It is worked from left to right by a right-handed person, and the work should be kept on a flat surface while sewing. The needle is inserted pointing towards the finished stitching and the stitch is worked parallel to the folded edge. When sewing a hem, the stitches in the single thickness of fabric should only pick up one or two threads so that they barely show on the RS. To avoid forming a ridge in the material, the slack should only just be taken out of the thread when pulling up the stitch.

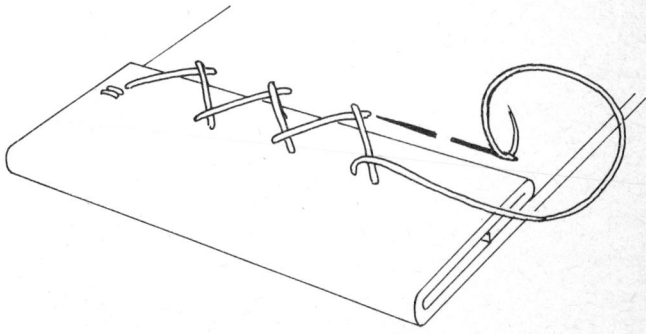

Catch stitch, which is similar to herringbone stitch, is used for holding the edges of interfacing in place. The stitch should be worked from right to left by a right-handed person, and the work kept on a flat surface while stitching. Fasten the thread on, and take a small stitch in the interfacing only, not more than 3 mm ($\frac{1}{8}$ in.) from the edge. Pick up one or two threads of garment fabric at the edge of the interfacing so that only a tiny stitch shows on the RS. Take another stitch in the interfacing and continue, forming a zigzag line of evenly spaced stitches, and taking care not to pull the thread quite tight.

A chain tack is used when parts of a garment need to be loosely connected together, for example when linking the side seams of the loose lining to a garment. The stitch is formed in a similar manner to chain stitch. Start with three back stitches, and form a loop about 3 mm ($\frac{1}{8}$ in.) in diameter. Holding this loop, pass the needle through it and over the thread. Pull the thread up to form a second loop of the same size. Repeat until sufficient length of chain has been formed.

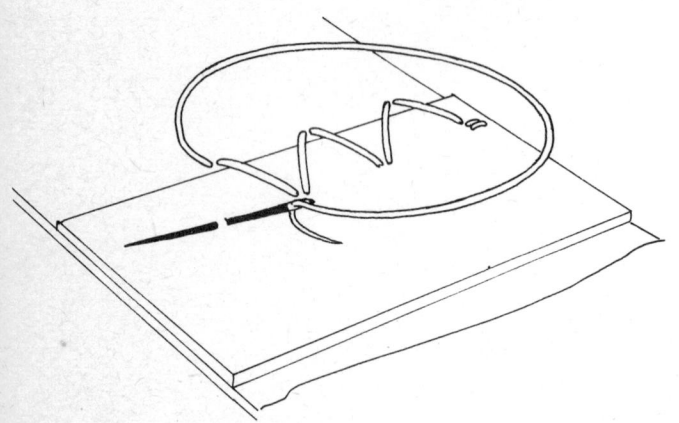

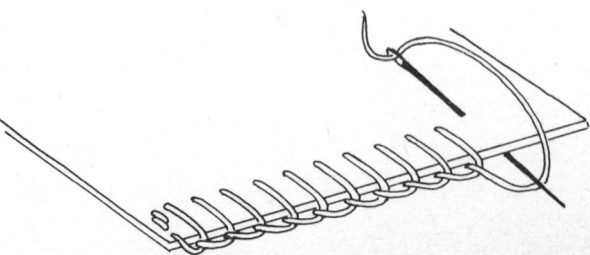

Stab stitch or **prick stitch** is most often used when putting in zips by hand, where the stitching should be strong but unobtrusive. It is worked in a similar manner to backstitch, but the stitches on the RS are short and detached, returning over only one or two threads in the material. The amount of space left between each stitch will be influenced by the thickness of the fabric, but it is usually about 4 mm ($\frac{1}{8}$ to $\frac{3}{16}$ in.).

Loop stitch which is also called blanket stitch, is used for finishing raw edges when a firm, flat finish is required. It can be worked over a group of threads to form thread loops and belt carriers (see page 108). The edge of the fabric should be towards the sewer and the stitch should be worked from left to right by a right-handed person so that the free hand can control the setting of each stitch. To start, fasten on and bring the needle out on the upper surface of the fabric close to the edge. The stitches should be placed about 2 to 3 mm ($\frac{1}{8}$ in.) apart for a firm neat effect. One should not need to make the stitches more than 5 mm ($\frac{3}{16}$ in.) deep even on the most fraying fabric: the normal amount is about 3 mm ($\frac{1}{8}$ in.).

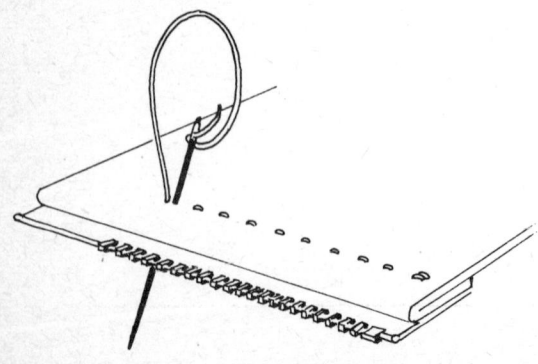

Hemming is a strong stitch used for finishing cuffs, collars, waistbands and underwear. It is not used today on the hems of outer garments because the stitches, however small, would still show on the RS of the material. The edge is held at right angles to the sewer, and the stitches are worked towards the body. The folded edge is held with the thumb and third finger on top, and with the separated index and second fingers underneath supporting and tensioning the work. Start with tiny backstitches. Pick up one or two threads of the single thickness of fabric and bring the needle out through the fold. The needle should not take up more than 1 mm ($\frac{1}{32}$ in.) of the fold and the stitch should slope at about 45°. The space between the stitches depends on the weight of the material, but it should never be more than 2 mm ($\frac{1}{16}$ in.). and on fine fabrics should be 1 mm ($\frac{1}{32}$ in.) or less, or the effect will be coarse.

inside the fold. The length of this stitch, which is really a spacing stitch, should never be more than 8 mm ($\frac{3}{8}$ in.) or the hem will not be strong enough; 5 mm ($\frac{3}{16}$ in.) is a good average. The thread should pass from fold to single thickness and back to fold with as little thread as possible showing on either side of the garment.

Slip stitch is used to draw two folded edges together in places where there will be very little strain. (When securing the hem fold of the front facing to a garment and when closing the ends of tie belts, for example.) The work is held with the folds towards the sewer and the stitches are worked between them by being made in each fold alternately. The stitches should be short and of equal length and should not pick up the outer layers of fabric.

Slip-hemming is used to attach a folded edge to a flat piece of material, when a firm but unobtrusive stitch is required. It is most commonly used to secure hems on outer garments. The work should be held in the same way as it is for hemming. The thread must never be pulled tight or a ridge will be formed on the RS of the fabric, where the single thickness of material is pulled in over the folded upper edge of the hem. Start with backstitches, and pick up one or two threads of the single thickness of the fabric close to the fold. Pull the needle through, and make the next stitch by passing the needle along

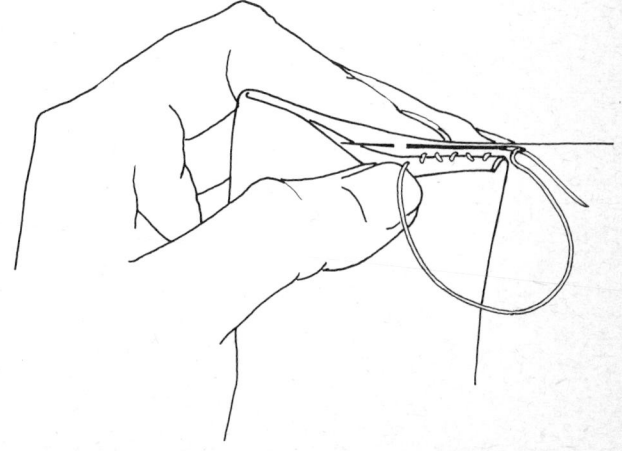

Before using a sewing machine on a garment, set it up with the correct size of needle, and with the thread you intend to use. Sew a sample seam in a piece of the scrap material to check that the machine is stitching properly. Examine both sides of the fabric. The knots between the stitches should not show more on one side of the fabric than on the other. Look not only for faults which may be corrected by adjusting the machine, such as loops of thread and skipped stitches, but also for any difficulty which may arise from the qualities of the fabric, such as a tendency to slip, twist or buckle. All the machine sewing techniques which will be used on the garment, such as zigzag stitching, pin-tucking and blind-hemming should be tested, because if any one proves to be unsatisfactory the method of making up the garment may have to be changed.

Sheer and very fine, soft fabrics, such as organdie, chiffon, crêpe and voile, require a fine needle, size 70 or 80 metric (9 or 11 imperial) and are usually sewn with a fairly long stitch – 2 to 3 mm (8 to 10 stitches per in.). These fabrics may have to be sewn with paper underneath to give the material body, and to prevent it from puckering. When doing this, always use clean, crisp, tissue paper; never use newspaper because the ink can offprint onto the fabric.

For fine, firmly woven and light-weight fabric such as poplin, lawn and taffeta, use a needle size 90 metric (14 imperial), and a shorter – 2 mm stitch (12 stitches per in.).

Medium and thicker fabrics, such as denim, corduroy, suitings and brocade will need a 90 or 100 metric needle (16 imperial), and a 2 mm stitch (10 to 12 stitches per in.). Very thick coatings and tweeds may need a 100 to 110 metric needle (16 to 18 imperial), and a 2 mm stitch (10 to 12 stitches per in.).

When sewing jersey, bonded jersey and other knitted fabrics, a short 1·5 to 2 mm stitch (12 to 14 stitches per in.) is used with the size of needle appropriate to the thickness of the jersey. The seams will need to be stretched slightly as they are sewn to prevent them from puckering: experiment to discover how much stretch is required.

The needle must always be sharp, because a blunt or damaged needle is liable to catch and pull threads. Synthetic fibres can blunt needles quickly, and when sewing even quite thin, closely woven fabrics made from hard, synthetic fibres, skipped stitches may occur. If the sharpness of the needle is not at fault, the trouble can almost always be cured by changing the needle for one which is a size larger.

Faults found when stitching by machine

Faults found when stitching by machine	Can be caused by
Loops of thread forming underneath material	Incorrectly threaded top thread Machine used with raised presser foot
Loops of thread forming on top of material	Top tension too tight Incorrectly threaded bobbin
Threads entangled in spool or race	Wrong type of bobbin Bobbin case incorrectly inserted Thread not passed through take-up lever No fabric under the presser foot End of the thread not being held when beginning to sew
Top thread breaks	Needle wrongly inserted Knot in the thread Upper thread jammed Balance wheel being turned backwards Stitching too fast when starting to sew
Bottom thread breaks	Bobbin wound unevenly Bobbin too full
Needle comes unthreaded when beginning to stitch	Take-up lever not at the highest point

Faults found when stitching by machine

Faults found when stitching by machine	Can be caused by
Needle breaks	Presser foot loose Pins Needle loose, or wrongly inserted Pulling the material so that the needle is bent and hits the needle plate
Skipped stitches	Blunt needle Needle too fine for the material or the thread Tight upper tension
Needle does not move although the balance wheel turns	Loose stop motion screw (sometimes called a clutch knob).

When unpicking, a good light is essential, especially when working with dark materials. Never use a method of removing stitches which might cut or pull the threads of the fabric. Use the head end of a pin, or the eye of a needle when unpicking stitches in napped and fine fabrics, where a pointed instrument would be liable to catch in the weave. The fine point of a stitch ripper is a useful tool for loosening the first few stitches in a seam and it, or a finely pointed pair of scissors, can then be used to cut the thread every few stitches, to enable short lengths of thread to be pulled out easily. Do not cut the stitches by sliding the ripper along the seam between the layers of material because there is a risk of cutting the fabric, and there will be a great many short ends to remove. In strong fabrics the stitches can be ripped out by unpicking stitch by stitch until one has a loose thread long enough to grasp. If this end is held tightly and pulled back sharply over the remaining line of stitches, several stitches will

be undone before the thread breaks off. Turn the work over and repeat. After undoing a seam which has been stitched and pressed open, the creases must be pressed out because they will prevent the pieces of fabric from being accurately rejoined.

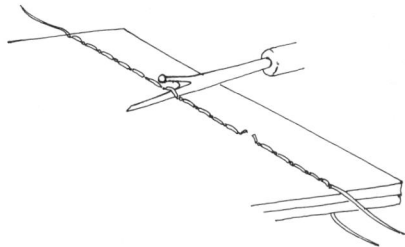

Using a stitch ripper to cut threads

Stay stitching is a line of machine stitching placed on the seam allowance 2 mm or less ($\frac{1}{16}$ in.) from the seam line. In this position it cannot show when the garment is assembled. It is primarily used to prevent bias cut edges from stretching, and it also limits the extent of fraying in such places as corners, where most of the seam allowance has to be trimmed away. Because it runs close beside the seam line, stay stitching can be used as a register when placing two pieces of fabric together (when making a continuous strip opening in a slash for example). It may be used as a guide when clipping and notching curved edges and also when stitching them.

After taking off the pattern and separating the layers of material, any curved or bias cut edges should be stay stitched, using the normal length of stitch for the fabric, and stitching with the grain. Slashes are always stay stitched before being cut. When the edge also needs to be interfaced, the interfacing may be basted into position first and the stay stitching used to hold the pieces together. This technique will not only hold the interfacing firmly in position, but will make the edge more resistant to stretching.

3 Seams

Seams are used to join two or more pieces of material, and are usually machine stitched, although hand stitched seams are strong and more flexible. The seam allowance of 1·5 cm ($\frac{5}{8}$ in.) must be accurately observed unless alterations have been made to the garment during fitting. The raw edges of seam allowances should always be brought exactly together. The balance marks and tailor tacks should be matched and pinned together before the rest of the seam is pinned. When pinning and basting, keep the work flat on a table, except when the seam is curved. The pins should cross the seam line at right angles, because it is easier to baste in a straight line along a cross-pinned seam, than along one in which the pins lie along the seam line. Pin a straight seam at 5 cm (2 in.) intervals, but make the intervals smaller if the seam is curved. All seams can be used to join simple curved edges – that is, edges in which the curves match when the pieces to be joined are placed RS together (for example the joins between the facing and garment at the neck and armhole). The seam allowances of these seams will need to be clipped or notched to enable them to lie smoothly. When the curved edges are markedly different, one concave and the other convex (these occur for example in shaped yokes), refer to page 36 for the instructions on handling curved seams.

Pressing presents few problems with fabrics made from natural fibres, but some fabrics made from synthetic fibres are so crease resistant that it can be difficult to press their seam allowances flat. The pressing temperature for these fabrics is fairly critical: if too low they will not press at all, if too high they may without warning, shrivel, melt or change colour permanently. The controls on some irons name only a few types of fibre, and the correct pressing temperature of an unnamed fibre must be established by experiment.

While working on the garment have a spare piece of fabric available to test the iron on, because fluctuations in voltage can cause a noticeable variation in the temperature of an iron, even if it has a heat control. In general it will be found that a thick fabric will withstand a greater amount of heat than a thin one (eg the type of industrial nylon used for overalls will melt less readily than nylon chiffon), and all fabrics will withstand a greater amount of heat when steam is present than when they are dry.

When pressing the iron is raised and lowered as it is moved from one place on the fabric to another. It is not slid as it is in ironing. Whenever possible, all fabrics should be pressed from the WS. If pressing from the RS is unavoidable, a dry wool pressing cloth should be used to prevent a shine developing, especially when pressing dull surfaced fabrics. The wool cloth may be used with a steam iron, or a damp cotton pressing cloth may be placed on top of the wool one. Slip a piece of brown paper or a sheet of thin cardboard beneath such places as pocket flaps and the edges of pleats to prevent them from leaving an imprint on the layer of fabric underneath.

All seams should have the basting stitches removed before final pressing. If this is not done the basting threads which lie on the surface of the material can leave marks, and in the case of an open seam, and any of its derivatives, the basting will prevent the seam from being pressed quite flat. When a seam has been pressed from the WS the seam line should be checked from the RS in case a fold of fabric has developed over the stitching line. Most seams should be pressed on a seam roll so that the weight of the iron bears only on the seam line, because if the edges of the seam allowances are pressed against the garment fabric they may show as lines on the RS. All curved seams should be pressed over a tailor's ham, but if one is not available the extreme end of the sleeve board can be used instead.

In some seams both seam allowances have to be pressed in the same direction, in a lapped or top-stitched seam for example; and the way they are turned is a matter of convention. The seam allowances are usually pressed towards the CF if they occur in the front of the garment, towards the CB if they occur at the side or back, and upwards if they form part of a horizontal seam such as a yoke.

When intending to use steam on a garment, try the technique out on a spare piece of the fabric first. A pressing cloth should be only just dampened, because too much moisture may watermark the fabric. Although steaming may be combined with pressure, a more subtle application is to hold the steam iron just above the area in order to heat the fabric with steam. Use this technique to set a rolled edge or unpressed pleats. Pat the edge into shape while it is still very hot. When working with wool fabrics, subtleties in shaping may be achieved by shrinking limited areas with the aid of a hot iron and a damp cloth. This kind of work is usually carried out over a padded shape called a ham, or over a sleeve roll. The areas most often involved are the ends of darts, the seam allowance of a sleeve head, and eased hems.

Fabrics with a pile, such as velvet, require special treatment. Seams may be pressed by running the seam allowances across the edge of an iron which is held, or stood vertically. In this way no pressure is placed on the pile on the RS of the fabric. Fabric with a pile may also be pressed RS down on a needleboard. If this is not available, a fine bristled clothes brush gives good results, or another piece of velvet may be used, placed RS up, with its pile interlocked with that of the piece being pressed. When using any of these methods it must be stressed that the pressure of the iron should be very light to reduce the risk of marking the pile.

Finishing or neatening is required on the raw edges of most fabrics. The factors influencing the choice of method include the thickness of the fabric, its readiness to fray, the amount of friction which the edge is likely to receive, and whether the garment will be laundered or dry-cleaned. The garment will look well finished inside if all the seam allowances are treated in the same way, but two methods are often necessary.

Pinking is a quick method of finishing which gives a flat edge and is suitable for all types of seams in closely woven materials which do not fray easily. It is suitable for lined garments which will be dry-cleaned rather than washed. Pinking shears should not be used for cutting out, because the outline they provide is not accurate enough to work from when making up the garment.

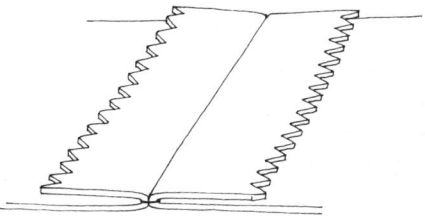

Edge stitching is excellent for finishing thin opaque fabrics, but the fold in the seam allowance creates too much bulk in medium and thick materials. This method is strong and will withstand machine washing. The extreme edge of the seam allowance is turned towards the WS of the material and stitched, without basting, close to the folded edge.

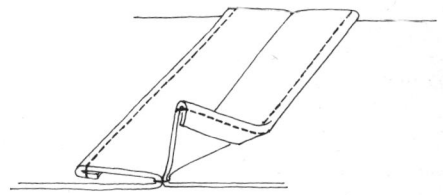

Binding is the best way of finishing edges of fabrics which fray readily. It adds little bulk to medium-weight and thick fabrics and it can be used on garments which will not be lined, and which may be washed. After the seam allowances are pressed open each edge should be bound separately with bias binding, but if the seam allowances point in the same direction, as in a lapped seam, they may be bound together. The binding should be stitched to the RS of the seam allowance and slip-hemmed to its WS.

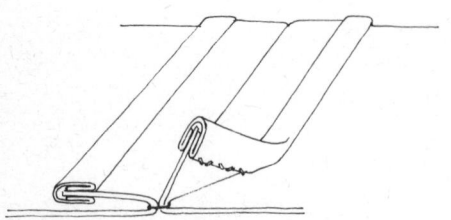

Overcasting and **loop stitch** both make flexible flat finishes, but it requires practice to achieve a really neat effect. They are especially suitable for soft fabrics that unravel easily where extra machine stitching would stiffen the seam unduly. They are often used to finish the edges of lapped and top stitched seams, as well as curved seams which have been trimmed close to the stitching line. For details of these stitches see pages 17 & 18.

Zigzag stitch is a quick method of finishing which has the advantages of being applicable to a wide range of fabrics and of being able to withstand machine washing. The width of the setting used will vary; coarse weaves will need a wide stitch, finer weaves a narrower one. On

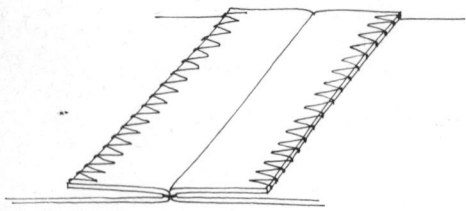

thin fabrics it may be found that the stitch buckles the raw edge of the material. This can be avoided if the edge of the seam allowance

is folded as it would be for an edge stitched finish, and the zigzag stitching used to trap the raw edge.

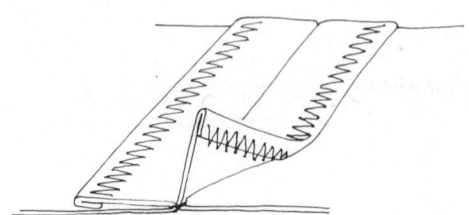

Self finishing can be used as an alternative to a French seam when working in light-weight and sheer fabrics. It is also particularly suitable for finishing arm-hole seams because it withstands washing and friction well. Trim one seam allowance to 4 mm ($\frac{1}{8}$ in.) and enclose this edge with the untrimmed seam allowance which has been folded into thirds. Slip-hem the folded edge to the line of machine stitching.

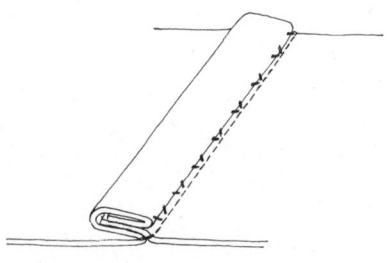

Grading or layering is used to reduce bulk where two or more seam allowances lie together. Trim the seam allowances but leave the one which will lie against the WS of the show fabric untrimmed. In this way the imprint of the trimmed edges will not show on the RS when the seam is pressed. Always grade before clipping if both are necessary.

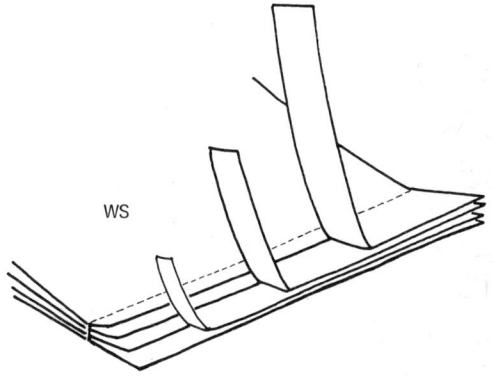

WS

When curved seam allowances are pressed, either open or to one side, it will be found that one edge may have too much material, and therefore pucker, and the other may have too little, and pull. To remedy this the edge is either clipped to release tension, or notched, to remove excess material. The seam allowances should be snipped deeply, but the stay stitching should not be cut. Seam allowances in fabrics which tear easily may, instead of being snipped at right angles to the edge, be cut at forty-five degrees. Alternatively the seam allowances may be trimmed to 5 mm ($\frac{3}{16}$ in.), and their edges finished.

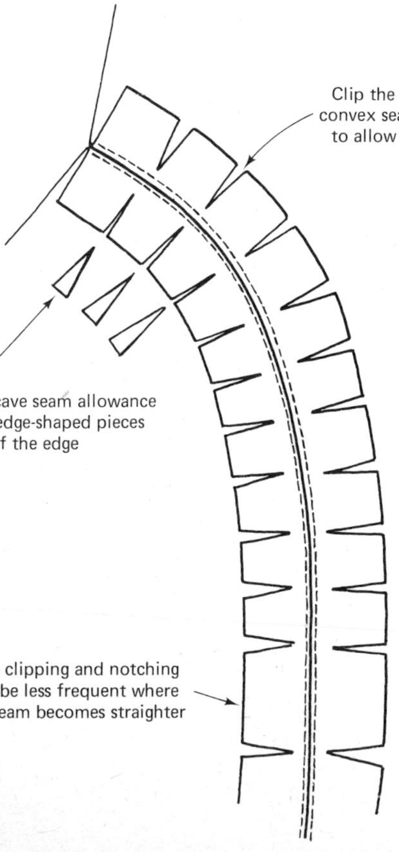

Clip the edge of the convex seam allowance to allow it to spread

n the concave seam allowance taking wedge-shaped pieces out of the edge

The clipping and notching can be less frequent where the seam becomes straighter

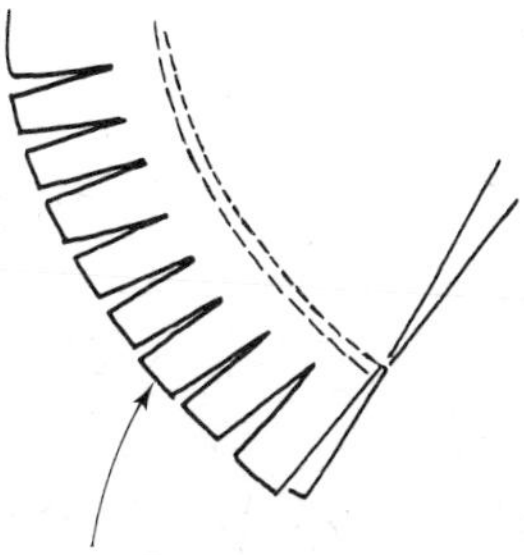

If the seam allowance of a sharp curve still pulls, clip more often

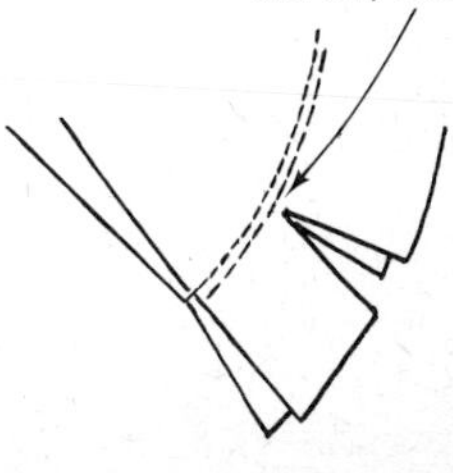

Leave 1-2 mm ($\frac{1}{16}$ in.) between the end of cut and stay stitching

Intersecting seams present a problem when working in medium-weight and heavier fabrics. Because of the additional thicknesses of seam allowance, a lump is liable to occur where two or more seams meet. A typical place is where the bodice and skirt side seams meet at the waist seam. Much of this bulk can be removed by trimming away the seam allowance of the first two seams, from the point where the third line of stitching will cross them to the raw edge. Finish the edges of the first two seams before joining them with the third, because it will be more difficult to do so afterwards.

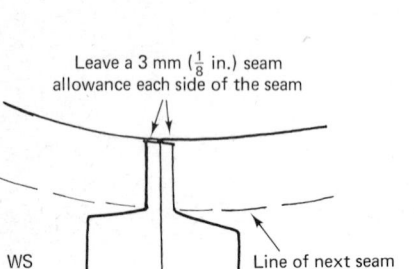

Leave a 3 mm ($\frac{1}{8}$ in.) seam allowance each side of the seam

WS

Line of next seam

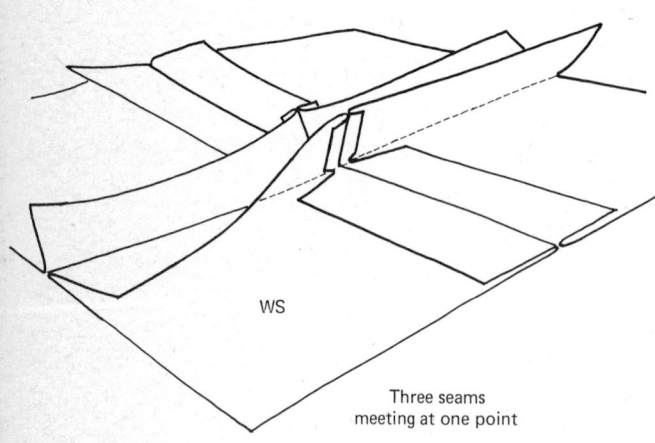

WS

Three seams meeting at one point

A plain seam is also known as an **open** or **dressmakers' seam**, and can be used to join straight or curved edges. It is the seam most commonly used in dressmaking and is also the basis of many others.

Stage 1   Place the RS of the pieces together, cross-pin, and baste firmly on the seam allowance 1mm ($\frac{1}{16}$ in.) from the seam line.

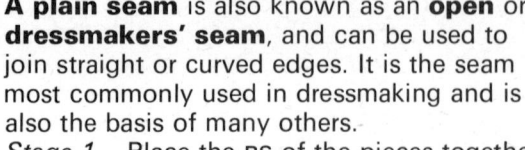

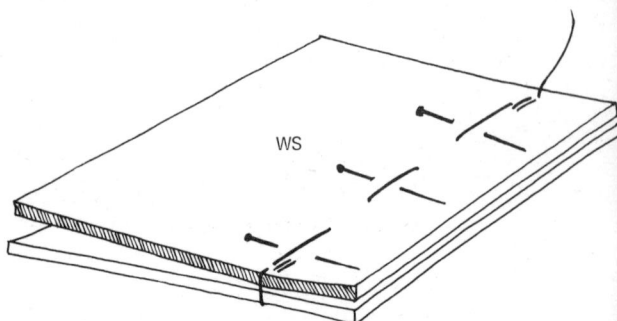

WS

Stage 2   Remove the pins and stitch on the seam line.
Stage 3   Remove the basting and press the seam open from the WS using a seam roll.

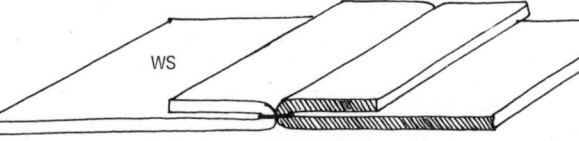

WS

Stage 4   Finish the raw edges using a method suitable for the material.

A lapped seam can be straight or curved and is often used as a decorative junction for shoulder yokes, skirt panels, etc.
Stage 1   Place the RS of the pieces together, cross-pin, and hand or machine baste along the seam line. Remove the pins.

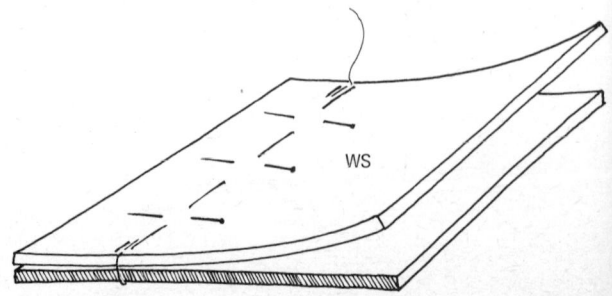

WS

Stage 2 Open the material out flat, and working from the WS, press both seam allowances to one side over a seam roll. After pressing, check from the RS that the basting is against the fold.
Stage 3 Baste the seam allowances to the main fabric 6 mm ($\frac{1}{4}$ in.) from the seam line.

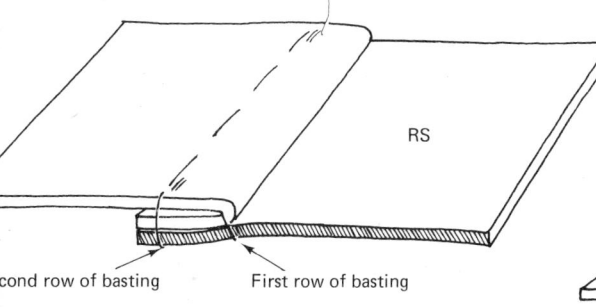

cond row of basting   First row of basting

Stage 4 With the work RS up, stitch through all three layers, 1 to 2 mm ($\frac{1}{16}$ in.) from the fold.
Stage 5 Remove the basting and finish the raw edges.

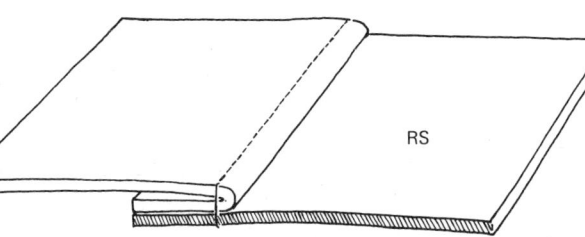

When making this seam keep the stitching an even distance from the fold, and take care with curved sections that the seam allowances are snipped or notched at stage 2 so that they lie flat. (See section on curved seams page 25.)

Lapped seam (alternative method).
Stage 1 Mark the seam line on the underlap piece with basting.

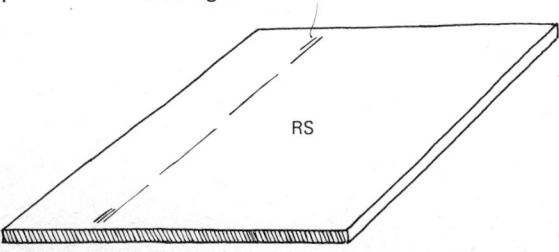

Stage 2 Fold the seam allowance of the lapped piece to the WS, press the fold and baste it into place.
Stage 3 With both pieces RS up, bring the fold of the lapped piece to the marked line on the underlap. Cross-pin, baste the two pieces together and remove the pins.
Stage 4 Stitch 1 to 2 mm ($\frac{1}{16}$ in.) from the folded edge through all three layers.

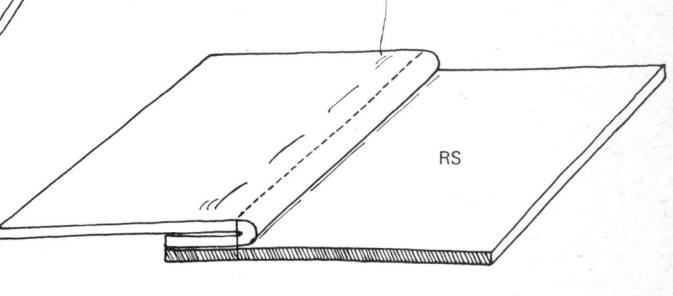

Stage 5 Remove the basting stitches and finish the raw edges.
The distance of the stitching from the fold on a lapped seam should not be greater than 2 mm ($\frac{1}{16}$ in.). When this distance is exceeded the seam changes its character and its name, and it is known as a **tucked seam**. In this form it should not be used where it will come under tension because the tuck will set badly.

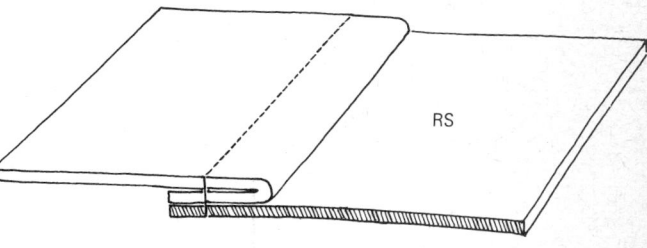

A lapped seam
finished as a tucked seam

A top-stitched seam is similar to a lapped seam. It can be straight or curved, and forms a very strong flat join. It may be made a design feature of the garment by using a thick thread or one of contrasting colour for the second row of stitching.

Stage 1   Place the RS of the fabric together, cross-pin, and baste firmly on the seam allowance 1 mm ($\frac{1}{16}$ in.) from the seam line. Remove the pins.

Stage 2   Stitch on the seam line and remove the basting.

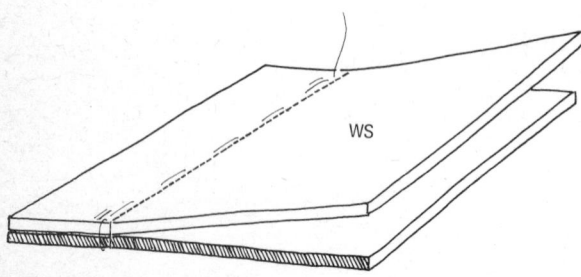

Stage 3   Open the fabric out flat, and working from the WS, press both seam allowances in the same direction over a seam roll. After pressing, check from the RS that the line of stitching is against the fold.

Stage 4   Baste the seam allowances to the main fabric and stitch from the RS through all layers. The distance of the second row of stitching from the seam is determined by the design.

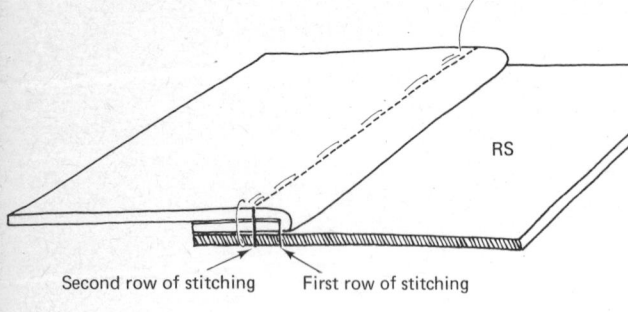

Second row of stitching   First row of stitching

Stage 5   Remove the basting stitches, finish the raw edges and press.

Because of the decorative nature of this seam it is important that the second row of stitching should be parallel to the fold.

A double-top-stitched seam is a strong flat seam which is especially useful for holding the seam allowances of springy synthetic fabrics. It is a variation of the top-stitched seam, and may be used for joining straight or curved edges. The two rows of stitching may be made more pronounced by using buttonhole twist for the top thread, or a colour may be used which contrasts with the main fabric. The distance of the rows of stitching from the seam line should depend on the thickness of the fabric and the scale of the garment.

Stage 1   Make a plain seam, and press the seam allowances open, from the WS, over a seam roll.

Stage 2   Unless the material is very firm, baste each seam allowance to the main fabric to prevent it from slipping during stitching.

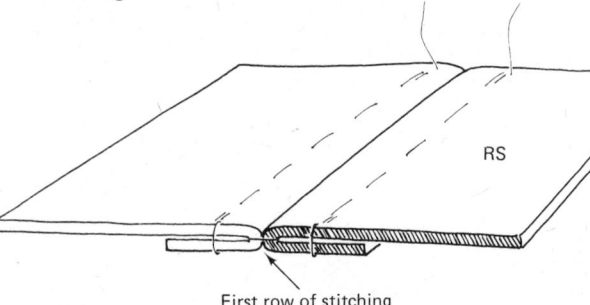

First row of stitching

Stage 3   With the fabric RS up, stitch through both layers along each side of the join. Use the edge of the presser foot or a quilting guide to keep the two lines of top stitching parallel with the seam.

A welt seam is a strong decorative seam, and is often used to give a tailored effect to garments. It is also suitable for clothing which has to withstand hard wear.

Stage 1   Make a plain seam, and press the seam allowances open from the WS.

Stage 2   Trim the raw edge on the side towards which the seam allowances will be pressed to 5 mm ($\frac{3}{16}$ in.).

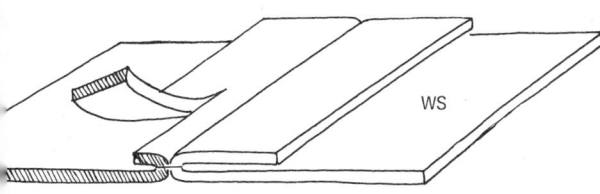

Stage 3   Using a seam roll and working from the WS, press the untrimmed seam allowance over the trimmed one. Check, from the RS, that the stitching is against the fold.

Stage 4   Baste the untrimmed seam allowance to the garment fabric to prevent it from twisting during stitching.

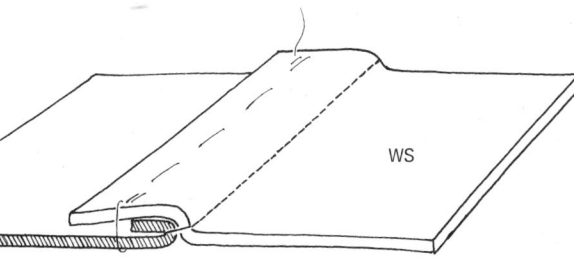

Stage 5   With the fabric RS up, stitch parallel to the join (usually about 6 mm − $\frac{1}{4}$ in. from it). Buttonhole twist may be used as a top thread if desired. Remove the basting.

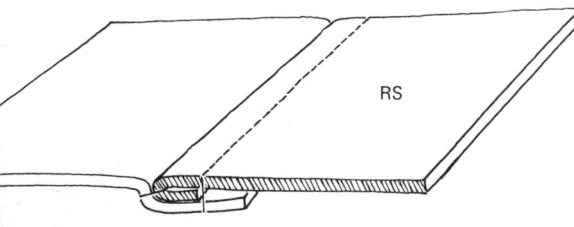

A double-machined seam, also known as a **double-stitched seam**, is a self-finished seam, worked from the RS of the garment. It is often used for shirts, pyjamas, and work or play clothes such as jeans and overalls, all of which require frequent laundering.

Stage 1   Place the WS of the material together, and make a plain seam. Press the seam allowances open over a seam roll from the RS.

Stage 2   Trim the raw edge on the side towards which the seam allowances will be pressed to 5 mm ($\frac{3}{16}$ in.).

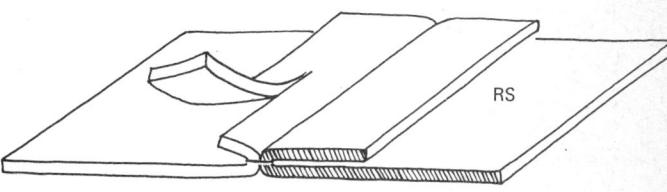

Stage 3   Fold the untrimmed seam allowance in half, WS together, and crease it with an iron.

Stage 4   Press the folded seam allowance so that it lies on the trimmed one.

Stage 5   Enclose the trimmed edge with the fold. Cross-pin, and baste along the folded edge.

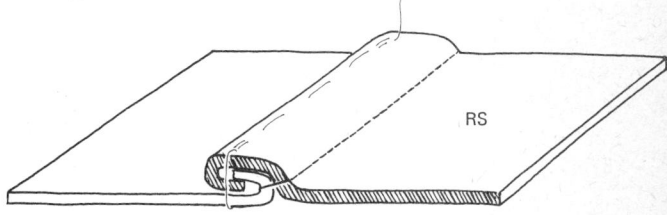

Stage 6   Working from the RS, edge-stitch 2 mm ($\frac{1}{16}$ in.) from the fold. Remove the basting and press.

When making this seam take care that the distance between the lines of stitching is equal on all seams.

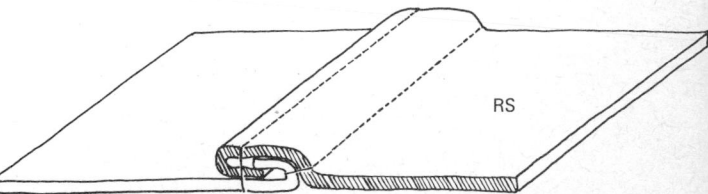

A run-and-fell seam is a strong, self-finished seam, which because it is hand stitched is soft and flexible. This makes it suitable for underwear and baby clothes which require frequent laundering, but it is not used on outer garments because the row of hemming shows on the RS. The seam may be worked on either the RS or WS of the fabric.

Stage 1　Place the WS of the fabric together (if the seam is to be made on the RS), cross-pin, baste, and sew along the seam line with small running stitches.

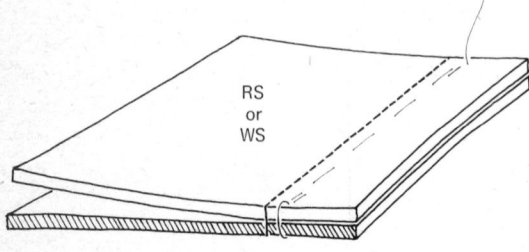

Stage 2　Remove the basting, open the fabric out flat and press the seam allowances open over a seam roll. Trim the raw edge on the side towards which the seam allowances will be pressed to 3 mm ($\frac{1}{8}$ in.).

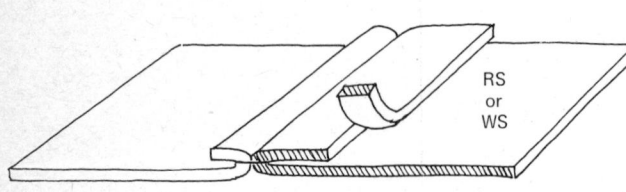

Stage 3　Trim the other seam allowance to 1 cm ($\frac{3}{8}$ in.). Fold it in half lengthways, and crease the fold with an iron.

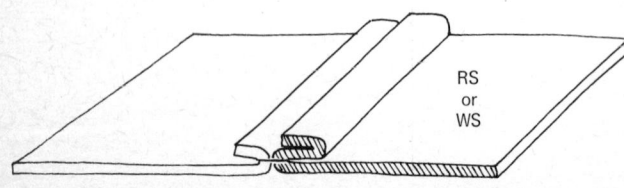

Stage 4　Fold the creased seam allowance over, enclosing the narrower one. Baste it into place and hem the folded edge to the garment fabric with small stitches.

Stage 5　Remove the basting and press.

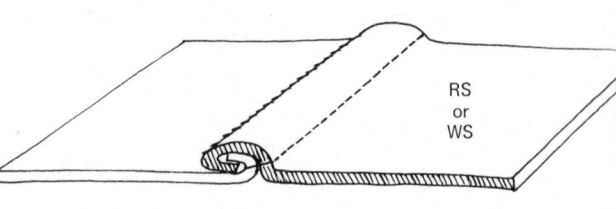

A french seam is a strong, self-finished seam used on thin materials which fray easily, and on sheer fabrics. It is usually made by machine, but may also be made by hand using running stitch.

Stage 1　Place the WS of the fabric together. Cross-pin, baste, and stitch 1 cm ($\frac{3}{8}$ in.) from the raw edge.

First row of stitching only 1 cm ($\frac{3}{8}$ in.) from edge

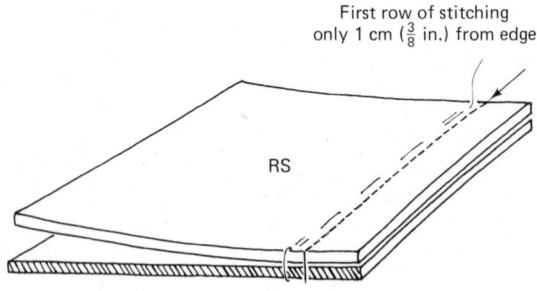

Stage 2　Remove the basting, and trim the seam allowances carefully to 3 mm ($\frac{1}{8}$ in.). Open the pieces out flat, and press both seam allowances to one side over a seam roll.

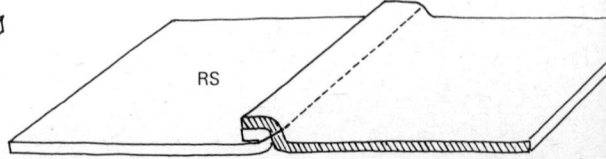

Check after pressing that the fold is exactly on the stitching line, and then press the RS of the pieces together enclosing the seam allowances.

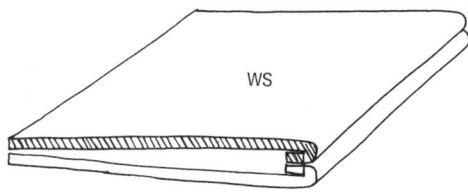

Stage 3   Pin, baste and stitch on the WS 6 mm ($\frac{1}{4}$ in.) from the fold.
Stage 4   Press the seam to one side over a seam roll, but avoid pressing the free edge of the seam against the WS of the fabric.

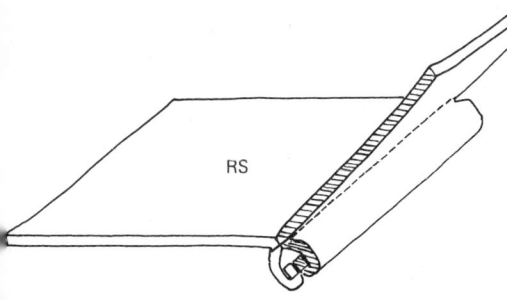

When making this seam there are several points to remember. The two lines of stitching should be parallel. There must be no threads from the raw edge projecting through the second line of stitching. When joining two french seamed pieces together, eg the side and sleeve seams at the armhole of a blouse, the seam allowances should be arranged to lie in the same direction.

A mantua makers' seam can be used as an alternative to a french seam. It is easier to use when joining shaped sections because there is only one line of stitching, and the seam is made and finished in one operation. If this seam is made entirely by hand the first fold is placed against the seam line at stage 3, and then hemmed through all layers.
Stage 1   Place the RS of the material together and baste firmly along the seam line. Do not press the seam allowances open.

Stage 2   Trim one seam allowance to 5 mm ($\frac{3}{16}$ in.).

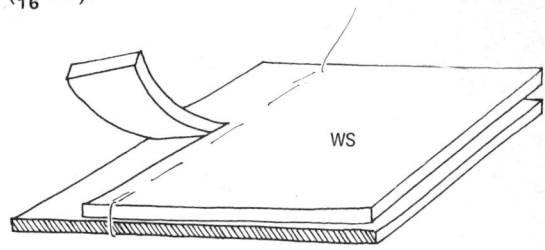

Stage 3   Fold the edge of the untrimmed seam allowance so that it almost meets that of the trimmed one, and press the fold.

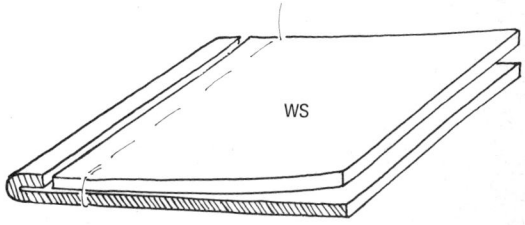

Fold this side again so that the first fold just crosses the seam line. Press the second fold.
Stage 4   Baste and stitch on the seam line catching the folded edge of the seam allowance.

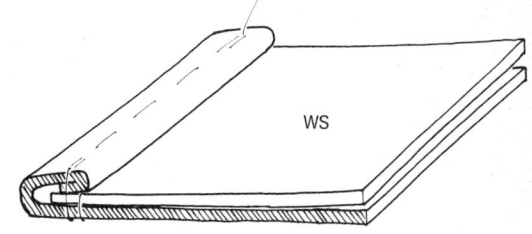

Stage 5   Remove the basting threads, and press the seam to one side over a seam roll, but avoid pressing the free edge of the seam against the WS of the fabric.

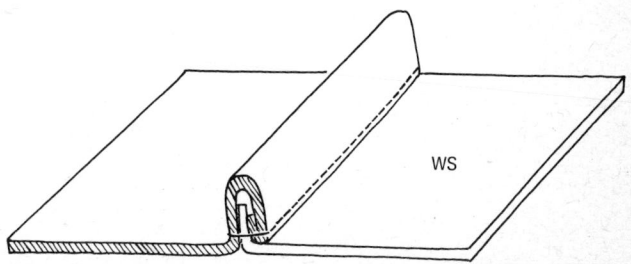

A slot seam is a decorative seam which is used on the CF and CB of skirts, coats and dresses, sometimes in conjunction with an inverted pleat. The distance between the rows of top stitching is determined by the design of the garment.

Stage 1 Cut a strip of fabric a little wider than twice the width of a seam allowance.

Stage 2 Mark the centre line on the RS along the length of the strip with uneven basting.

Stage 3 Turn the seam allowance of each garment piece towards the WS. Press and baste.

Stage 4 Lay out the strip RS up. Place one of the prepared pieces on it WS down with its folded edge against the marked centre line, and the ends level. Pin and baste it firmly into place.

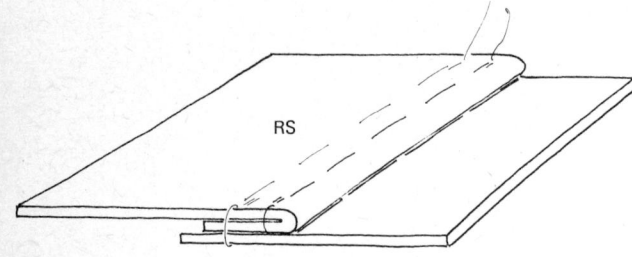

Stage 5 Take the second piece and pin it in position against the first. With the work flat on a table, baste the two pieces together with herringbone stitch. Then baste the second piece to the strip.

Stage 6 Top-stitch the pieces to the strip. Each row of stitching should be parallel with the centre line, and the same distance from it.

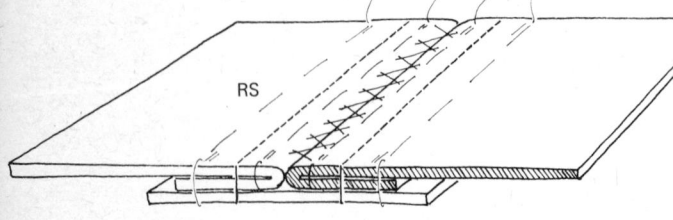

Piped and corded seams, often made with contrasting fabric, can be used to emphasize cut by giving added interest to the seams, and also to the edges of the garment. Piping cord should be pre-shrunk if it is to be used in a garment which may be washed. When making these seams, the seam allowances are pressed so that they all point in the same direction, and because of this, it must be decided which piece is to be the underlap, before setting the piping or cord into the seam.

A piped seam

Stage 1 Cut a strip of fabric on the true bias the same length as the seam, by twice the width of the finished piping, plus twice the seam allowance.

Stage 2 Fold the strip in half lengthwise, WS together, and press lightly. Take care not to pull the strip during pressing, or it will become narrower.

Stage 3 Place the folded strip on the seam allowance of the underlap piece with their raw edges exactly together. Cross-pin and baste. Stitch the two pieces together along the seam line. The stitching must be parallel with the folded edge of the piping so that it will project from the seam by an even amount when it is finished. Remove the basting.

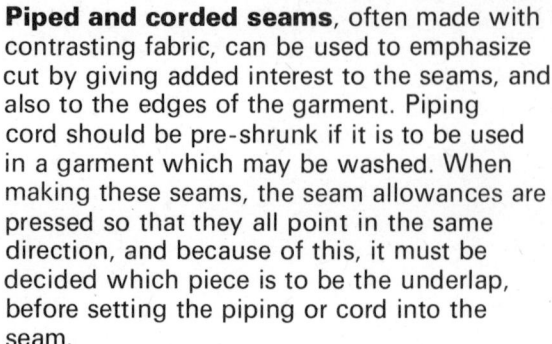

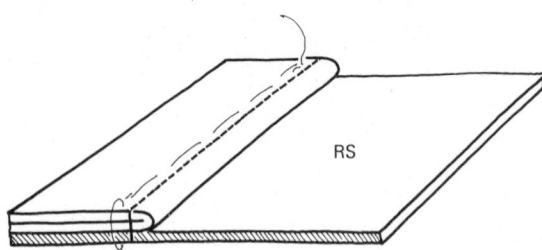

Stage 4 Place the other garment piece on the underlap so that their RS are together. The raw edges should be exactly level. Baste firmly.

Stage 5 With the underlap piece on top, stitch through all layers exactly on the first row of stitching. Remove the basting. Using

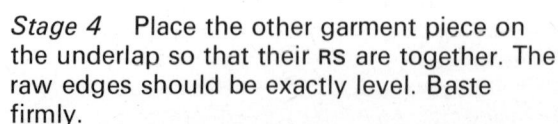

a seam roll, and working from the RS, carefully press the fold of the lapped piece.

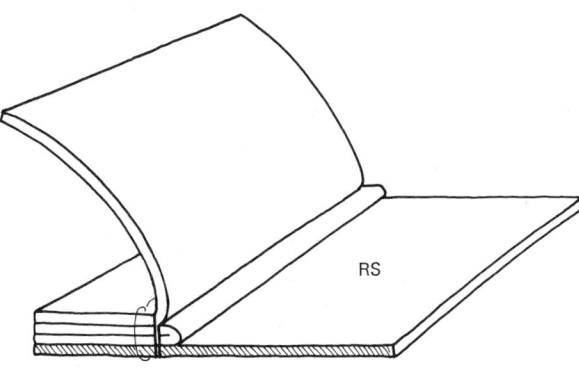

Grade and finish the seam allowances.

The seam may be top stitched by sewing close beside the piping.

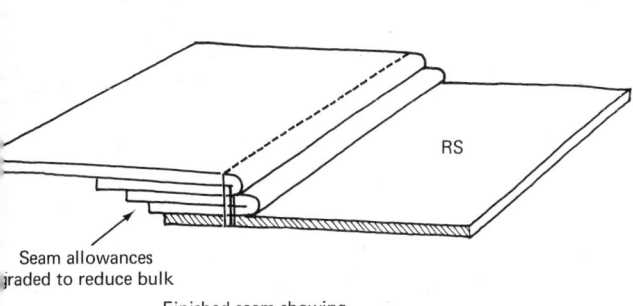

Seam allowances graded to reduce bulk

Finished seam showing top-stitched finish

A corded seam

Stage 1   Cut a strip of fabric on the true bias, making its width equal to the circumference of the cord plus twice the seam allowance.
Stage 2   Fold it in half lengthwise, WS together, and press it very lightly. Place the cord in the fold, and pin the corded strip to the seam allowance of the underlap piece with all three raw edges exactly together. Baste firmly.
Stage 3   Using the right size of cording foot, and stitching just behind the cord, stitch the strip to the garment. If a cording foot is not available, a zip foot may be used, but care

must be taken to keep the cord against the side of the foot whilst stitching.

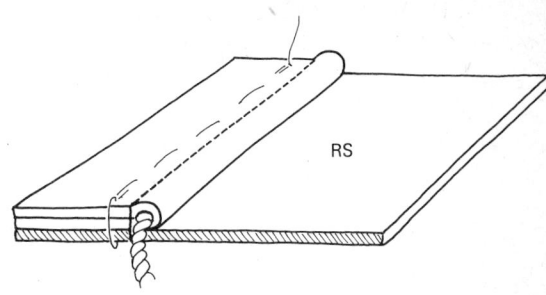

Stage 4   Place the other garment piece on the underlap so that their RS are together. The raw edges should be exactly level. Baste firmly.
Stage 5   With the underlap piece on top, stitch through all layers, exactly on the first row of stitching. Remove the basting.

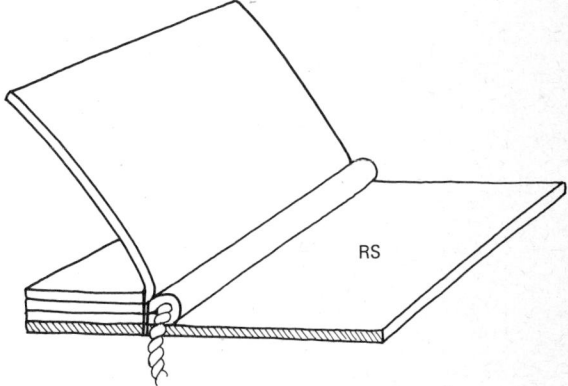

Stage 6   Using a seam roll, and working from the RS, carefully press the fold of the lapped piece beside the cord, but avoid pressing the cord itself. Grade and finish the seam allowances.

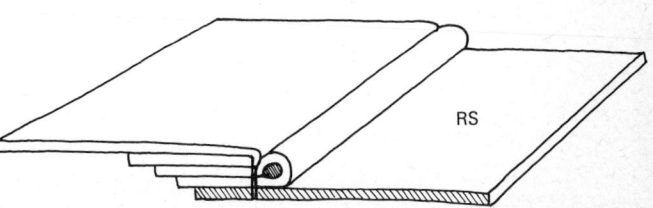

Angled pieces may be joined with an open seam, and they are sometimes used instead of darts to provide shaping in the bodice of a garment. The art of making this junction successfully lies in stitching the angle accurately, and in not catching the pleats which develop at the point.

Stage 1 Stay-stitch the angled sections on the seam allowances, 2 mm ($\frac{1}{16}$ in.) from the seam line.

Stage 2 On the piece which contains the internal angle, snip across the seam allowances from the corner towards the angle in the stitching line. Cut up to, but not through, the stay stitching.

Stage 3 Place the pieces RS together, and match the angles in the stitching lines carefully. Cross-pin the seam lines together, beginning at the angle. Use extra pins at the corner to control the fullness evenly.

Stage 4 Baste firmly. Remove the pins, except at the angle where they will help to hold the fabric during stitching.

Stage 5 With the pleated side uppermost, machine sew, shortening the stitch length to 1 to 2 mm (16 stitches to the inch) for 2 cm ($\frac{3}{4}$ in.) on either side of the angle, and taking care that the pleats are not caught by the stitching.

Stage 6 After removing the pins and basting, press the seam open from the WS over the end of a sleeve board.

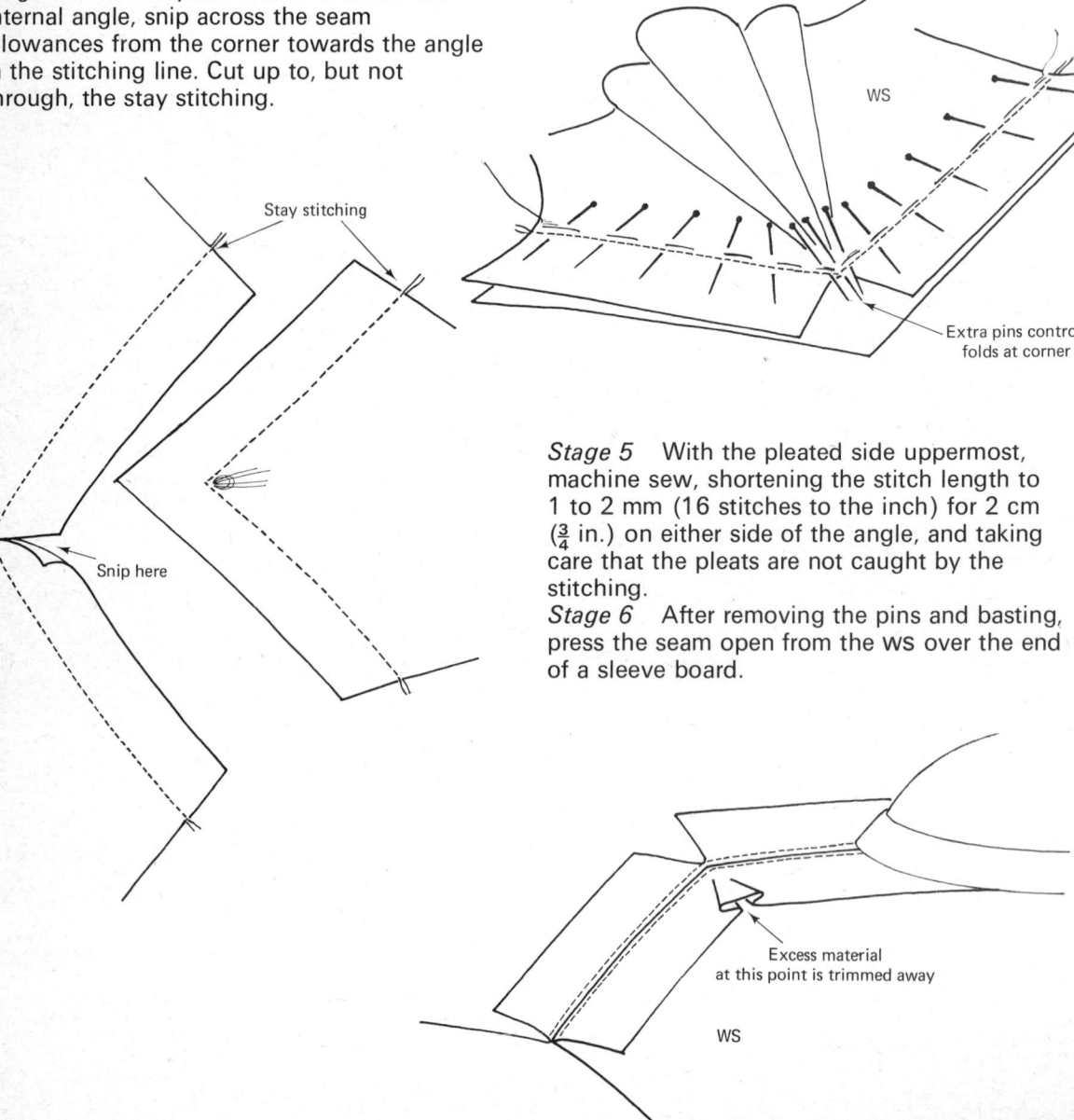

Stay stitching

Snip here

WS

Extra pins control folds at corner

Excess material at this point is trimmed away

WS

Stage 7 Overcast the edges of the slash to finish and strengthen them. The other seam allowance may be notched, so that it lies flat, and the raw edges of the notch overcast together.

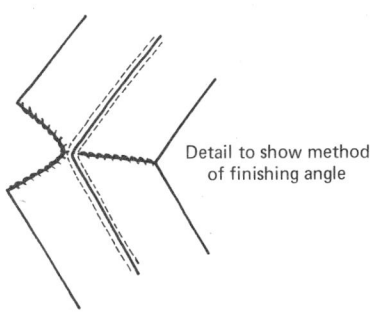

Detail to show method of finishing angle

When an angle occurs in a lapped or top-stitched seam, it is made in exactly the same way as one in an open seam, but the seam allowances are pressed to one side.

When the lapped piece contains the internal angle the edges of the slash may be neatly overcast to the underlap seam allowance to provide the slash with extra support.

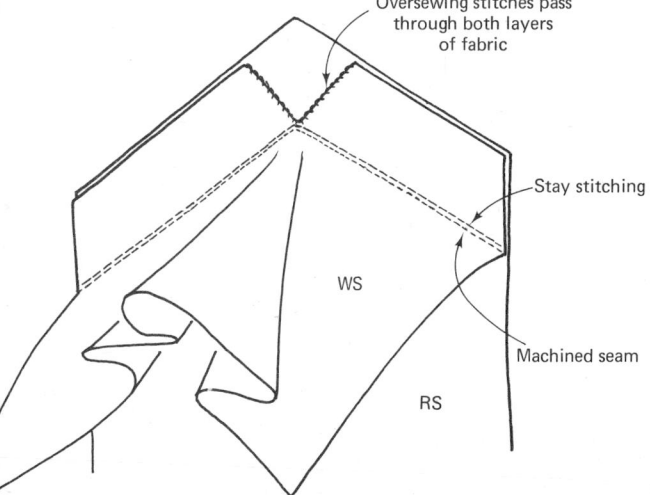

Oversewing stitches pass through both layers of fabric

Stay stitching

WS

Machined seam

RS

When the lapped piece contains the external angle, the two edges of the slash will come together after pressing. The pleat formed at the angle may be cut and finished as shown in the diagrams.

Top-stitch the seam from the RS.

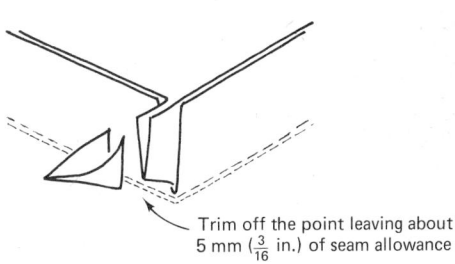

Trim off the point leaving about 5 mm ($\frac{3}{16}$ in.) of seam allowance

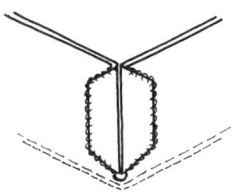

Snip the fold and oversew the cut edges to the seam allowance

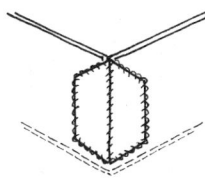

Oversew the centre folds together to strengthen the corner

Curved seams have one edge concave (hollow) and one edge convex (rounded), and need special care in joining if they are to set well. This is one of the few occasions in dressmaking when the seam must be pinned and basted over the hand.

Stage 1   Stay-stitch both curved sections on the seam allowance, 2 mm ($\frac{1}{16}$ in.) from the seam line.

Stage 2   If the curve is sharp, put an easing thread along the middle of the seam allowance of the convex edge.

Stage 3   Place the pieces RS together, and holding the work over the hand with the convex piece on top, match and cross-pin each pair of balance marks and tailor tacks.

Take care that the raw edges do not twist out of line.

Stage 4   Gently pull up the easing thread, and distribute the fullness until the top seam allowance lies evenly on the under one.

Stage 5   Continue to cross-pin, keeping the raw edges exactly level, and dividing the remaining spaces into halves, quarters, and, if necessary, eighths. The pins may finally be spaced only 6 mm ($\frac{1}{4}$ in.) apart on a sharp curve.

Stage 6   Baste with short stitches. Remove the pins and tailor tacks. The two seam lines should lie smoothly together without any tendency to pleat.

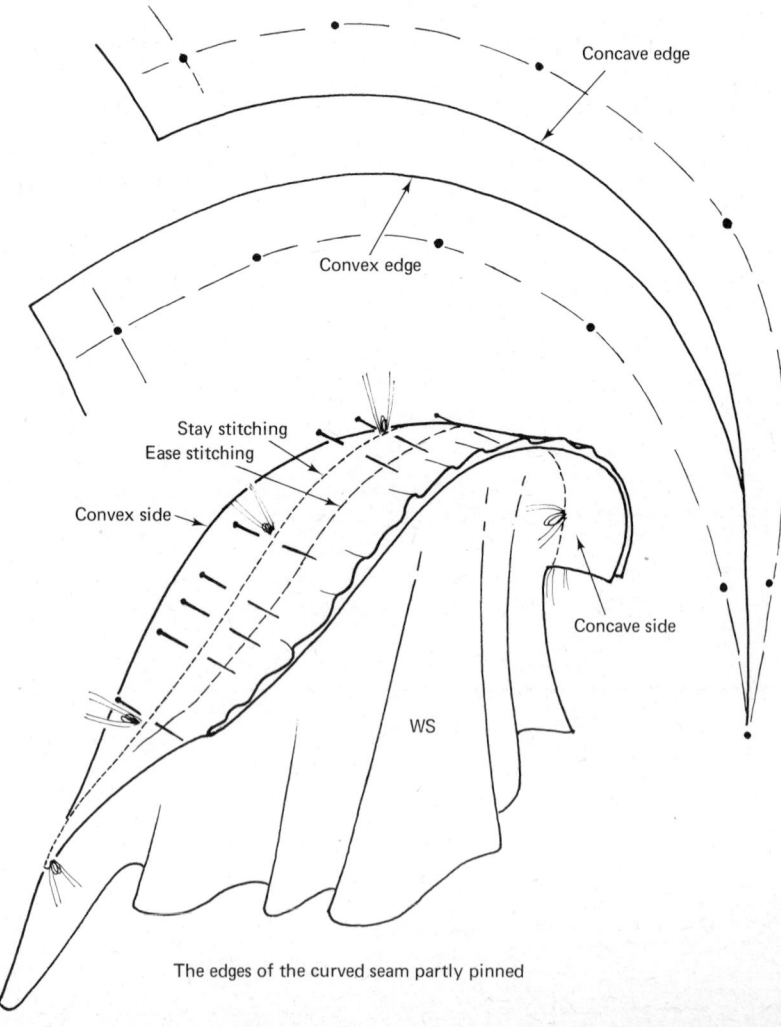

A typical curved seam ending in a dart

Concave edge

Convex edge

Stay stitching
Ease stitching
Convex side
Concave side

WS

The edges of the curved seam partly pinned

Stage 7 Clip the seam allowance of the concave edge at intervals so that the curve may be flattened to make stitching easier. Stitch and remove the basting and easing threads.

If the join is to be left as a plain seam, press the seam open from the WS over a tailor's ham, and, if the seam allowances tend to pull or pleat, clip and notch them as shown in the 'treatment of curved seam allowances' page 25.

If the seam is to be top stitched, the seam allowances should be pressed to one side (they may need further clipping to allow them to lie flat against the WS of the garment), and should be basted to prevent them from pleating up during stitching. Be careful not to let the fabric pucker under the presser foot during top stitching.

When making a curved lapped seam: after basting, at stage 6, clip and notch the seam allowances so that they can be pressed one way. Press them to one side, and baste them to the garment. Edge-stitch from the RS, keeping the fabric under the presser foot as flat as possible.

When making seams in reversible garments the seam allowances have to be concealed between the layers of the material. A form of open seam which is finished as a double-top-stitched seam may be used, or if the fabric is not too bulky, a double-stitched seam makes a strong and decorative join.

Open seam for reversible garments
This seam is suitable for joining straight sections, and curved ones because the seam allowances can be clipped or notched.
Stage 1 Separate the layers at the edges for twice the width of the seam allowance.

Stage 2 Place the RS of one pair of matching layers together, pin and baste, keeping the other pair of layers folded back out of the way. (The same sides of the garment should be placed together for all seams in any one garment.)

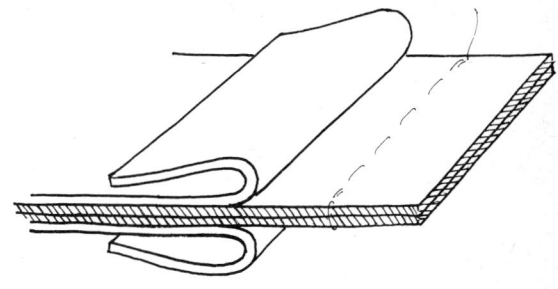

Stage 3 Stitch the basted pair and trim away half the width of their seam allowances. Remove the basting and press the seam allowances open over a seam roll.

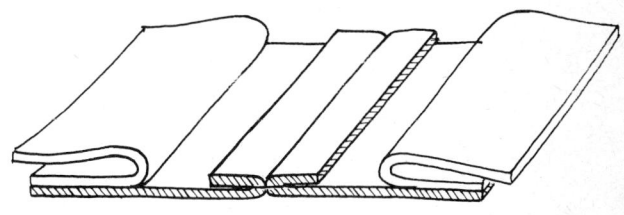

Stage 4 Turn in one of the free edges of the other layer so that its fold is on the seam line. Baste it to the layer beneath. Turn the remaining free edge in so that its fold lies against the one just formed, and baste it into place.
Stage 5 Slip-stitch the two folds together firmly, and finish the seam with a line of top stitching on each side of the join. Remove the basting and press.

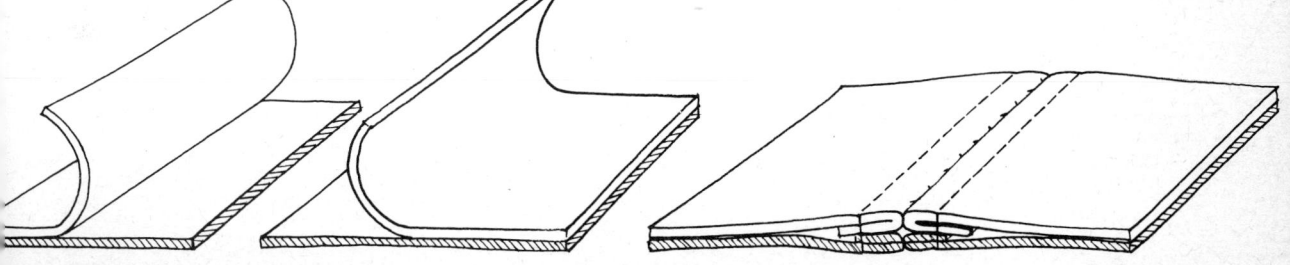

Double-Stitched seams for reversible garments.

Stage 1   Place two matching sides of the fabric together, and make an open seam. (The same sides should be placed together for all seams in any one garment.)

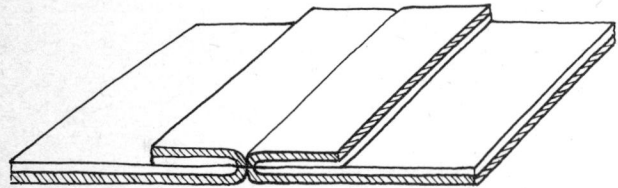

Stage 2   Separate and grade the seam allowances, leaving the one which will be used to cover the others untrimmed, make the next one 9 mm ($\frac{3}{8}$ in.), and the shortest one 3 mm ($\frac{1}{8}$ in.).

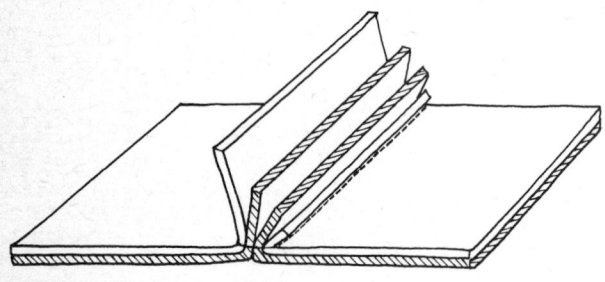

Stage 3   Fold in 5 mm ($\frac{3}{16}$ in.) of the edge of the untrimmed seam allowance, enclosing the three trimmed layers. Baste, and stitch 2 mm ($\frac{1}{16}$ in.) from the fold.
Stage 4   Remove the basting and press.

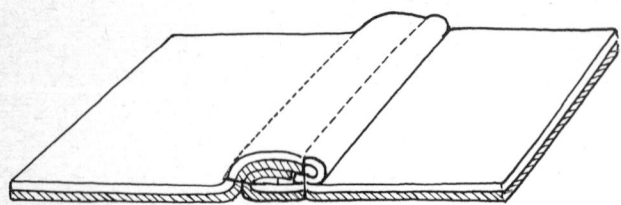

The edges of reversible garments may be finished simply by trimming away the seam allowance and applying a braid or binding which will blend with the colour of both surfaces. Another way of finishing the edge is to separate the layers to a depth of twice the width of the seam allowance, trim one side to 1 cm ($\frac{3}{8}$ in.), and turn the two seam allowances in towards each other, so that their edge folds are level. Baste the edges together through all four thicknesses, and stitch 2 mm ($\frac{1}{16}$ in.) from the fold. An additional row of stitching may be placed further from the edge for a decorative effect.

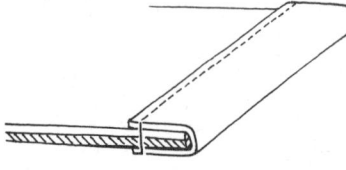

Braided or taped

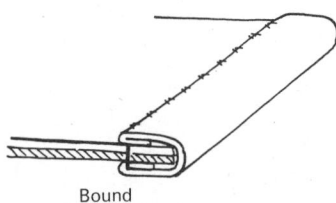

Bound

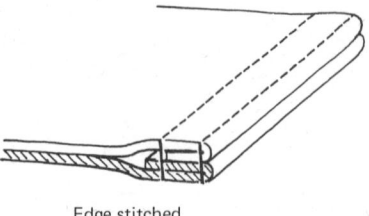

Edge stitched

4 Bindings, casings and hems

Bindings

The raw edges of a garment are sometimes enclosed and strengthened by binding them, either with a strip of fabric cut on the true bias, or with purchased bias binding. As a binding not only appears on the WS but also on the RS, it is possible for it to contribute to the decorative effect, and the use of self or contrasting dress fabric, rather than purchased binding, can provide an attractive detail in the finish of a garment.

Although on a straight edge a binding may be made any width to suit the design of the garment, it should be remembered that the wider the binding, the more difficult will it be to persuade it to follow around curves smoothly. In practice a binding of more than 1 cm ($\frac{3}{8}$ in.) finished width will be difficult to apply to even a shallow curve. When binding several edges on a garment, plan the use of the strips so that any short distance, such as an armhole, will be bound with a single length of binding, and arrange the joins so that they occur in inconspicuous places. If a striped garment is bound with self fabric, the slanting stripes of the binding can make a very decorative edge, but when joining the strips ensure that all the stripes slope in the same direction, and that the joins slope in the same direction as the stripes.

When marking out strips on the true bias, take a piece of fabric which still has at least one of its selvages, because if it has none it will be difficult to find the true bias.

Press out any creases. Straighten one weft edge, and the edge opposite to the selvage. Then fold the weft edge over so that it lies along the selvage. The sloping fold of the right-angled triangle will lie in the direction of the true bias of the material. Use tailor's chalk or pins, and a ruler to measure and mark the cutting lines for the strips parallel to the sloping fold. The strips should normally be made four times the width of the finished binding. For sheer fabrics, where double binding is used, cut the strips six times the finished width.

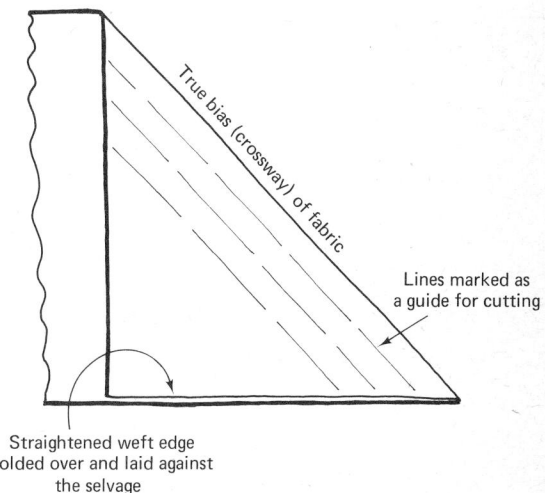

True bias (crossway) of fabric

Lines marked as a guide for cutting

Straightened weft edge folded over and laid against the selvage

Strips cut on the true bias can be joined to form a length of binding, and where more than one bias strip join has to be made, they should all slope in the same direction. Provided that the edges of the fabric were properly straightened, the ends of each strip will automatically be formed by a single warp or weft thread.

Stage 1   Place the two strips to be joined with their RS together, and at right angles to each other (as shown in the diagram), so that

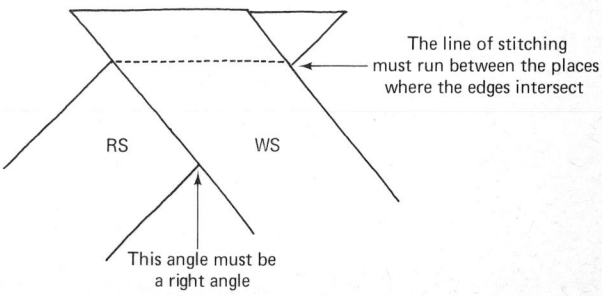

The line of stitching must run between the places where the edges intersect

RS   WS

This angle must be a right angle

their sides intersect about 6 mm ($\frac{1}{4}$ in.) from the ends. The stitching line must run between the angles which are formed where the strips cross. If the end of one strip slopes in the wrong direction, trim the end of this piece off at right angles to its cut end.

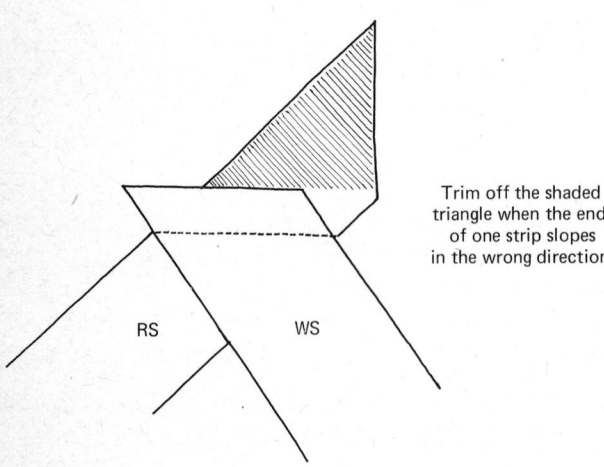

Trim off the shaded triangle when the end of one strip slopes in the wrong direction

RS   WS

Stage 2 Cross-pin. Stitch the strips together using a very short stitch, and press the seam allowances open.
Stage 3 Cut off the triangles of the seam allowances which project beyond the long edges.

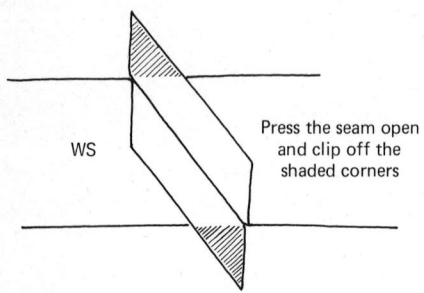

WS   Press the seam open and clip off the shaded corners

When binding the edge of a garment, unless the pattern specifies a bound edge, the edge of the garment piece will have a hem or seam allowance. Normally this allowance should be trimmed away before the binding is attached (the pattern can be used as a guide), but if the fabric unravels easily, it is better not to trim this allowance off until afterwards. When binding an edge before trimming it, the seam or hem line must be marked.
Stage 1 Place the RS of the garment and the binding together, with one edge of the binding level with the trimmed edge of the garment piece (or the marked line if the allowance has not been trimmed away). Cross-pin and baste the binding into place.
Stage 2 With the work RS up, stitch the binding to the garment. Use the edge of the presser foot or a quilting guide to keep the distance between the stitching and the edge equal to the width of the finished binding.

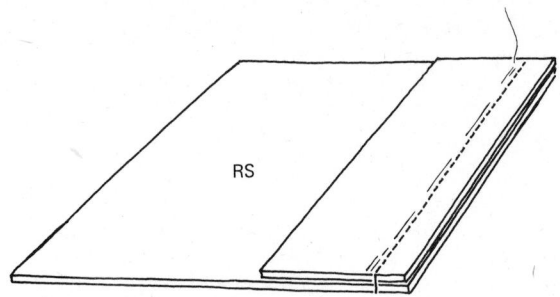

RS

Stage 3 Remove the basting. Trim the garment fabric along the seam or hem line if this has not already been done. Fold the binding at the stitching line, so that it lies across the raw edge, and crease it by running an iron outwards across the fold. If the iron were to be run along the fold, the binding might become stretched.

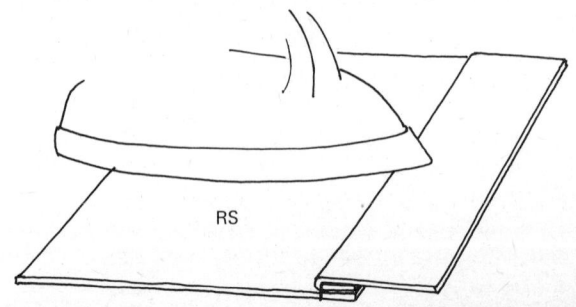

RS

Stage 4 Turn the work WS up, and fold the free edge of the binding towards the edge of the garment so that they almost meet. Press this fold into place and hem it to the line of stitching on the WS of the garment.

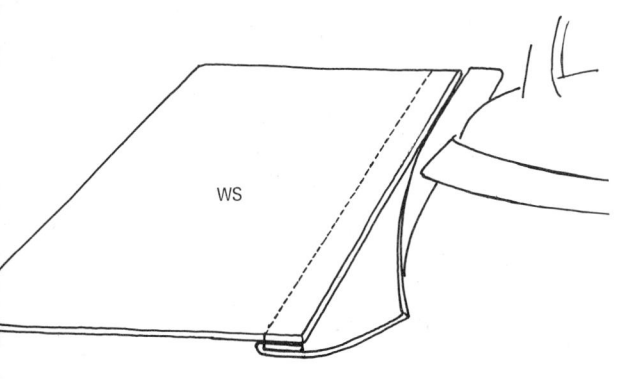

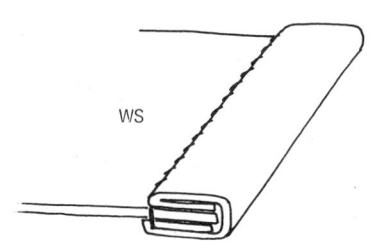

A double binding, which is also known as french fold binding, is used to make an opaque edge when binding a sheer fabric. The technique has much in common with ordinary binding, and the garment should be prepared in the same way.

Stage 1 Cut a strip of fabric on the true bias, six times the width of the finished binding.

Stage 2 Fold it in half lengthwise, WS together, and crease this fold, being careful not to stretch the binding.

Stage 3 Place the doubled binding on the RS of the fabric with its raw edges level with the trimmed edge of the garment (or the marked seam or hem line if the allowance has not been trimmed away). Cross-pin and baste the binding into place.

Stage 4 Hand sew, using small running stitches, or sew the binding to the garment by machine. Use the edge of the presser foot or a quilting guide to keep the distance of the

stitching from the edge equal to the width of the completed binding.

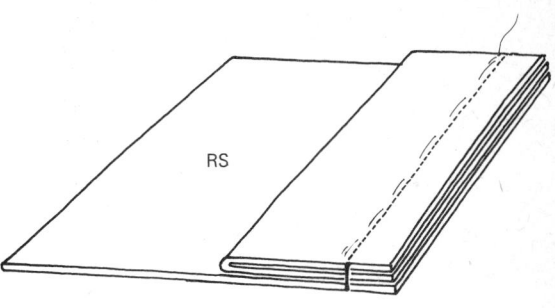

Stage 5 Remove the basting, and trim the garment fabric along the seam or hem line if this has not already been done. Fold the binding at the stitching line, so that it lies across the raw edge, and crease it by running an iron outwards across the fold.

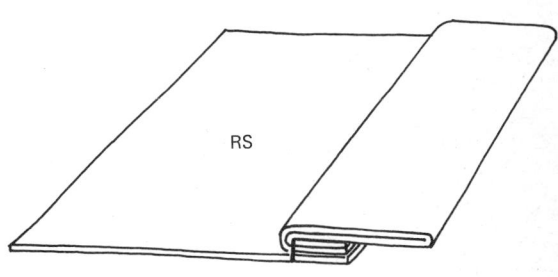

Stage 6 Bring the fold of the binding to the WS, and slip-hem it to the row of stitching. Press the finished edge.

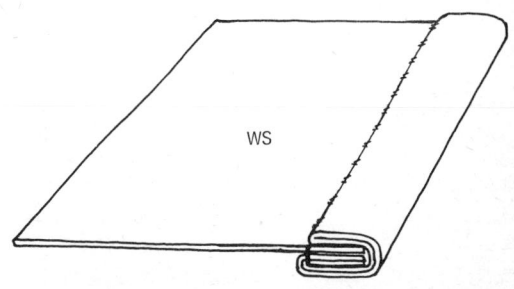

In order to make the final bias strip join in a circular edge, one needs a length of binding cut on the true bias which is equal to the length of the edge plus not less than three times the width of the unfolded binding.

Stage 1   Place the binding on the RS of the garment in the usual way leaving an end which is just longer than the width of the binding when opened out flat. Begin stitching the binding at the place where the join will be made, and continue round to the point where the stitching began, folding the free ends out of the way, so that they are not caught by the stitching.

Stage 2   Pin the binding to the main fabric on both sides of the join.

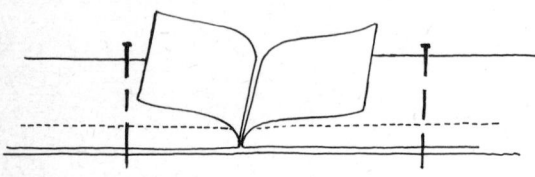

Stage 3   Fold and pin the free ends of the binding so that they lie at right angles to the raw edge of the fabric, with their sloping folds on the straight grain and just touching. (See diagram.) The join can be made to slope either way so that it matches other joins in the strip.

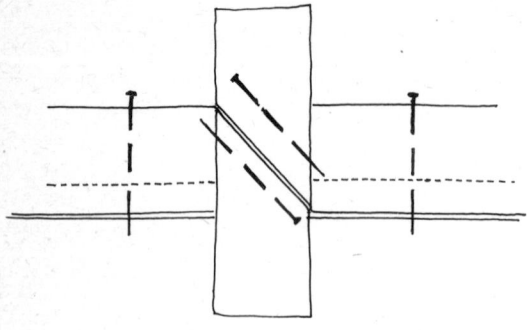

Stage 4   Oversew the folds together with small stitches, taking care not to catch the garment fabric. Press the join. Trim the free ends of the binding 6 mm ($\frac{1}{4}$ in.) from the

oversewing and also cut off the triangles so that the edges of the seam allowances do not project.

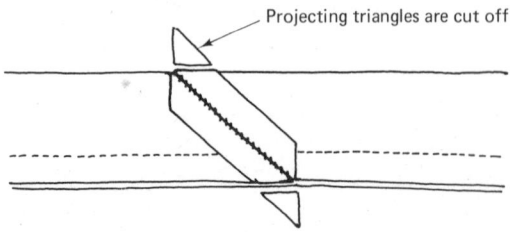

Projecting triangles are cut off

Stage 5   Attach the other edge of the binding in the normal way.

When binding an external angle both the stitching creases in the binding should have been made and pressed before beginning to attach it. If the sides of the angle do not lie on the straight grain, they should be stay stitched.

Stage 1   Bring the raw edges of the angle together to form a fold in the fabric. This fold will bisect the angle and should be creased, or its line marked with a thread.

Stage 2   Open the fabric out flat again, and place the binding on it RS together in the usual way. Sew the binding to the fabric working towards the corner, and stopping exactly at the mark made in stage 1. Make the last stitch a backstitch and take the needle through to the WS of the fabric.

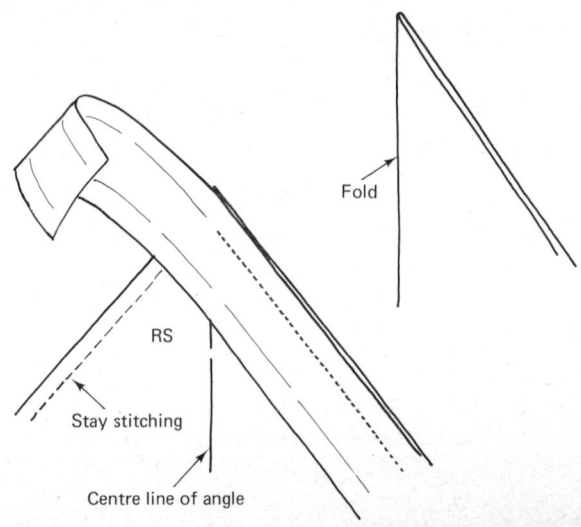

Fold

RS

Stay stitching

Centre line of angle

Stage 3   Fold the free end of the binding outwards so that a mitre fold is formed at the angle which exactly coincides with the line marked in stage 1. Pin this fold.

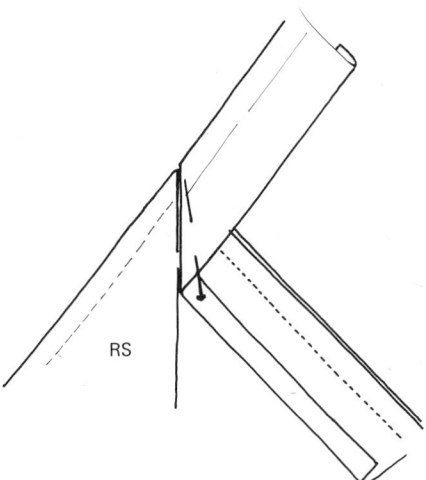

Stage 4   Fold the binding back over the fabric so that its edge lies on the seam or hem line of the unbound edge, and a small triangle is formed at the corner. Pin this triangle.

Stage 5   Bring the needle up through the fabric, make a backstitch, and continue stitching so that the line of sewing is unbroken, and the triangle at the corner is left free. Remove the pins. Trim the garment along the seam or hem line if this has not already been done.

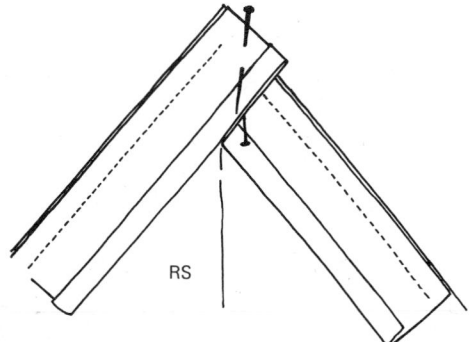

Stage 6   Turn the free edge of the binding to the WS of the fabric, and slip-hem its fold against the line of stitching. Fold the triangle

at the corner as shown in the diagram, and for firmness, hem the mitre fold on the WS of the garment.

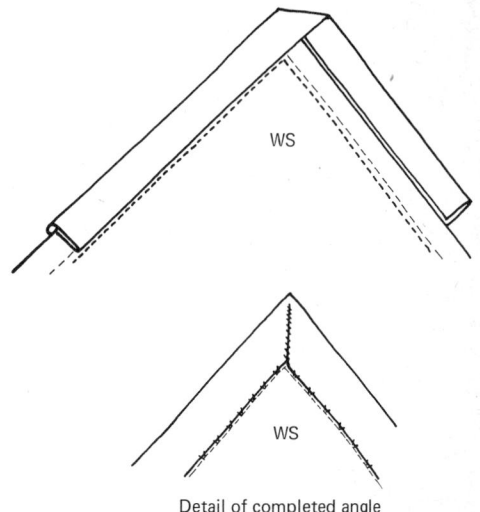

Detail of completed angle

When binding an internal angle, both the stitching creases in the binding should have been made and pressed before beginning to attach it. If the sides of the angle do not lie on the straight grain, they should be stay stitched.

Stage 1   Bring the two sides of the angle together to make a fold in the fabric. The line of this fold will bisect the angle, and should be either creased or marked with thread.

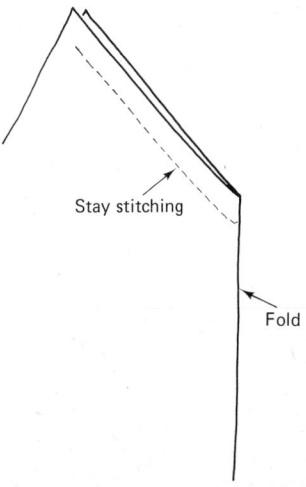

Stage 2 Open the fabric out flat again, and place the binding on it RS together in the usual way. Sew the binding to the garment working towards the angle and stopping at the line marked in stage 1. Finish with a backstitch and pass the needle through to the WS of the fabric.

Stage 3 Lay the binding back exactly over itself so that a crosswise fold is formed where the stitching ends. Crease this fold.

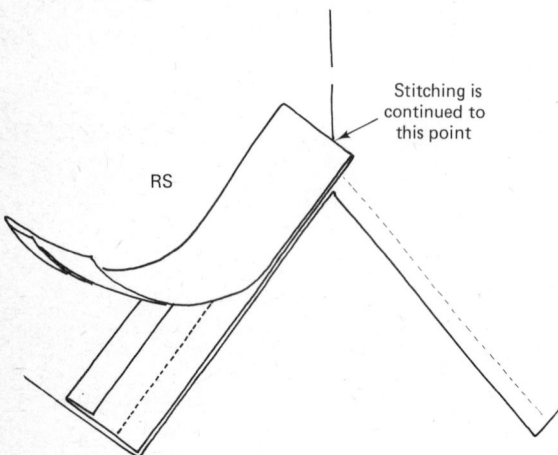

RS

Stitching is continued to this point

Stage 4 Snip the garment piece at the corner as far as the stay stitching. Place the edge of the binding on the seam or hem line of the unbound side, so that the binding stands up at right angles to the surface of the fabric. Make sure that the pleat which will form at the corner of the binding is wholly inside the angle.

Stage 5 Bring the needle up through the fabric, and starting with a backstitch, sew the binding along the second side of the angle.

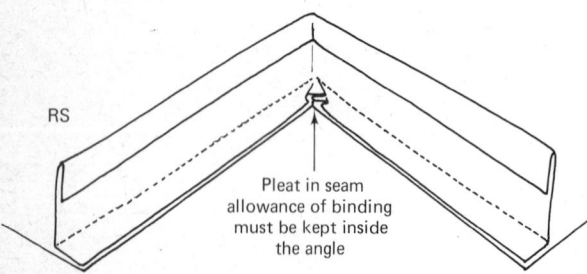

RS

Pleat in seam allowance of binding must be kept inside the angle

Stage 6 Trim the garment along the seam or hem line if this has not already been done, and

snip the pleat in the binding to remove bulk if necessary.

If the internal angle is a right angle or greater continue with stages 7 and 8. If the angle is less than a right angle carry out stage 9 to 12.

The final stage of binding an internal angle which is a right angle or greater.

Stage 7 With the work RS up, fold the binding as shown in the diagrams to form a mitre. Pin this on the RS to hold it in place.

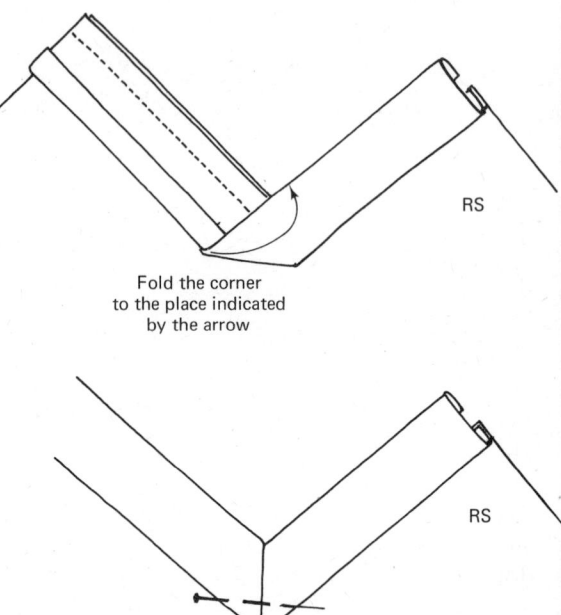

RS

Fold the corner to the place indicated by the arrow

RS

Stage 8 Turn the work WS up, and carefully bring the binding at the corner to the WS without allowing the mitre to unfold itself. Slip-hem the binding to the WS of the garment except for 1 cm ($\frac{3}{8}$ in.) on either side of the corner where hemming will be firmer. Hem the mitre fold in the binding on the WS to prevent it from unfolding.

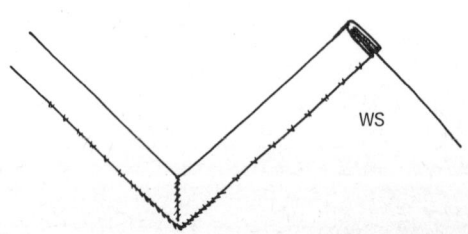

WS

The final stage of binding an acute internal angle.

Stage 9 Line up the crease at the corner of the binding with the mark made in stage 1 (see diagram) and press.

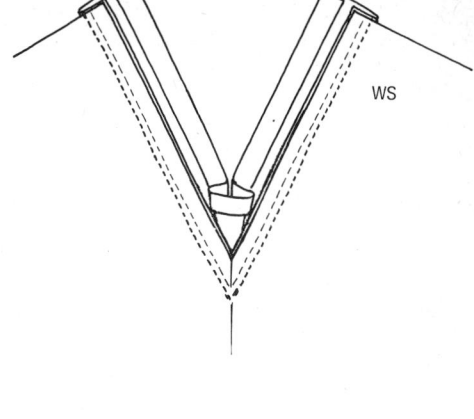

WS

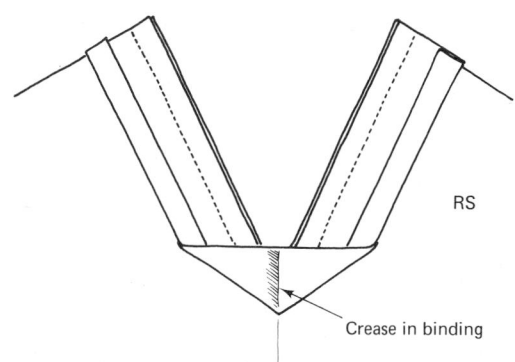

RS

Crease in binding

Stage 10 Carefully fold the binding along the lines of stitching so that the two creases pressed in at stage 9 lie together on the line bisecting the angle. Pin these folds into place.

Stage 11 Turn the work over, and bring the binding to the WS. Pull the central pleat through the slash first and then arrange the folds in the binding at the corner so that the mitre fold is continued on the WS.
Stage 12 Slip-hem the fold in the binding to the WS except for 1 cm ($\frac{3}{8}$ in.) on either side of the corner, which should be hemmed. Hem the mitre folds together on the WS of the work.

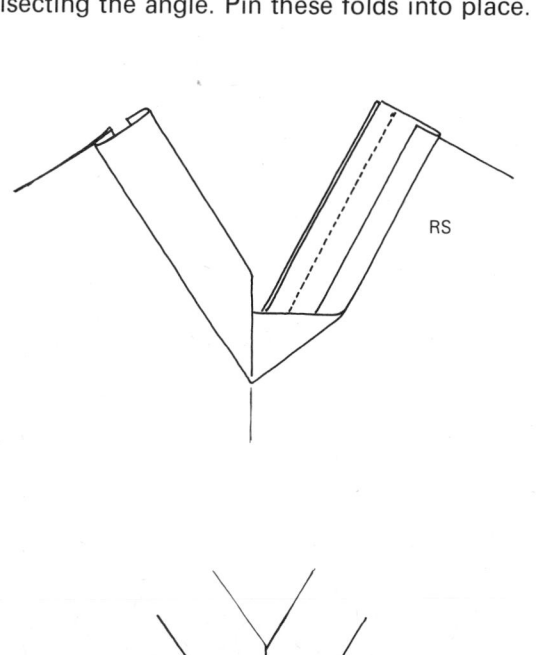

RS

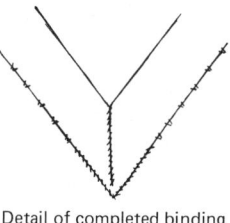

Detail of completed binding

When completing a binding at the bottom of a slash, because there is no space at the point in which to fold the binding, the strip is merely slightly stretched around the tip of the slash.

Casings

These must be made a little wider than the ribbon or elastic they will contain. A casing may be made from a seam allowance, which must be wider than normal if a heading is required, from a hem allowance, from a shaped facing or from a strip cut on the true bias. Although a purchased binding can be used to make a satisfactory casing, a bias strip can be cut from fabric chosen for its hardwearing properties.

Before making the casing, plan where the opening will need to be to enable the ribbon to be threaded in and tied. Loop-stitched or faced slots must be made before the casing is completed, and should be about two thirds of the finished width of the casing. Elastic should be threaded through a small gap left in the stitching, which can be closed afterwards with backstitches.

Making a casing at an edge from a strip cut on the true bias.

Stage 1   Cut and join the strip, making it the finished width of the casing plus two 6 mm ($\frac{1}{4}$ in.) seam allowances, by the length required for the edge plus about three times the full width of the strip to allow for the bias join.

Stage 2   Trim the garment seam allowance to 6 mm ($\frac{1}{4}$ in.).

Stage 3   Place the strip and garment with their RS together, with one of the raw edges of the strip level with the raw edge of the garment. Cross-pin, baste and stitch 6 mm ($\frac{1}{4}$ in.) from the raw edges.

Stage 4   Crease the strip along the stitching line so that it lies over the raw edge. If the casing is likely to receive hard wear, understitch it to the seam allowances just beside the fold. Alternatively edge-stitch it through all layers at stage 7.

Stage 5   With the work WS up, turn in and crease a 6 mm ($\frac{1}{4}$ in.) seam allowance in the free edge of the strip. If a slot is required for a ribbon make it at this stage.

Stage 6   Fold the whole of the casing to the WS along the seam line, and press.

Stage 7   Cross-pin and baste the free edge of the casing to the garment fabric, and then either machine stitch or hand sew the fold to the garment. When using elastic, remember to leave an opening for threading.

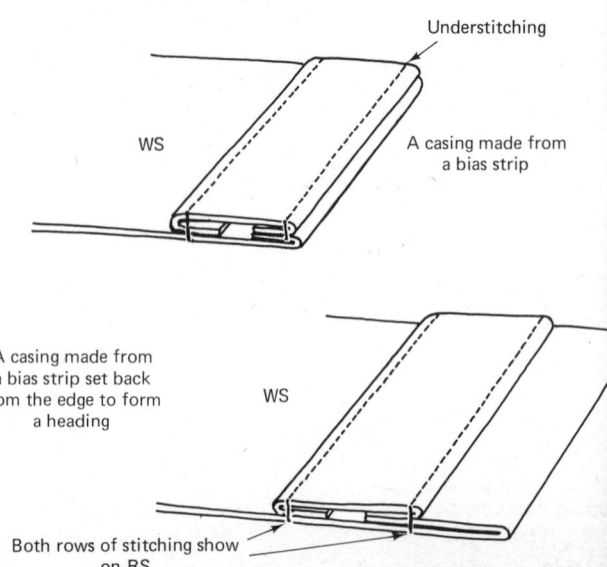

Understitching

WS

A casing made from a bias strip

A casing made from a bias strip set back from the edge to form a heading

WS

Both rows of stitching show on RS

A casing can be made from the hem
only when the edge of the garment is straight.
Stage 1   Trim the hem allowance to the width of the casing plus one 6 mm ($\frac{1}{4}$ in.) seam allowance.
Stage 2   Fold in a 6 mm ($\frac{1}{4}$ in.) seam allowance to the WS and crease it with an iron.
Stage 3   Turn the casing to the WS and crease the hem fold. This fold may be edge stitched to strengthen it.
Stage 4   Cross-pin, and baste, and leaving a small space for threading, sew the free edge of the casing to the garment.

When a casing is made a little way back from the edge so that a heading is formed, the distance between the hem line and the raw edge must be made equal to the depth of the heading plus the width of the casing plus one 6 mm ($\frac{1}{4}$ in.) seam allowance.

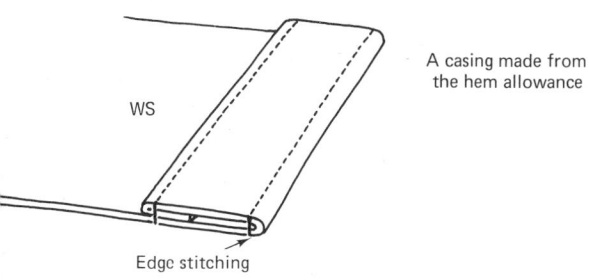

WS

A casing made from the hem allowance

Edge stitching

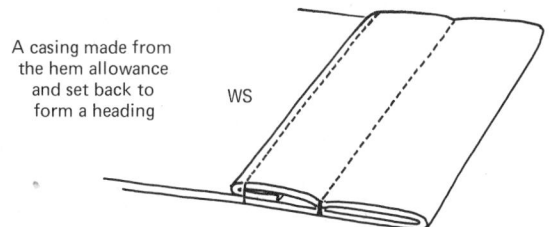

A casing made from the hem allowance and set back to form a heading

WS

Hems

A hem is used to finish the lower edge of a garment, and to give that edge weight so that it will hang well. Turning it up is usually the last process in making a garment. The method of finishing the hem will depend on whether it is straight or curved, and on the weight and type of the garment fabric.

Before turning up the hem of any garment which has bias areas or seams in the skirt, it should be hung for at least a day to give the fabric time to drop. The hems of straight-cut skirts can be turned up immediately.

When a garment is being fitted, appropriate underclothes and shoes should be worn. A marked change in heel height can alter the posture, and affect the level of the hem. If a belt will be worn with the garment, this also should be put on for the fitting.

It is well worth spending a little time experimenting with the exact height of the hemline. Although the pattern will indicate a level, the hem needs to be considered in relation to the proportions of both the wearer and the garment.

Although there are devices which enable the wearer to mark her own hemline, by far the most satisfactory method is to get someone else to mark it. Having decided on the hem level, this height should be marked on a marking stick, with an elastic band or sticky paper for example. The task of marking the hem will be made much easier if the marking stick has its own stand, leaving the fitter with both hands free for pinning. If possible, the wearer should stand on a stool or table so that the fitter can work with the hem at her eye level. The wearer must stand up straight, keep still, and not look down.

The stick should be vertical, and the pins put in horizontally, level with the mark, and at about 10 cm (4 in.) intervals all the way round the skirt. The fitter should go round a second time to check the height of each pin. No attempt should be made to turn up the hem while the garment is still on.

Lay the garment on a flat surface, RS out, and mark along the line of pins with a basting thread. Slight deviations in the level of the pins should be averaged. Remove the pins and try the garment on again to check the level.

The depth of hem allowance required will depend upon the way in which the hem is to be finished, but, unless the possibility of letting it down is envisaged, it should not exceed 6 cm (2½ in.). Make a hem marker out of card, and use it to mark the cutting line.

A hem marker

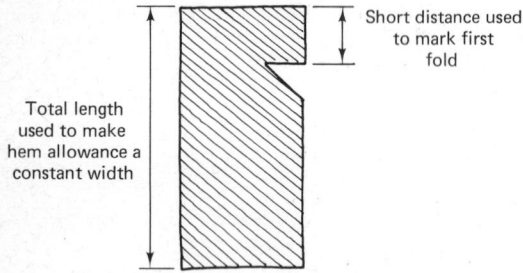

Short distance used to mark first fold

Total length used to make hem allowance a constant width

Trim the seam allowances of the long seams to 6 mm (¼ in.), from just on the garment side of the hem line to the raw edge of the hem allowance. This will prevent the seam allowances from causing a bulge in the fold.

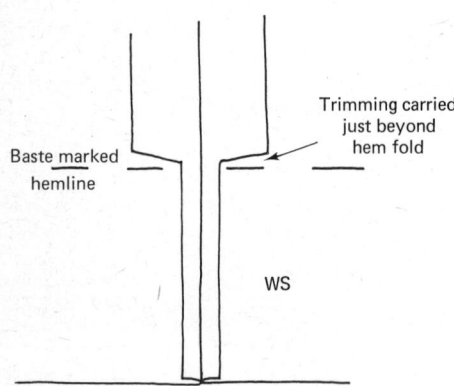

Trimming carried just beyond hem fold

Baste marked hemline

WS

When hand sewing the hem, pick up only one or two threads of the garment fabric so that the stitches hardly show on the RS. The needle can be slid through the back of thick fabrics so that the stitches do not appear on the RS at all. Never pull the thread quite tight, because this has the effect of forming a ridge at the top of the hem which shows on the RS.

Always press the hem fold from the WS. If the hem has to be pressed from the RS, place it on two thicknesses of terry towelling, and use a pressing cloth under the iron.

A straight or plain hem is suitable for use on light-weight fabrics.

Stage 1   After marking the hemline, trim the hem allowance to an even depth – usually between 5 and 6 cm (2–2½ in.). Trim the seam allowances of the long seams to 6 mm (¼ in.), from just on the garment side of the hemline to the raw edge.

Stage 2   Make the first fold of the hem 6 mm (¼ in.) from the raw edge. Crease this fold to the WS.

Stage 3   Turn the hem allowance to the WS along the baste-marked hemline. Pin, and baste 1 cm (⅜ in.) from this line.

Stage 4   Working from the WS, press the hem fold only to set it.

Stage 5   Baste, and slip-hem the hem allowance into place. Remove the basting.

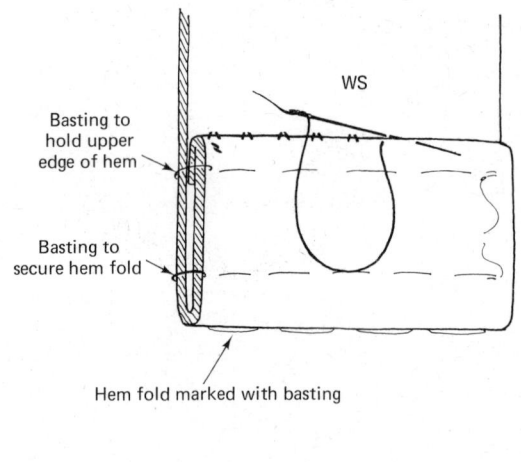

WS

Basting to hold upper edge of hem

Basting to secure hem fold

Hem fold marked with basting

A deep hem is used on sheer fabrics to avoid more than one tone showing in the hem. It is made in the same way as a straight hem except that at stage 2 the hem allowance, which should have been trimmed to an even depth, must be folded in half towards the WS. Because sheer fabrics are often soft and slippery, extra care should be taken to ensure that the fabric does not slip or twist during sewing, and, if the hem is wide, an extra row of basting should be used to hold the upper edge of the hem in place during slip-hemming.

Stage 2   Take a sufficient length of bias binding and place it and the hem allowance with their RS together, and their raw edges level. Cross-pin, baste, and stitch the binding to the hem allowance. Join the ends of the binding with a bias-strip join.

Stage 3   Turn the hem allowance to the WS along the marked line and baste about 1 cm ($\frac{3}{8}$ in.) from the fold.

Stage 4   Turn the binding so that it lies over the raw edge and baste and slip-hem its free fold to the garment.

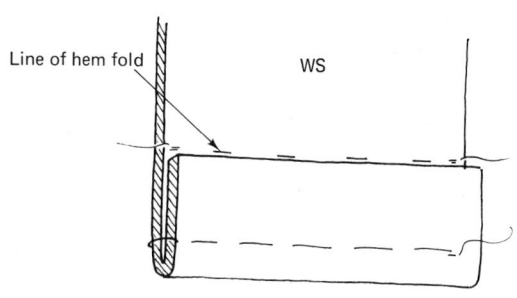

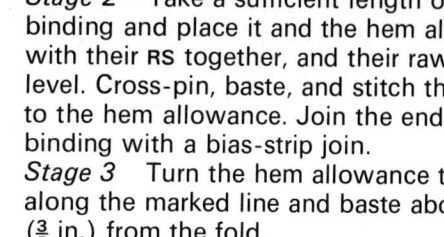

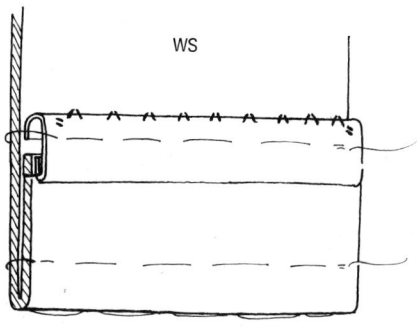

Hem bound with bias binding

Alternatively, seam binding may be creased in half lengthwise, and the raw edge of the hem allowance placed in the fold. Both edges of the binding are then stitched to the hem allowance in one operation. Care must be taken when using this method to keep the tension on the binding and the fabric even during stitching, or one or the other may buckle.

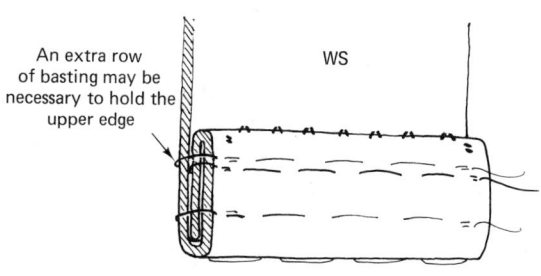

A bound hem is used on medium- and heavy-weight fabrics where a turned-in edge to the hem allowance would be too bulky. It may also be used on fabrics which unravel easily.

Stage 1   Trim the hem allowance to a convenient depth, usually about 5 cm (2 in.). Trim the seam allowances of the long seams to 6 mm ($\frac{1}{4}$ in.), from just on the garment side of the hemline to the raw edge.

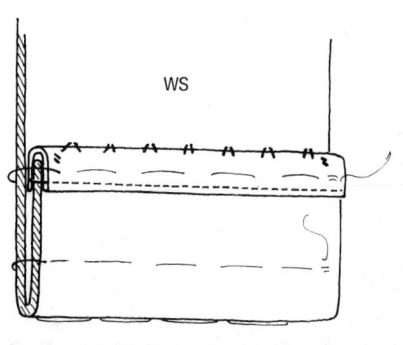

Hem bound with straight binding

A herringboned hem gives a flat finish in thick fabric and is recommended for bonded and stretch fabrics, where an elastic stitch is an advantage.

Stage 1   After marking the hemline, trim the hem allowance to an even depth, usually about 5 cm (2 in.). Trim the seam allowances of the long seams to 6 mm ($\frac{1}{4}$ in.), from just on the garment side of the hemline to the raw edge.

Stage 2   Turn the hem allowance to the WS along the marked line, pin, and baste 1 cm ($\frac{3}{8}$ in.) from the hem fold. With the work WS up, press the fold only.

Stage 3   Baste the hem to the garment 1 cm ($\frac{3}{8}$ in.) from its raw edge.

Stage 4   Sew the hem using herringbone stitch, taking care not to pull it too tight. Remove the basting.

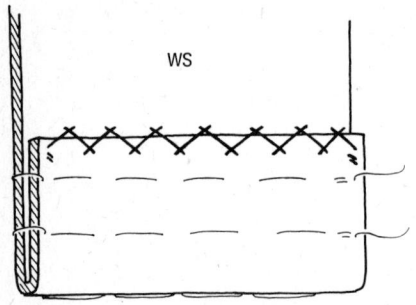

WS

A blindstitched hem is also called **a french dressmaker's hem.** It makes a flat finish suitable for medium- or heavy-weight fabrics. If the blindstitching is to be done by machine, test the stitch on a spare piece of fabric before working on the garment.

Stage 1   After marking the hemline, trim the hem allowance to an even depth, sufficient for a single fold, usually about 5 cm (2 in.). Trim the seam allowances of the long seams to 6 mm ($\frac{1}{4}$ in.) from just on the garment side of the hemline to the raw edge. Finish the raw edge of the hem allowance.

Stage 2   Fold the hem allowance to the WS. Pin and baste 1 cm ($\frac{3}{8}$ in.) from the hem fold. Working from the WS press the fold only.

Stage 3   Keeping the garment WS out, fold the hem line against the RS of the garment, so

that 1 cm ($\frac{3}{8}$ in.) of the edge of the hem allowance projects beyond the new fold. Baste through all layers to hold the turned-back hem in place.

Stage 4   Blindstitch the new fold, either by hand or machine, to the single thickness of the hem allowance. Remove the basting and press again if necessary.

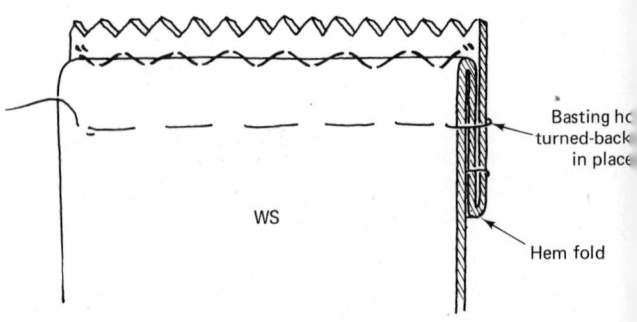

WS

Basting ho
turned-back
in place

Hem fold

A machine-stitched hem is used on garments such as aprons, jeans, and overalls. It is often made quite narrow, and in this form it can be used on a curved edge.

Stage 1   Trim the hem allowance to the depth of the finished hem plus 6 mm ($\frac{1}{4}$ in.). Trim the seam allowances of the long seams to 6 mm ($\frac{1}{4}$ in.) from just on the garment side of the hem fold to the raw edge.

Stage 2   Make the first fold of the hem 6 mm ($\frac{1}{4}$ in.) from the raw edge. Crease this fold to the WS and edge-stitch it.

Stage 3   Turn the hem allowance to the WS. Pin and baste.

Stage 4   Press the hem fold to set it into place, and stitch the hem from the WS, 3 mm ($\frac{1}{8}$ in.) from the first fold. Remove the basting.

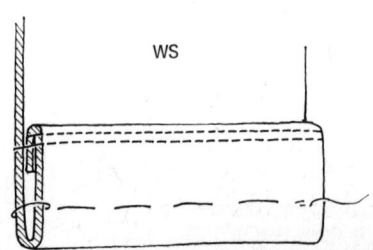

WS

A loop and blindstitched hem is
particularly suitable for jersey and soft fabrics.
The stitch forms an elastic knot which cannot
pull and indent the fabric.
Stage 1   After marking the hem line, trim the
hem allowance to an even depth, usually
about 5 cm (2 in.). Trim the seam allowances
of the long seams to 6 mm($\frac{1}{4}$ in.), from just on
the garment side of the hemline to the raw
edge. If necessary, finish the raw edge using
overcasting, loop stitch or crochet to prevent
fraying.
Stage 2   Turn the hem allowance to the ws,
and baste through both layers, 1 cm ($\frac{3}{8}$ in.)
from the fold. Press the fold only.
Stage 3   Baste the hem to the garment 6 mm
($\frac{1}{4}$ in.) from the finished edge. When the
fabric is very soft, to prevent the finished edge
from falling under its own weight, it should be
basted only 3 to 4 mm ($\frac{1}{8}$ in.) from the edge.
Stage 4   Turn back the free edge of the hem
allowance as far as the basting will permit,
and, holding it with the left thumb, fasten on
(see diagram). Place the thread under the left
thumb, and picking up one thread of garment
fabric close to the fold, pass the needle over
the loop of thread. Again place the thread
under the thumb, and taking a small stitch,
this time in the fold, pass the needle over the
loop. Make the stitches 6 to 8 mm ($\frac{1}{4}$ in.)
apart and do not pull them tight.

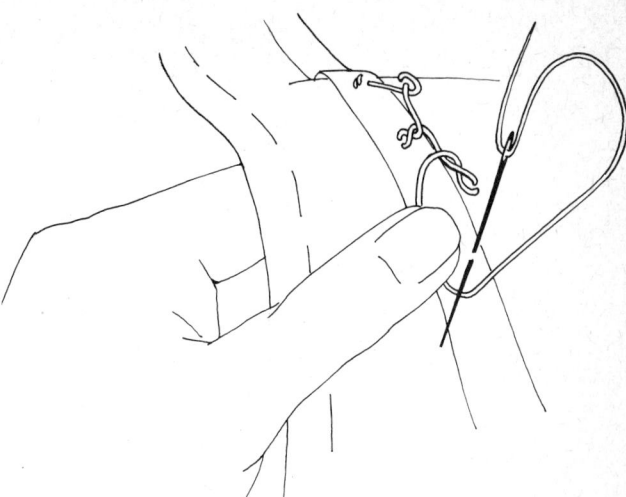

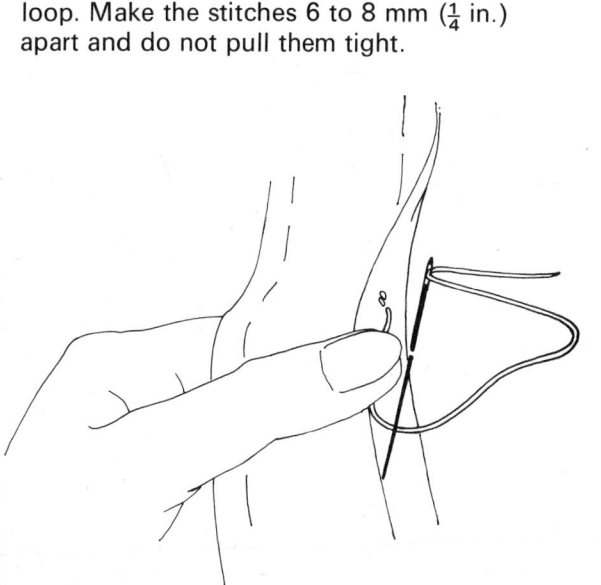

A hand-rolled hem is used to make a narrow
finish on straight or curved edges in sheer
fabrics. Although this hem requires a very
small allowance, it should not be trimmed
before it is machine stitched and the paper is
removed, as otherwise these operations will be
made more difficult.
Stage 1   Using a machine, stitch along the
hem allowance 3 mm ($\frac{1}{8}$ in.) from the hemline,
using tissue paper beneath the fabric to
prevent it from puckering. Remove the paper.
Stage 2   Trim the hem allowance 1 to 2 mm
($\frac{1}{16}$ in.) from the stitching.
Stage 3   Roll a short length of the edge to
the ws between the thumb and index finger so
that the line of stitching is just concealed, and
slip-hem the roll into place.

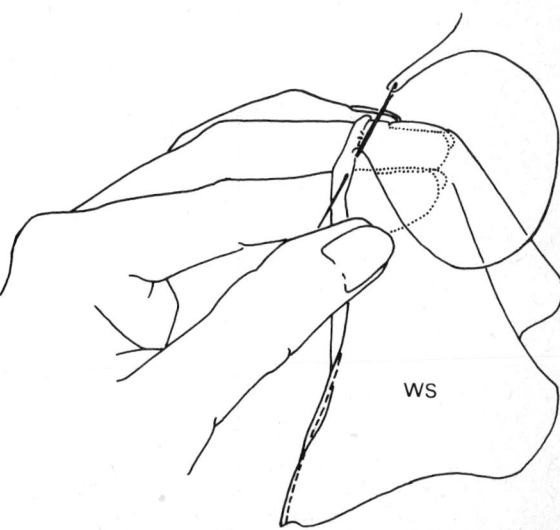

ws

The problem of a curved hem is that the distance along the convex edge of a piece of material is greater than any line parallel to it, to which that edge, when turned up, could be sewn. The art of making a successful curved hem lies in losing evenly and neatly, the difference between these lengths. This can be accomplished either by easing the edge or by darting the hem allowance. Another solution is to trim away almost the whole width of the hem allowance and finish the hem with a shaped facing, but it should be remembered that a hem treated in this way cannot be let down.

The width of the hem allowance, and the method by which it is handled, depends upon the amount of flare in the skirt. A 5 cm (2 in.) hem allowance can be eased satisfactorily if the skirt is a quarter circle or less. If the skirt is larger, the extra length will be more easily lost if the hem allowance is made narrower. A greater difference in length can be lost by darting than by easing, and this may be relevant if it is intended to let the skirt down at a later date.

An eased hem is suitable for garments made from wool, where some of the fullness can be shrunk away: it is equally satisfactory for light-weight materials.

When making this hem in thin fabric the raw edge of the hem allowance may be turned in and edge-stitched with a slackened top tension, so that the stitching not only finishes the edge but provides the easing thread. In thicker fabrics this technique would be too bulky, and a flatter finish can be achieved by ease-stitching through the single thickness 3 mm ($\frac{1}{8}$ in.) from the edge, and applying bias binding to finish the hem.

Stage 1 After marking the hemline, trim the hem allowance to an even depth. Trim the seam allowances of the long seams to 6 mm ($\frac{1}{4}$ in.), from just on the garment side of the hemline to the raw edge.

Stage 2 With the ws of the hem allowance uppermost put in the ease-stitching (see above).

Stage 3 Turn the hem allowance to the ws along the marked line, matching and pinning together the seam lines of the skirt and hem allowance. Baste 1 cm ($\frac{3}{8}$ in.) from the fold, and press the fold only.

Stage 4 Gently pulling up the easing thread in several places, adjust the folds, which should lie at right angles to the hemline, until the hem allowance lies flat and the fullness is evenly distributed. Care must be taken not to pull the edge up too much. Fasten off the loose loops of the easing thread with backstitches.

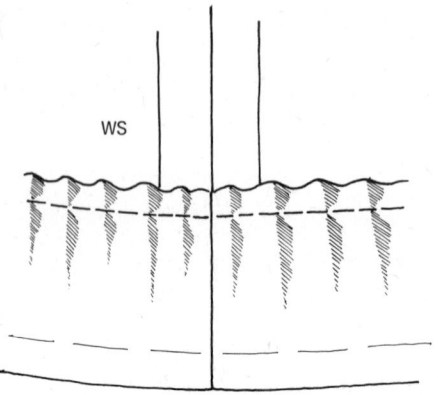

Stage 5 Apply the binding if the edge is to be bound.

Stage 6 Baste the hem allowance to the garment close to the eased edge, and slip-hem the fold into place.

Stage 7 Remove the basting and press the hem gently from the ws. Turn the work over, and press from the RS using a pressing cloth on top, and two layers of towelling underneath.

A darted hem may be made in light- and medium-weight fabrics, and should always be finished with a binding.

Stage 1 After marking the hemline, trim the hem allowance to an even depth. Trim the seam allowances of the long seams to 6 mm ($\frac{1}{4}$ in.), from just on the garment side of the hemline to the raw edge.

Stage 2 Turn the hem allowance to the ws along the marked line, matching and pinning together the seam lines of the skirt and hem allowance. Baste 1 cm ($\frac{3}{8}$ in.) from the fold and press the fold only.

Stage 3 Arrange and pin small darts in the hem allowance so that they lie flat against the ws of the skirt, and are at right angles to the hemline. (See diagram). Any dart which is large enough for its point to reach the hemline should be divided.

Stage 4   Baste each dart firmly to its underlap (not to the body of the garment), and hem along the outer fold of each dart. The inner fold may be snipped, and the dart pressed open if the fabric is bulky, but this should not be done if the skirt may need to be let down.

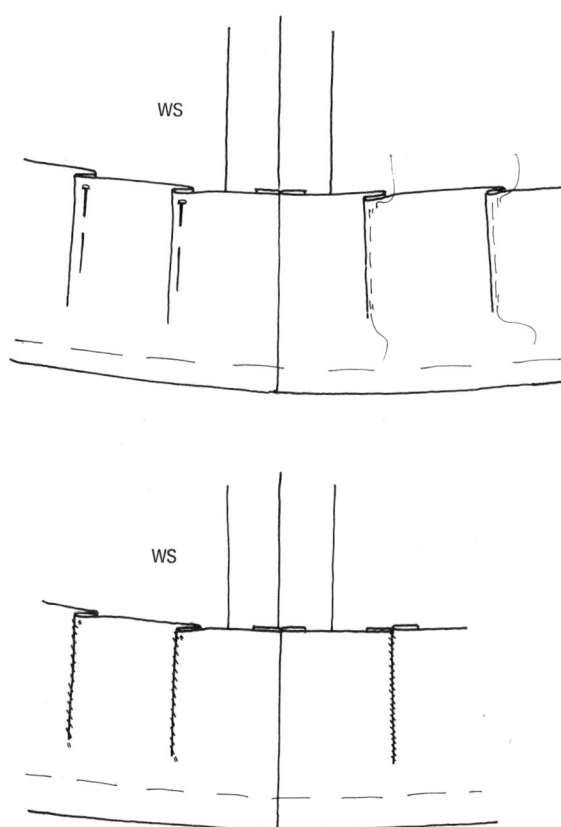

Darts finished by being pressed to one side

Darts finished by being pressed open

Stage 5   Apply bias binding to the raw edge of the hem allowance. Baste and slip-hem the free fold of the binding to the garment.

Stage 6   Press the darts lightly from the WS. Turn the work over, and press from the RS using a pressing cloth on top, and two thicknesses of towelling underneath.

A shaped facing is the best method of finishing strongly curved hems. A strip cut on the true bias may be used, but it should not be more than 1·2 cm ($\frac{1}{2}$ in.) wide when finished. When a wider facing is required, it must be cut to the same curve as the hem line. When working with thick fabrics the facing should be cut from thinner matching material.

Stage 1   After marking the hemline, trim the hem allowance to 1 cm ($\frac{3}{8}$ in.). Trim the seam allowances of the long seams to 6 mm ($\frac{1}{4}$ in.), from just on the garment side of the hemline to the raw edge. Zigzag stitch or overcast the raw edge if the fabric frays easily.

Stage 2   Cut out the facing and join all but one of its seams, or join sufficient lengths of bias strip. In either case they must be wide enough for 6 mm ($\frac{1}{4}$ in.) seam allowances to be formed on each long edge. Crease these seam allowances to the WS.

Stage 3   Place the RS of the facing and garment together with their raw edges level. Cross-pin and baste, leaving enough overlap at each end to make a join.

Stage 4   Attach the facing to the hem allowance by stitching in the crease, remove the basting and make the final join.

Stage 5   Fold the hem allowance and the facing to the WS along the marked line, and baste 1 cm ($\frac{3}{8}$ in.) from the fold. Press the fold only.

Stage 6   If the facing is more than 2 cm ($\frac{3}{4}$ in.) deep, baste again close to its upper edge. Slip-hem the turned-in edge of the facing to the garment and remove the basting.

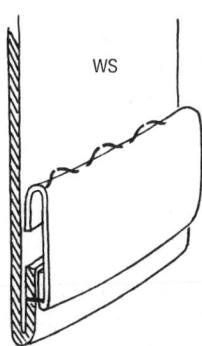

5 Fullness

Darts

Darts are tapered pleats which are used to shape a flat piece of fabric so that it will follow the contours of the body. A simple dart is pointed at one end and its other end is crossed by a seam. A double-ended, or contour, dart is pointed at both ends, and is used most frequently for shaping the waist section of a garment.

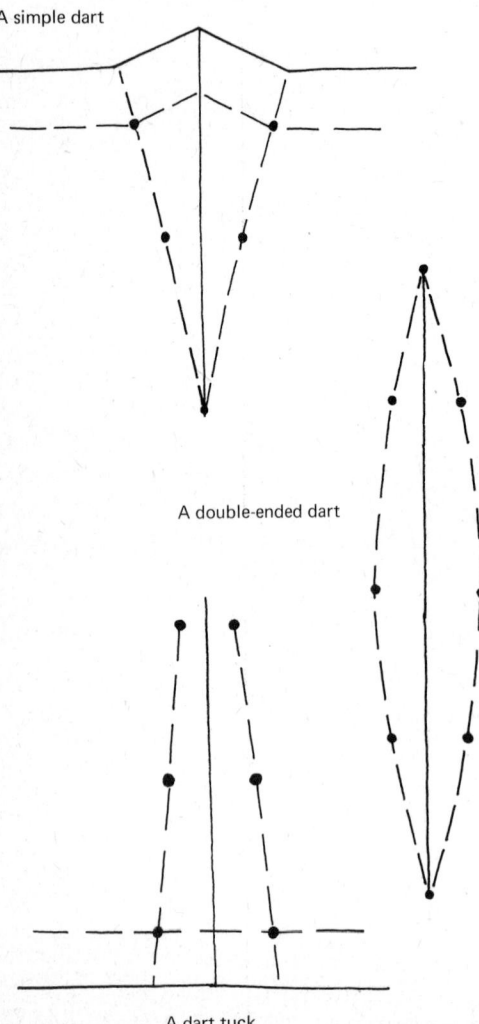

A simple dart

A double-ended dart

A dart tuck

Stage 1   Fold the fabric RS together along the centre line of the dart. Stab through each pair of tailor tacks with a pin to match them exactly before cross-pinning the stitching lines together.

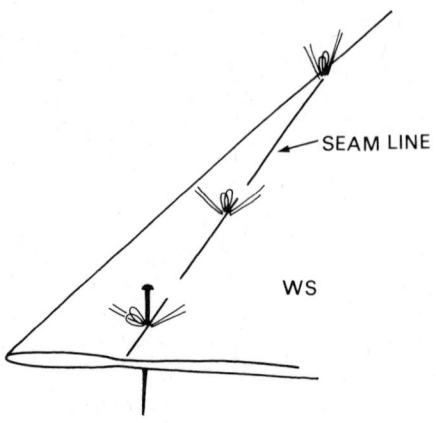

SEAM LINE

WS

Stage 2   Baste firmly 1 mm ($\frac{1}{16}$ in.) on the fold side of the stitching line, and remove the pins and tailor tacks.

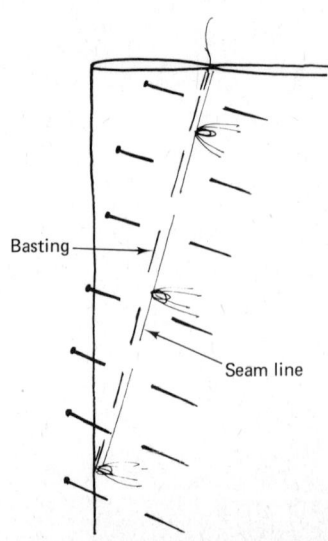

Basting

Seam line

Stage 3 Stitch just beside the basting (from the wide end if the dart has only one point). To make a smooth point, continue stitching along the fold for two or three stitches beyond the point of the dart. Sew in the thread ends and remove the basting.

fabrics darts are pressed so that their fullness is distributed equally on either side of the stitching line. Darts in bulky fabrics are cut along the fold line towards, but not quite to, the point. Stop cutting where the width of the dart fold narrows to about 4 mm ($\frac{3}{16}$ in.), and finish the cut edges.

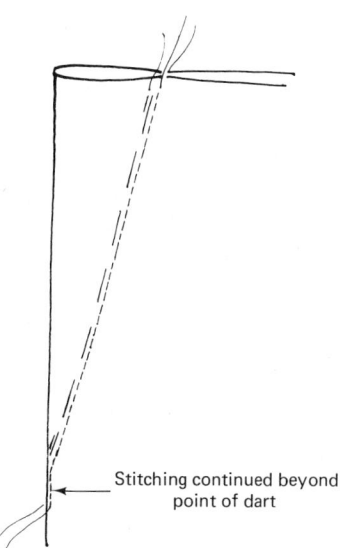

Stitching continued beyond point of dart

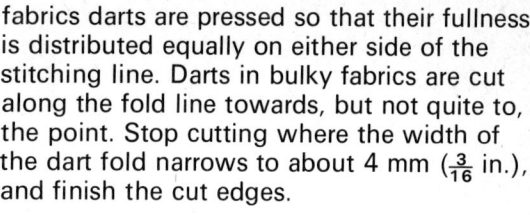
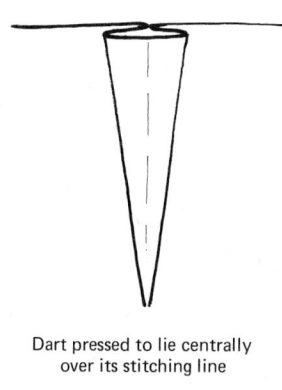

Dart pressed to lie centrally over its stitching line

Darts should always be pressed from the WS over a tailor's ham. Check from the RS that no fold has developed beside the stitching line. In most fabrics darts are pressed to one side. In the front of the garment they are pressed so that the fold of the dart points towards the CF, and in the back so that it points towards the CB: but unlike seam allowances, horizontal darts are pressed so that the fold points downwards. In sheer

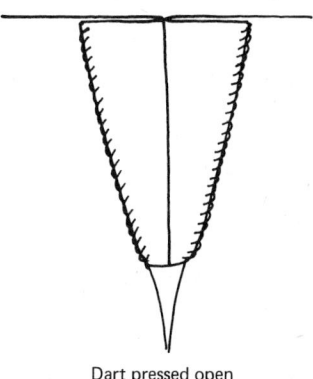

Dart pressed open

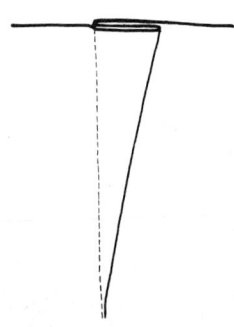

Dart pressed to one side

Double-ended, or contour, darts must be clipped at intervals from the fold towards the stitching line to release tension along the fold. They may be pressed to one side, or pressed open if the fabric is bulky.

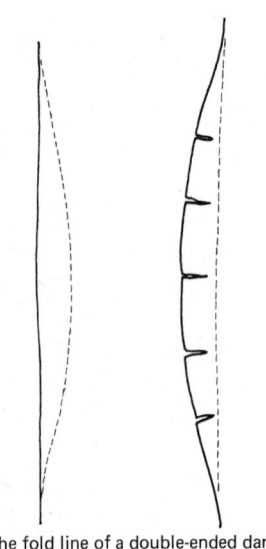

The fold line of a double-ended dart snipped to release tension

Dart tucks do not come to a point and are usually only slightly tapered. They are made in the same way as simple darts and are used to create a bloused effect. If the fold is to be pressed to one side the stitching may be finished either by pivoting through 90° and continuing to the edge of the fold, or by reversing the stitching at the end of the dart. This last technique should be used if the fullness is to be distributed equally on each side of the stitching line.

Curved darts are sometimes used to shape the bust or hip sections of a garment. For details of how to handle them refer to 'curved seams', page 36.

Tucks

Tucks are a simple way of decorating part of a garment. They are often used on children's clothes where they can be let out to allow for growth. In adult clothing, tucks are very much subject to fashion, and depending on the current 'look', they may be made on the straight grain of the fabric or on the bias, and may be wide or narrow.

Before attempting to make tucks on a garment for the first time, practise making some on a spare piece of material. In a large group of tucks there is a much greater chance of developing a cumulative error, than in a small one.

When planning to add blind tucks to a pattern, the breadth of the area to be tucked must be increased by three times to allow sufficient extra fabric, because a tuck has a show side and an under side, and needs a piece of the same width to lie on. When adding spaced tucks to a pattern, each tuck will require three times its width plus the distance from the fold of one tuck to the stitching line of the next.

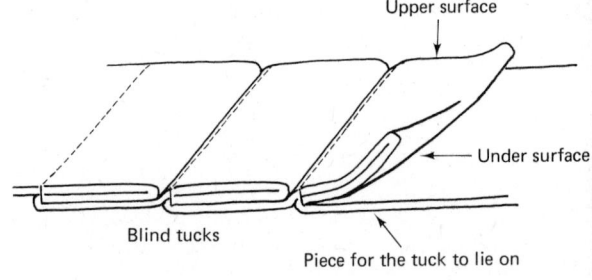

Upper surface

Under surface

Blind tucks

Piece for the tuck to lie on

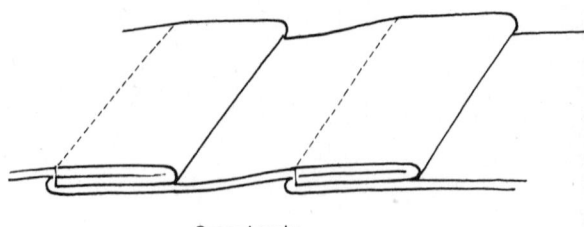

Spaced tucks

When making tucks accuracy is essential. A gauge cut from thin, stiff cardboard will be found very useful if a number of tucks have to be made. Each tuck fold in turn should be marked with fine pins. Tucks on the straight grain may be marked in some fabrics by pulling a single thread in the material at each outer fold. Always try this on a spare piece of the material first to see if it will be satisfactory. When marking tucks which are quite short, 5 to 10 cm (2 to 4 in.), it is sufficient to mark them at each end; longer ones should be marked every 10 cm (4 in.), and bias tucks every 5 cm (2 in.).

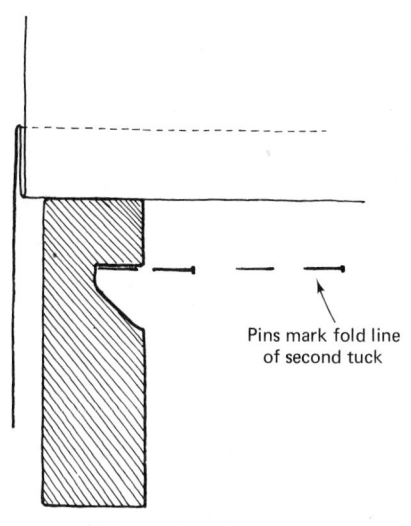

Pins mark fold line of second tuck

Using a tuck marker

Tucks are normally made in a garment piece before seaming it to any other, and always before any seam which runs across their ends is made. Begin working from the back edge of the group. For example, if the tucks are vertical ones, and will be pressed so as to point away from the CF, begin with the tuck nearest to the CF. This way of working makes it easy to keep a check on the distance between the previous fold and the new one.

Stage 1   Working from the RS mark the fold line of the first tuck. Fold the material WS together on this line and place it on an ironing board with the show side of the tuck downwards. Pin the fold to the board at each end to keep the fabric taut. Crease the tuck fold with an iron.

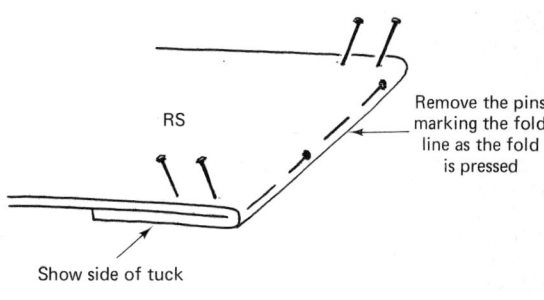

RS

Remove the pins marking the fold line as the fold is pressed

Show side of tuck

Stage 2   Unpin the material from the board, and cross-pin the tuck at intervals. The distance between the pins may be as much as 5 cm (2 in.) for crisp fabrics folded on grain, or as little as 1 cm ($\frac{3}{8}$ in.) for bias tucks in a soft fabric.

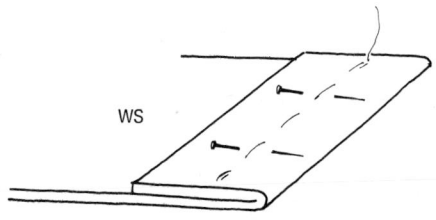

WS

Stage 3   Baste the tuck firmly the required distance from the fold. Remove the pins.

Stage 4   The tuck may be sewn by hand using small running stitches. Alternatively, use a quilting guide to keep the machine stitching parallel to the fold. Remove the basting.

A pintuck is a very narrow form of tuck, which is often hand sewn with running stitch, and which is never more than 3 mm ($\frac{1}{8}$ in.) wide. They give a delicate texture to light-weight and sheer fabrics.

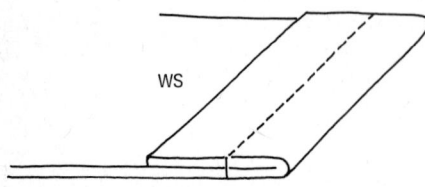

WS

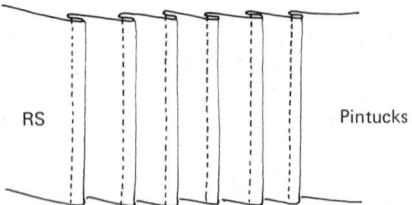

RS

Pintucks

Stage 5   Place the fabric on the ironing board, and press the material still to be tucked over the line of stitching so that it covers the tuck fold. Turn the work RS up and mark the next tuck fold. Repeat stages 2 to 6 until all the tucks are made.

This method will be found to work for soft and slippery fabrics as well as for firmer ones. In crisp fabrics such as poplin or gingham, it is quite possible, and quicker, to fold, press and baste all the tucks, and to stitch them as a group afterwards.

When making tucks check the evenness of the total width of the group after making each tuck, and take care that the material is not puckered by the parallel rows of stitching. When working in slippery fabric it will help to prevent a twist developing in the tucked area if each row is stitched in the opposite direction to the previous one.

Released tucks are used to provide a sudden burst of fullness, and may be arranged to release it at one or both ends. They are formed on the WS of the fabric, and the material at the ends is never creased to continue their line. To finish off the stitching of a tuck which will be pressed to one side, pivot through 90° at the end of the tuck and continue to the edge of the fold. Alternatively the stitching may be reversed for a short distance. This last method must be used when the fullness is to be equally distributed on either side of the stitching line.

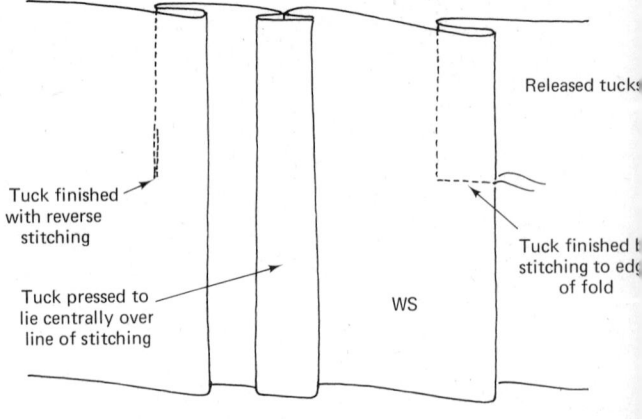

Released tucks

Tuck finished with reverse stitching

Tuck pressed to lie centrally over line of stitching

Tuck finished b stitching to edg of fold

WS

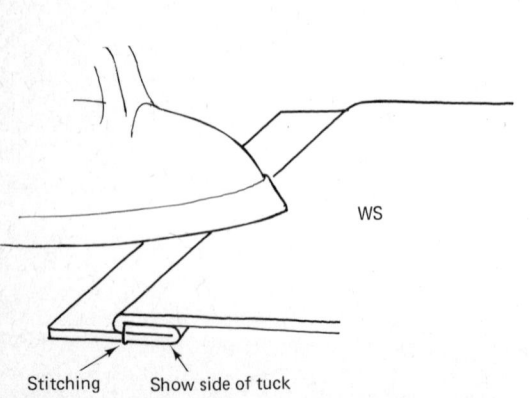

WS

Stitching   Show side of tuck

Shell tucks are always narrow — not more than 5 mm ($\frac{3}{16}$ in.) wide — and spaced. They are not pressed to one side, but are left to stand up, and are caught at regular intervals — 6 to 10 mm ($\frac{1}{4}$ to $\frac{3}{8}$ in.) — with pairs of stitches which pass over the tuck and catch it down giving a scalloped effect. The stitches must be evenly spaced so that the shell shape is regular. The thread running from one pair of stitches to the next is concealed inside the tuck.

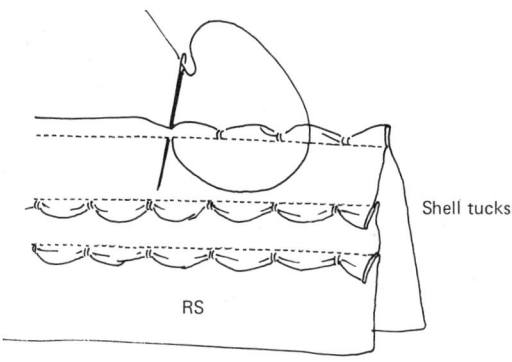

Shell tucks

RS

Cross tucks are always made spaced and at right angles to each other. The fabric is tucked before the garment piece is cut from it, the horizontal tucks being made first and pressed downwards: the vertical tucks are made second, and care must be taken to ensure that they are pressed in the correct direction.

Pleats

Pleats in their most basic form are parallel folds of material pressed to one side. These are called knife, or side pleats when they are arranged so that all the pleats lie in the same direction. A box pleat is a pair of knife pleats turned so that their outer folds point away from one another, and an inverted pleat is formed when they are turned to point towards one another. When estimating the amount of fabric required, allow three times the finished width of the pleats.

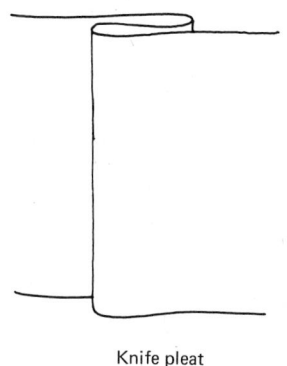

Knife pleat

Box pleat

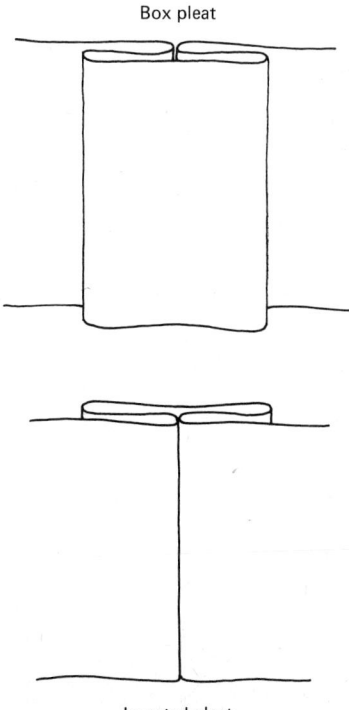

Inverted pleat

The simplest way of making pleats is merely to press them, but they can only be left in this state if no shaping is involved (as might be the case if they were attached to a hip yoke). Where pressed pleats are used, they must be stitched over the hip section to hold them in place if a smooth-fitting effect is required.

Accordion pleats, which are the only exception to this rule, are not pressed to one side because they are very narrow, but are left to stand up. Material can be purchased which has been pre-pleated in this way, but it may prove difficult to find if accordion pleats are not in fashion. It may also be possible to find a firm who will pleat a short length.

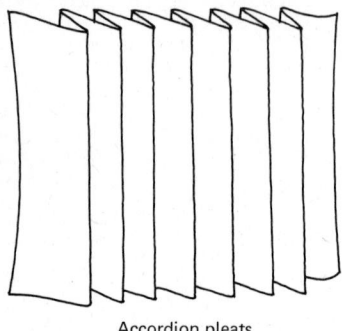

Accordion pleats

When marking pleats the most important parts are the fold line (known as a roll line in an unpressed pleat), and the placement line (see diagram). Pleat lines must be marked accurately because with a run of pleats it is easy to develop an error. The marking should extend for the full length of the pleats, except in the case of unpressed pleats which need to be marked for the top 15 cm (6 in.) only — just enough to make sure that they are correctly aligned.

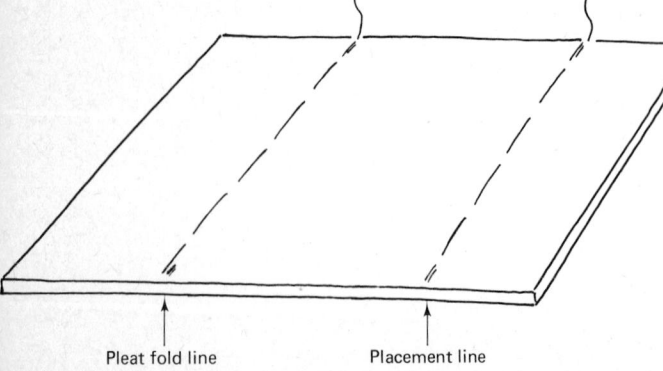

Pleat fold line   Placement line

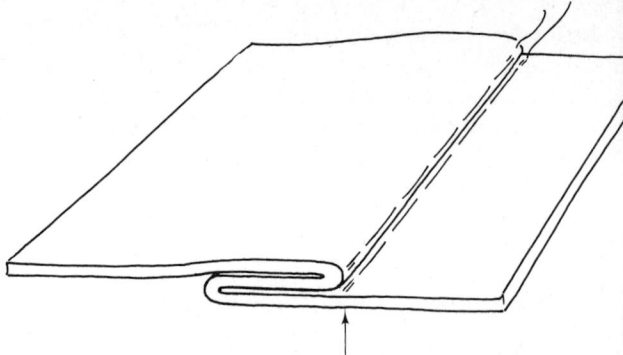

Pleat fold and placement lines brought together

If pleats are to be stitched, mark where the stitching will end, on the RS if the pleats will be top or edge stitched, and on the WS if the stitching will be concealed inside the garment. The outer fold line of each pleat must be exactly on the straight grain of the material, otherwise the pleat will not hang well. It may be possible to follow a thread in the weave of the fabric, or the line of a stripe or check if the design is a woven one, and to baste mark to a thread in this way. If this is not possible, a ruler and the sharp edge of a piece of tailor's chalk may be used instead. The following methods of marking pleat fold and placement lines, have proved reliable and require little equipment.

Arrange the garment piece RS up on an ironing board, making sure that the fabric is perfectly straight. Take a piece of mending cotton or thin string, a little longer than the lines to be marked, and rub a piece of tailor's chalk several times along it. Fasten one end round a pin, and pin it firmly to the ironing board exactly in line with the end of the fold to be marked. Hold the other end taut so that the string lies just against the surface of the fabric, and exactly along the line of the fold. Lift the centre of the string about 2 cm ($\frac{3}{4}$ in.), and release it so that it snaps back against the fabric. A fine chalk line will be formed which should be marked with uneven basting. Repeat the process, marking each fold in turn on either the RS or the WS.

A good method to use on fabrics with a busy pattern which would make the chalk line difficult to see, is to mark the lines with the aid of a strip of brown paper. Arrange the garment piece on a smooth, hard surface, with the fabric perfectly straight. Take a piece of brown paper, the same length as the pleat fold, and about 20 cm (8 in.) wide, and fold it in half lengthwise. Place the folded edge of the paper against the line of the pleat, and cross-pin the paper to the fabric. Mark exactly beside the folded edge with a row of uneven basting. Unpin the paper, move it to the next pleat line, and repeat.

When preparing to make up pleats it will be necessary to plan where they will come in relation to the skirt seams. If the pleats occur in isolated groups which do not include a seam, make them up before joining the skirt pieces together. However, if the pleats form a continuous run which crosses the seams, work the skirt opening and its seam first, and then join all but one of the other seams, so that the skirt may be laid out flat for pleating.

When the skirt will include a number of pressed or stitched pleats, the hem should be turned up before making them. The easiest way of establishing the hem line is to transfer the CF, CB, and side seam lengths from another skirt which fits. Remember to add 1·5 cm ($\frac{5}{8}$ in.) for the waist seam allowance and about 5 cm (2 in.) for the hem. Mark and turn up the hem, and baste it into place, leaving about 20 cm (8 in.) on each side of the unjoined seam unfinished.

The hem of a pleated garment needs to be as flat as possible, so that bumps do not show on the RS when the garment is finished. Where a seam, pleat and hem all coincide they should be notched and trimmed as shown in the diagrams.

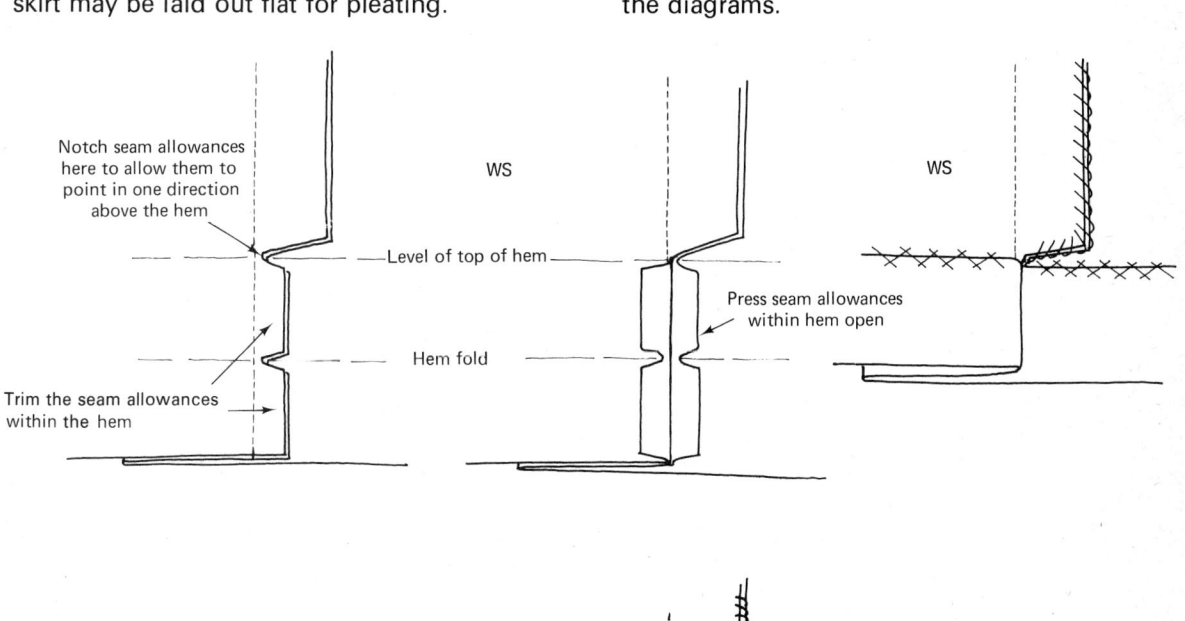

Notch seam allowances here to allow them to point in one direction above the hem

WS

WS

Level of top of hem

Press seam allowances within hem open

Hem fold

Trim the seam allowances within the hem

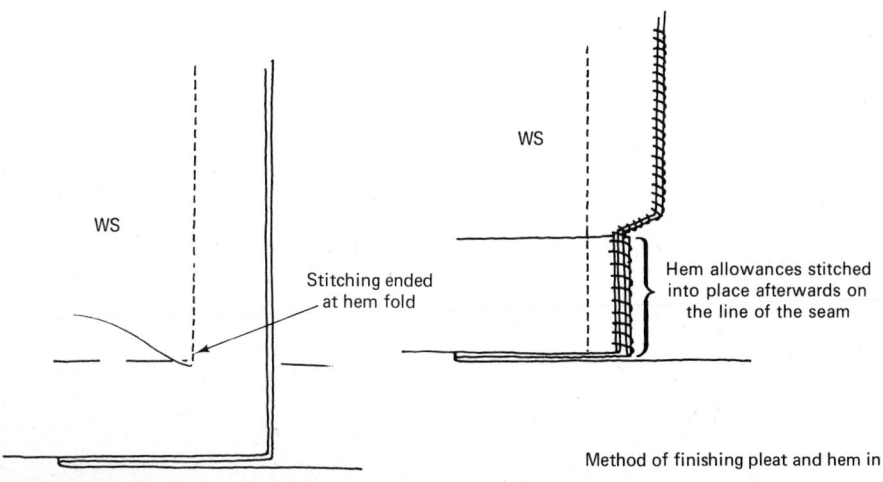

WS

WS

Stitching ended at hem fold

Hem allowances stitched into place afterwards on the line of the seam

Method of finishing pleat and hem in bulky fabric

Pressed and top-stitched pleats are used when a smooth-fitting hip section is required. The parts of the pleats which hang free may be merely pressed if the fabric is of a type which will retain pressed creases well, and the garment will be dry-cleaned. If this is not the case the pleats must be edge stitched (see next process) as well as being top stitched.

Stage 1   Baste mark the fold and placement lines on the RS of the fabric, and if there are a number of pleats in the skirt, mark and baste the hem.

Stage 2   Working from the RS form the fold line of each pleat, keeping the baste-mark exactly on the fold. Cross-pin, and baste each pleat fold about 5 mm ($\frac{3}{16}$ in.) from the edge. Remove the pins.

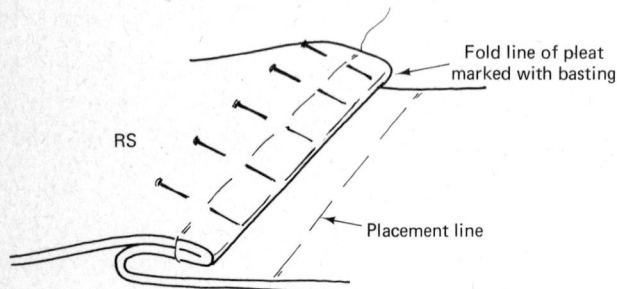

Fold line of pleat marked with basting

RS

Placement line

Stage 3   Arrange each pleat fold against its placement line, cross-pin, and baste it to its underlap for the length of the section which will be top stitched.

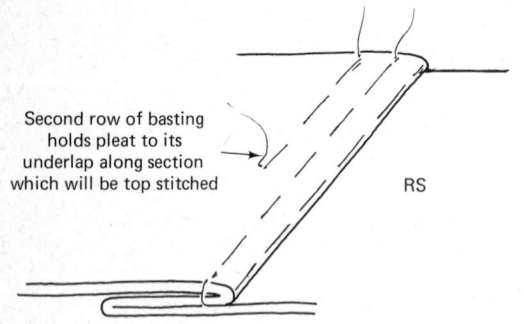

Second row of basting holds pleat to its underlap along section which will be top stitched

RS

Stage 4   Press the pleats lightly from both RS and WS.

Stage 5   Join the last seam and baste the remaining section of the hem.

Stage 6   Take a piece of petersham, or grosgrain ribbon, the same length as the waist measurement plus 5 cm (2 in.) for overlap, and baste it to the waistline seam allowance.

Stage 7   Fit the skirt (see section on adjusting pleats page 64).

Stage 8   After fitting, press any adjusted pleats into their new positions, and remove the temporary waistband.

Stage 9   If the pleats are to be top stitched: working towards the waist, stitch each pleat to its underlap along the edge of its outer fold. Finish off the thread ends firmly. If desired, bulk in the stitched section of the pleats may be reduced, and a stay fitted (see section on removing bulk page 65).

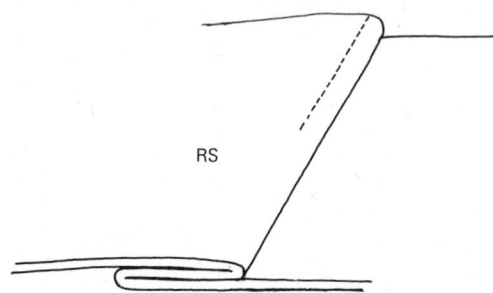

RS

Stage 10   Attach the waistband. Remove the basting and marking threads. Give the pleats a final thorough pressing from both RS and WS, slipping a strip of brown paper under the fold of each pleat to prevent its edge from marking the next one.

Edge stitching gives a crisp, permanent knife-edge finish, and is often used when materials are reluctant to retain pressed creases. The inner fold line of the pleat is stitched as well as the outer one, and the upper section of the pleat is top stitched. Experiment with edge stitching on a spare piece of material to arrive at a technique which will not pucker the fabric. A good result can usually be obtained if the fabric is kept under tension while stitching, but care must be taken with soft fabrics that the fold is not permanently stretched.

Follow the instructions for preparing pressed pleats as far as stage 8.

Stage 9   Turn the skirt WS out, and edge-stitch the entire length of each inner pleat fold, working from hem to waist.

Stage 10   Turn the skirt RS out. Edge-stitch each outer pleat fold from the hem line to 6 mm ($\frac{1}{4}$ in.) beyond the point where the top stitching will begin. Release the basting to allow this. Pull the thread ends through to the WS, and sew them in.

Stage 11   Still working up the skirt, top-stitch through each pleat and its underlap. Begin the top stitching at exactly the same level on each pleat, and overlap the end of the line of edge stitching. Draw the thread ends through to the WS and sew them in.

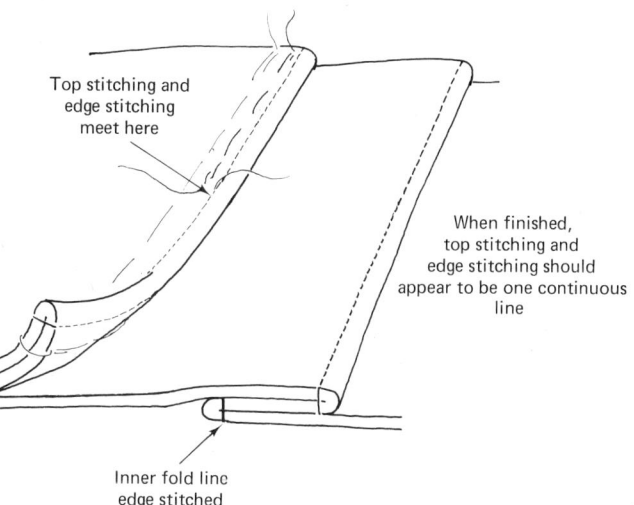

Top stitching and edge stitching meet here

When finished, top stitching and edge stitching should appear to be one continuous line

Inner fold line edge stitched

Stage 12   If desired, bulk in the top-stitched section may be reduced and a stay fitted (see page 65). Attach the waistband and remove all the basting and marking threads.

Pleats which are stitched from the WS
are sometimes used on the hip section of a skirt. Because the stitching is invisible they produce smoothness and shaping combined with a completely unfussy appearance.

Stage 1   Baste mark the fold and placement lines on the WS of the fabric, and if there are a number of pleats in the skirt, turn up the hem.

Stage 2   Folding the fabric RS together, match each fold line to its placement line, stabbing through with a pin to bring them exactly together. Cross-pin and baste each pleat along the line from the WS.

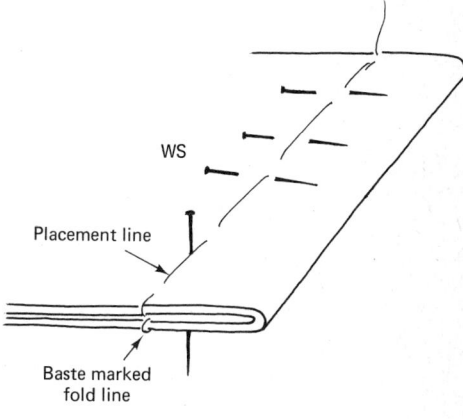

WS

Placement line

Baste marked fold line

Stage 3   Working from the WS, lightly press each pleat into place.

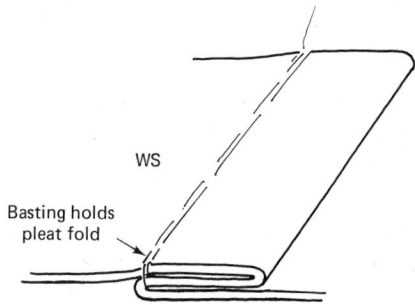

WS

Basting holds pleat fold

Stage 4   Join the remaining seam and complete the hem. Take a piece of petersham or grosgrain ribbon, the length of the waist measurement plus 5 cm (2 in.) for overlap, and baste it to the waistline seam allowance.

Stage 5   Fit the skirt (see page 64).

Stage 6   After fitting press any adjusted pleats into their new positions.

Stage 7   Remove the temporary waistband, and stitch the pleats from the WS along the fold/placement lines working up the skirt. In the case of an inverted pleat, the fold lines of a pair of knife pleats are stitched together from the WS.

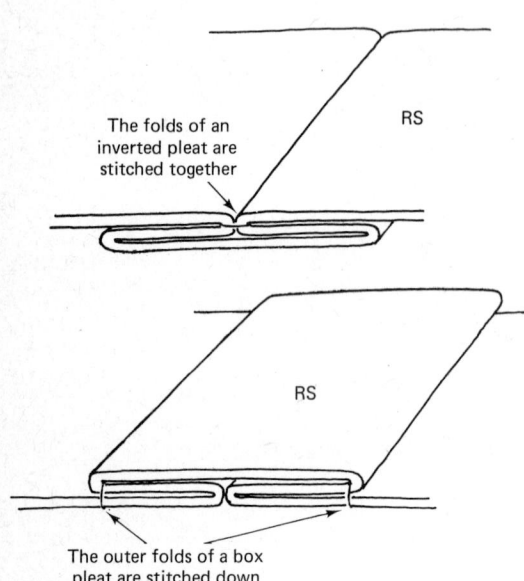

The folds of an inverted pleat are stitched together

RS

RS

The outer folds of a box pleat are stitched down

Stage 8   Remove the basting and thread marking before pressing. Take care when pressing inverted pleats treated in this way to distribute the fullness of the pleat equally on each side of the stitching line. If desired the pleat may be trimmed in the stitched section to reduce the bulk, and a stay fitted.
Stage 9   Attach the waistband.

Unpressed pleats must be made deep enough to hold their form for most of the length of the skirt. They look well in softly draping fabric, and are practical for garments which will be laundered. Join all the seams except one so that the skirt can be laid flat for pleating, but because the pleats are neither pressed nor stitched, the hem may be levelled and turned up last in the usual way.

Carry out stages 1 to 3 of making 'pressed and top-stitched pleats' (see page 62), confining the marking and basting to the top 15 cm (6 in.) of the pleats.
Stage 4   Baste firmly across the tops of the pleats along the waist seamline.

Stage 5   Join the remaining seam, and taking a piece of petersham, or grosgrain ribbon, the length of the waist measurement plus 5 cm (2 in.) for overlap, baste it to the waist seam allowance.
Stage 6   Try the skirt on and make any necessary adjustments. Remove the temporary waistband.
Stage 7   Stitch along the middle of the waistline seam allowance to hold the tops of the pleats in place. Attach the waistband, and remove all the basting and marking threads. Unpressed pleats may be set if the garment is put on a dress form, and the pleats steamed and smoothed into place.

When adjusting a pleated skirt at the hips or waist, release the basting which holds the pleat to its underlap, and move the pleat as a unit relative to its placement line. Never alter the position of the pleat fold in the fabric. When there are several pleats close together, make the adjustment by moving each of them by a small amount, so that the distance between the outer fold of one pleat and the next is only slightly altered. A skirt with stitched-down pleats should be a good fit over the upper part of the hips, but it should not be so tight that it pulls when the wearer is seated. If the hem was turned up before the pleats were made, check the hem level when trying on the skirt. If part of the hem is not level, mark the adjustment to be made with pins. Alter the level at the hemline; do not attempt to correct it by raising or lowering the pleats at the waist because their hang will be upset.

A pleat with a separate underlay is often used where the design includes a single inverted pleat, because it is more economical on material.
Stage 1   Baste the RS of the two skirt pieces together along the pleat fold lines, and use a machine to stitch the seam from the top of the pleat opening to the waistline. Press the seam and pleat allowance open.
Stage 2   Lay the garment WS up, and place the pleat underlay RS down on the pleat allowance, matching tailor tacks.
Stage 3   Pin and baste the underlay and pleat allowances together, working up the sides, and across the top stopping at the skirt seam. Stitch and remove the basting.

Stage 4   Turn the hem up. (For the treatment of seam allowances in hems, see page 61).
Stage 5   Stay the top edge, if the underlay has not been cut to include a stay.

come through to the RS. The edges of the pleats may be graded, as well as trimmed, to avoid forming a ridge.

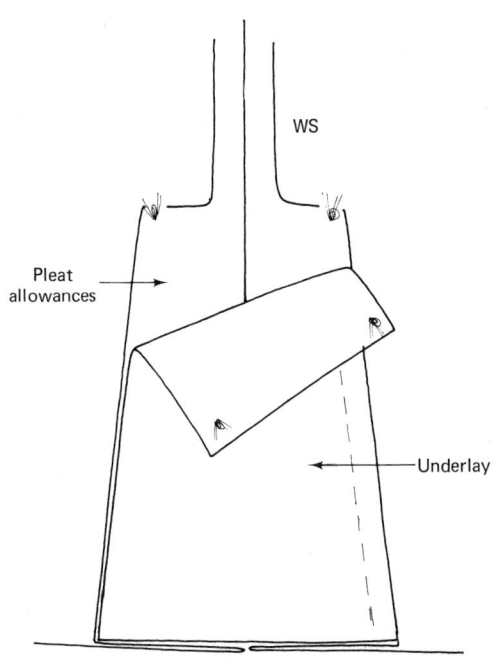

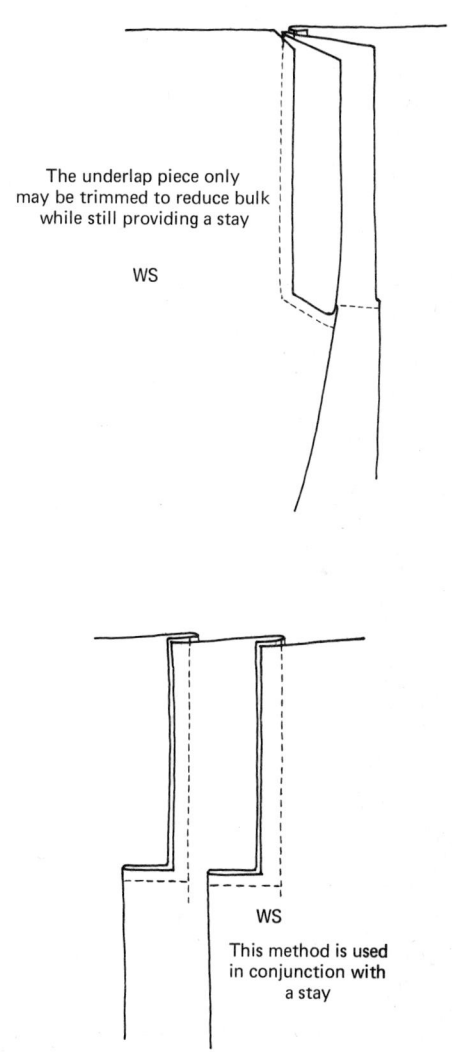

The underlap piece only may be trimmed to reduce bulk while still providing a stay

WS

WS

This method is used in conjunction with a stay

Pleats should be trimmed to reduce bulk before the waistband is attached. Groups of pleats which are stitched for part of their length may be reduced in bulk by trimming away part of the inside of the pleat as shown in the diagrams. The stitching, which runs across the pleat at the lower end of the trimming, holds the pleat only and does not

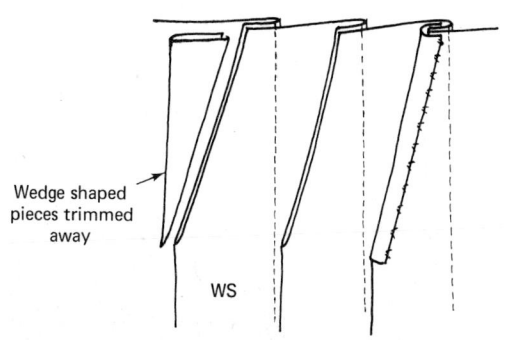

Wedge shaped pieces trimmed away

WS

This method of finishing knife pleats does not require a stay

Pleats must be stayed if it has been necessary to trim part of the top of the pleats away to reduce bulk. If the top of the pleat has not been trimmed the weight of the pleat is supported by the waistband. The stay should be constructed from lining material, making a narrow hand- or machine-sewn hem on the two vertical sides and across the lower edge. If the stay is a wide one, its top edge should be darted to follow the contour of the skirt. Baste the upper edge of the stay to the waist seam allowance, and its lower edge to the horizontal stitching which holds the pleats. It is important that the stay should not pull on the pleats because it will prevent them from setting properly; but neither should it be loose because then it will not provide the pleats with proper support. After trying on the skirt to check the set of the stay, its lower edge may be slip hemmed or herringboned to the pleats along the machine-stitched line.

Pleats should be strengthened at the point where their stitching ends if this comes below hip level. This is especially important in isolated pleats such as CB or side front ones. One method is to baste a small piece of tailor's canvas or strong tape to the WS at the point where the stitching ends, and stitch it with the pleat. Extra lines of stitching may be used instead. These can take the form of either a horizontal line about 1 cm ($\frac{3}{8}$ in.) long or a small triangle at the end of the stitched

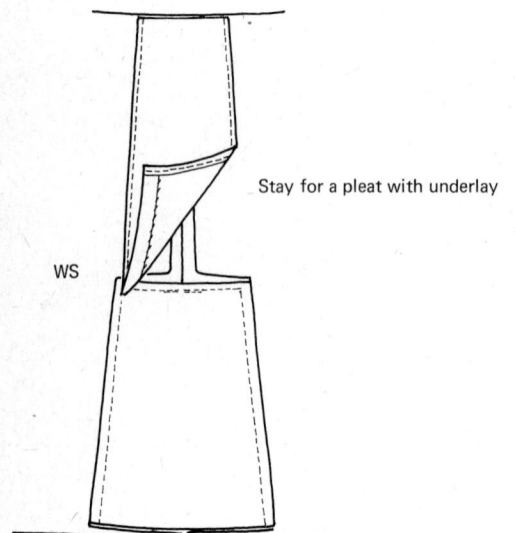

Stay for a pleat with underlay

WS

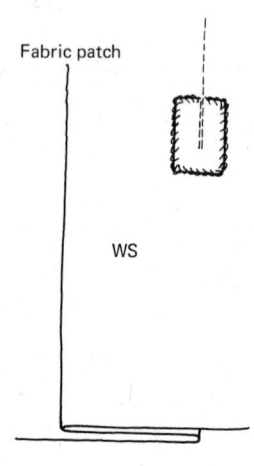

Fabric patch

WS

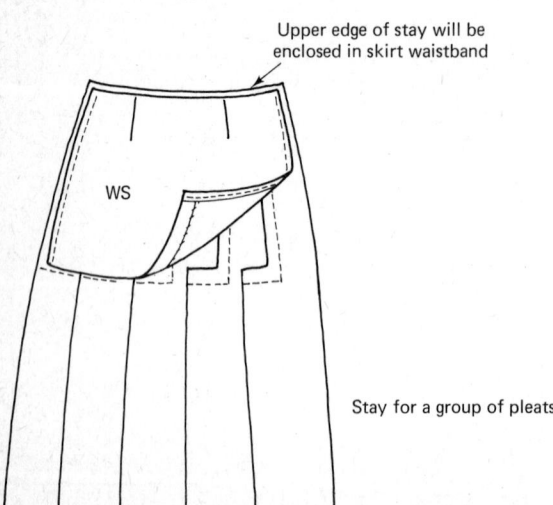

Upper edge of stay will be enclosed in skirt waistband

WS

Stay for a group of pleats

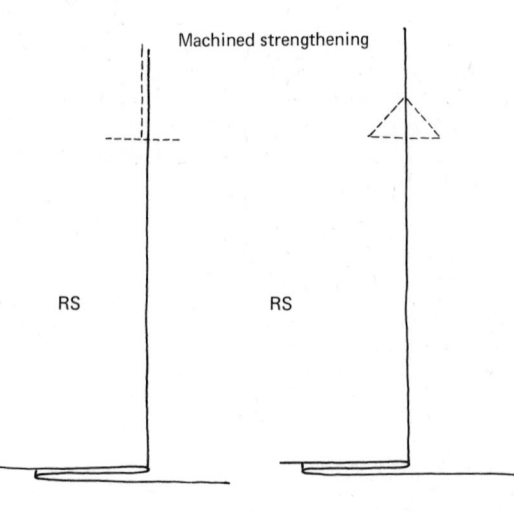

Machined strengthening

RS

RS

section of the pleat. The most decorative form of strengthening is to embroider an arrowhead on the RS, but this can only be used at the top of an inverted pleat or pleat with underlay where the outer surfaces are level. When making an arrowhead, outline the triangle with basting before beginning. The stitches should lie close together. as in satin stitch. Continue working the stitches until the triangle at the base is filled in. A bar tack may be used to strengthen the top of a knife pleat.

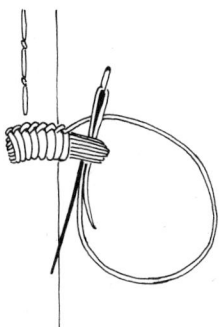

Bar tack.
Pass the needle under the threads eye-end first to avoid dividing the threads

Arrow head

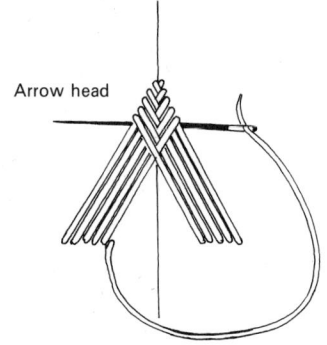

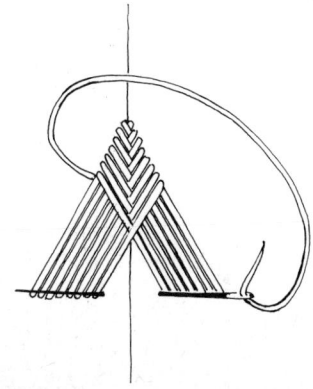

Easing and gathering

Easing and gathering differ from each other only in the amount of material which is drawn up – the technique used in each case is the same. An edge which has been gathered or eased is always set into a seam. Easing is used where subtle shaping is required; gathers, on the other hand, are used where sudden fullness is a feature of the design.

Put in two rows of stitching along the edge to be eased or gathered, one on the seam line and the other in the centre of the seam allowance. If the threads are to be put in by hand, fasten on firmly and sew with even running stitches. These stitches must line up in the two rows. If the material is fine use 2 mm ($\frac{1}{16}$ in.) stitches; if it is heavy use double thread and 4 mm ($\frac{1}{8}$ in.) stitches. In either case, each row of stitches must be made with a single length of thread which should be long enough for 5 cm (2 in.) of thread to be left after the row is completed, and before the material is pulled up.

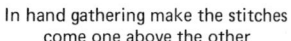

In hand gathering make the stitches come one above the other

If the stitching is done by machine use a stitch setting of 4 to 5 mm (5 to 6 stitches per inch), and slacken the top tension so that the fabric may be pulled up on the under thread. After putting in the rows of stitching bring all the ends through to the same side of the fabric and secure both rows of stitching at the same end.

Whether the stitching is put in by hand or machine, the fabric must be pulled up on the two rows of stitching at the same time, because once it has been pulled up on one thread, it is almost impossible to adjust the second one to the same tension. After pulling the fabric up to reduce the section to the correct length, but before attempting to distribute the fullness evenly, secure the free ends by twisting them, in the shape of a figure of eight, round a pin.

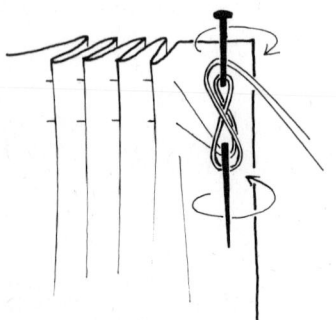

Making the gathering thread
fast round a pin

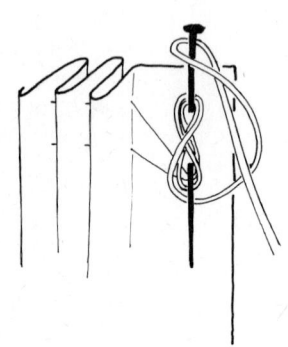

If a seam allowance were to be sewn in with a group of gathers, the double thickness of material would prevent their even distribution at this point. Therefore, when a seam runs into an edge which is to be gathered, put in the rows of gathering stitches right up to the seam, folding the seam allowance out of the way. Break off the threads leaving an end long enough to hold when pulling up the section. Fold the seam allowances the other way, and start the stitching again just on the other side of the seam. When using running stitch the seam allowance may be avoided without interrupting the stitching.

Distributing gathers and ease
Stage 1   Before gathering a long edge it should be divided into quarters, or even eighths, and the edge or band to which the gathers will be attached should be divided in

the same way. The divisions should be marked with tailor tacks, because these will remain clearly visible after the gathers are pulled up.
Stage 2   Draw up the fabric to the same overall length as the band or garment edge, and placing them RS together, adjust the gathers so that each pair of tailor tacks matches. Cross-pin these points together. It will then be easy to distribute evenly the short spans of gathers between the tailor tacks.
Stage 3   Cross-pin the gathered section to the band or garment edge at 1 cm ($\frac{3}{8}$ in.) intervals, and then baste firmly just beside the stitching line. Take care not to push the gathers out of place.
Stage 4   When possible, keep the gathered side uppermost during stitching so that it can be watched and prevented from becoming twisted. Always examine the seam from the RS after stitching to check that no unwanted pleats have formed. Remove the gathering threads if they show on the RS.
Stage 5   Because the bulk of tightly packed gathers can cause an unsightly ridge, the seam allowance of a gathered section which is to be enclosed within a band may be tapered off by a form of grading (see diagram). When it is not enclosed the best solution is to trim the gathered seam allowance to 6 mm ($\frac{1}{4}$ in.) and either bind it, or self-finish it using the other seam allowance.

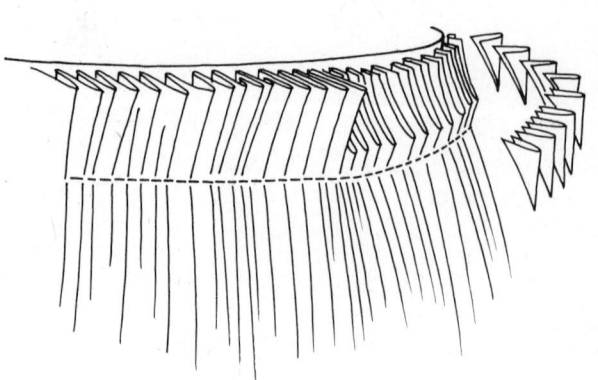

Grading gathers to reduce bulk

Shirring

This is a decorative method of controlling
fullness. It is popular on children's dresses
because it allows for movement and growth,
and on teenagers' summer dresses because a
fitted effect can easily be achieved without
elaborate cutting. Rows of shirring may be
evenly spaced, arranged in groups, or made to
cross each other to form diamonds or squares.

Fine, round shirring elastic can be
purchased in a variety of colours. Before
shirring a garment, experiment with a
measured piece of fabric to discover how
much it is reduced by different stitch lengths.
As a general guide, in light-weight cotton, a 2
mm stitch (12 stitches per inch) will reduce
the fabric to about three-quarters of its
unshirred width, and a 4 mm stitch (6 stitches
per inch) will reduce it to about half. Aim to
shirr the garment so that the elastic is only
slightly stretched when the garment is on.

Wind the shirring elastic onto the bobbin by
hand so that there is no tension on the elastic.
Test this by letting go of the end; if it springs
undone it is under tension and must be
re-wound. The fabric must be shirred RS up.
The lines to be shirred may be marked lightly
on the fabric, or a quilting guide may be used.
The fabric must be held taut under the presser
foot while each successive row of shirring is
put in. Always pull out a sufficient length of
elastic for fastening off at the end of each
row. If the elastic is under tension when it is
cut, its end will spring back through the hole
in the needle plate. Each row should be
finished off by firmly tying the thread to its
elastic on the WS of the fabric.

Rows of shirring should begin and end on a
seam allowance so that the ends of the elastic
are caught into the seam when it is made.
This means that these seams cannot be
stitched before the shirring is completed. Any
seams, however, which will be crossed by the
shirring must be joined; and the seam
allowances pressed open, their raw edges
finished, and basted to the garment fabric to
keep them flat; before the shirring is begun. If
the shirring comes close to a hem, as it might
at the end of a sleeve, make the hem before
shirring the area.

Sometimes the edge of a shirred area will
need to be joined to a piece which is not
shirred with a seam which will run parallel to
the rows of shirring. Place the last row of
shirring 6 mm ($\frac{1}{4}$ in.) from the seam line, and
stretch the shirred edge to make it the same
length as the plain edge when seaming the
two together.

Godets

Godets are triangular pieces of fabric which are used to give flared fullness to an edge, usually the hem of a skirt. They may be set into a slash or into a seam. A godet is usually cut with its centre line on the straight grain of the fabric, and with a normal seam allowance. The seam line on each straight edge should be equal to the length of the slash before the hem is turned up. The triangle at the tip may be trimmed off to leave a normal seam allowance above the place where the seam lines meet. The base of a wide godet should be cut to a shallow curve, to allow for its flared shape when the hem is turned up.

Sometimes godets are cut with their centre line on the bias for decorative effect. When this is done the godet should be suspended by a point 3 to 4 cm (1½ in.) below its upper end and allowed to hang for a day or two, so that the fabric can drop before it is inserted.

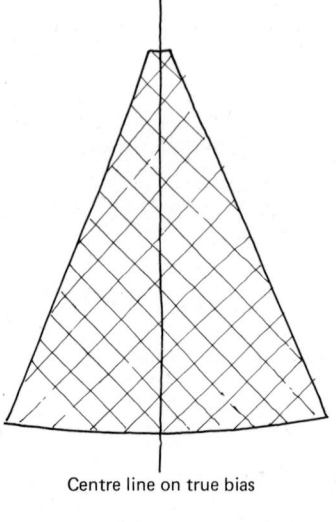

Centre line on true bias

Godet cut on the bias

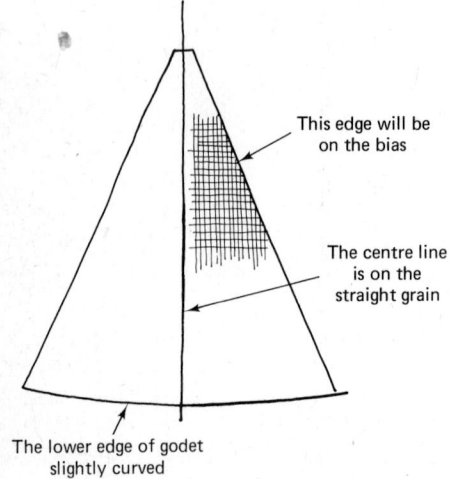

This edge will be on the bias

The centre line is on the straight grain

The lower edge of godet slightly curved

Godet cut on the straight grain

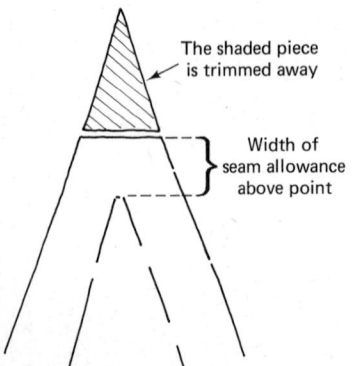

The shaded piece is trimmed away

Width of seam allowance above point

A godet must be set into a slash with care and precision if a good result is to be obtained. These instructions include a facing because most woven fabrics will fray enough to make the seam allowance, which is extremely narrow at the point of the slash, difficult to handle.

Stage 1 On the godet, mark the point at which the seamlines meet with a tailor tack, and stay-stitch its edges. On the garment piece, mark the end of the slash line with a tailor tack, and mark the line of the slash with a basting thread.

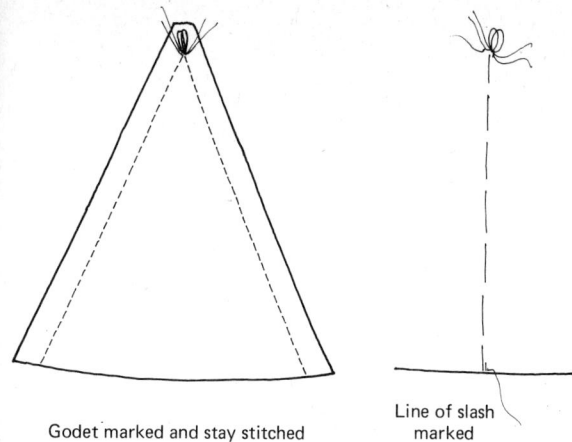

Godet marked and stay stitched

Line of slash
marked

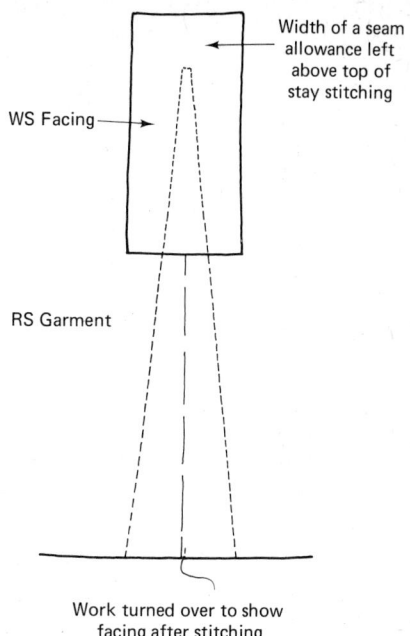

Width of a seam
allowance left
above top of
stay stitching

WS Facing

RS Garment

Work turned over to show
facing after stitching

Stage 2   Cut a strip of self fabric on the
straight grain, two seam allowances wide by
10 cm (4 in.) long, to form the facing, but if
the garment fabric is bulky, cut the piece
from thinner, matching fabric.

Stage 3   Place the facing and garment RS
together, with the facing positioned centrally
over the upper end of the slash line, and so
that it extends beyond the tailor tack by the
width of a seam allowance. Pin the facing
into place.

Stage 4   With the facing underneath, stay-
stitch on each side of the marked line. Begin
at the hem edge, where the stitching should
be the width of a seam allowance from the
marked line. The stitching should converge
with the slash line so that they are between 1
and 2 mm ($\frac{1}{16}$ in.) apart at the point. Shorten
the stitch to 1 mm (25 stitches per inch) for 2
cm ($\frac{3}{4}$ in.) on each side of the point. The
point cannot be a perfect one. Take 1 to 3
stitches across when turning to allow for the
width of the slash.

Stage 5   Cut along the line of the slash right
to the point but take care not to cut through
the stitching.

Stage 6   Working from the RS, press the
facing towards the slash so that the seam is
brought to the fold. Turn the facing to the WS,
easing it through at the point and gently
pulling it into shape until it lies flat. Press

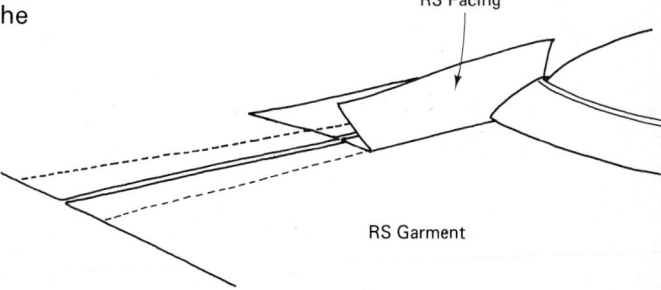

RS Facing

RS Garment

again, rolling the seam just to the WS. Press the rest of the seam allowance to the WS.

seam allowances together, turn the work so that the garment seam allowance is on top. Cross-pin working from point to hem. Match first the tailor tacks at the point and then the stay stitching. Baste. Match and baste the other edge similarly.

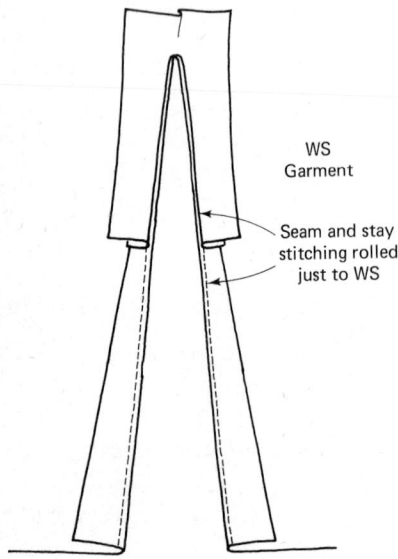

WS Garment

Seam and stay stitching rolled just to WS

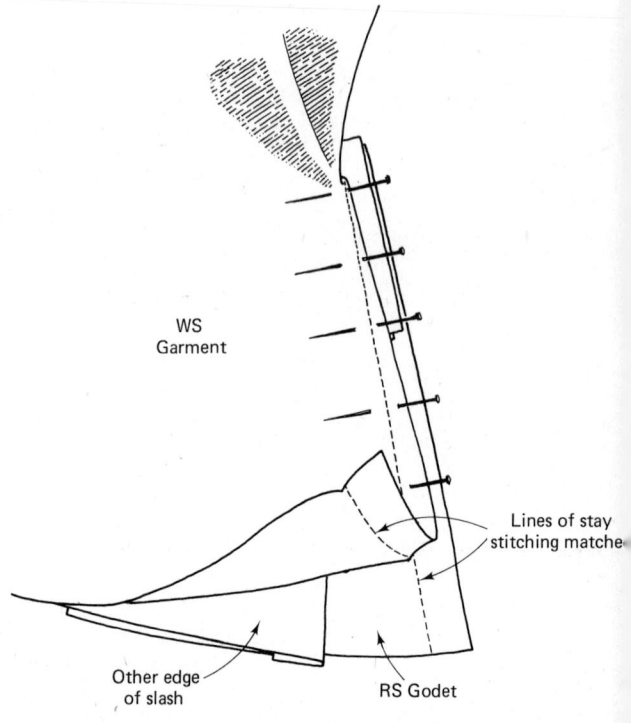

WS Garment

Lines of stay stitching matched

Other edge of slash

RS Godet

Stage 7 Lay the garment piece WS up, and the godet, also WS up, on it. Arrange the godet so that one of its seam allowances lies on the turned-back seam allowance of the corresponding edge of the slash. Holding the

Stage 8 With the godet underneath, stitch each side from point to hem on the garment side of the stay stitching and just touching it. Use a short stitch for the first 2 cm ($\frac{3}{4}$ in.). Remove the basting threads and press.

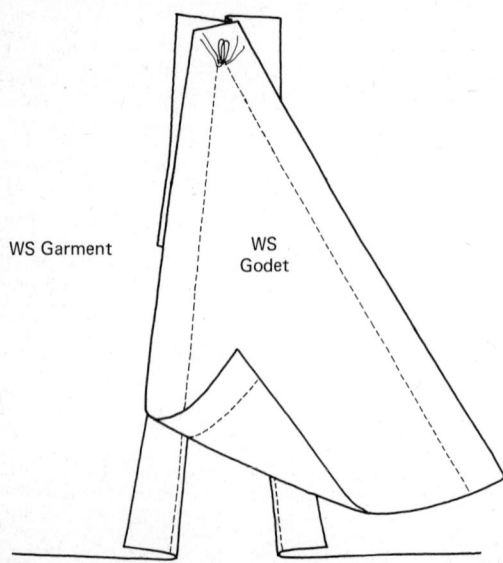

WS Garment

WS Godet

Stage 9 The godet seam allowances may be snipped 5 cm (2 in.) from the point and the seam allowances below this pressed open, above the snip they must be pressed away from the point. Alternatively the edge fold may be top stitched.

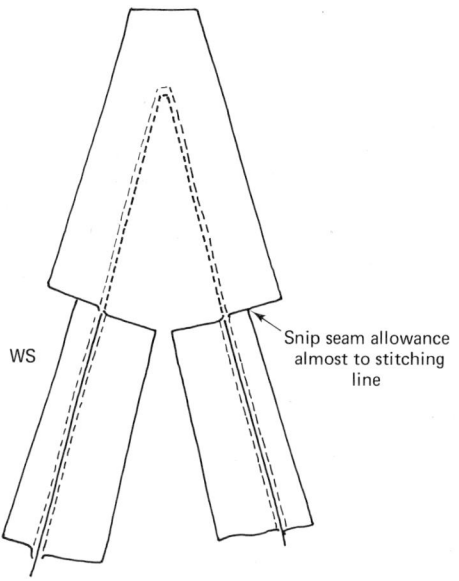

WS

Snip seam allowance almost to stitching line

Godets set into a seam are treated in much the same way as those set into a slash. No facing or stay stitching is required on the garment piece and its raw edges may be matched with those of the godet, because the normal width of seam allowance is present on both pieces. The godet, however, should be stay stitched.

Make the seam in the garment, ending the stitching at the point where the godet will begin. Finish off the thread ends. Press the seam open, and continue along the unjoined part of the seam pressing the seam allowances to the ws. Position and baste the godet into the seam as described in stage 7 above.

With the garment piece on top, stitch each side from point to hem, working in the crease and being careful to begin exactly where the stitching of the seam ends. Notch the seam allowances at the point as shown in the diagram.

A stay has the effect of throwing the fullness of a godet outwards, and it also relieves the point of the slash from strain. Cut a triangular piece of lining fabric or fine cotton 7 to 8 cm (3 in.) high, the width of its lower edge being a little less than the width of the godet at that point. The edges of the stay should be finished by hand so that they are soft and flat. Stitch the stay to the point of the completed godet, just on the seam allowance side of the stitching line. When fitting a stay, the seam allowances which it covers must be pressed so that they point away from the godet. The seam allowances below the base of the stay may be clipped and pressed open.

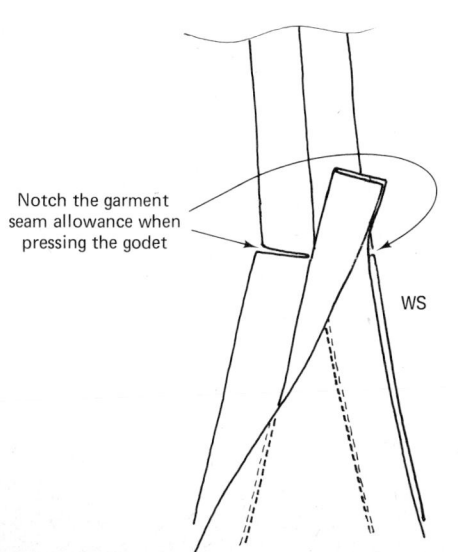

Notch the garment seam allowance when pressing the godet

WS

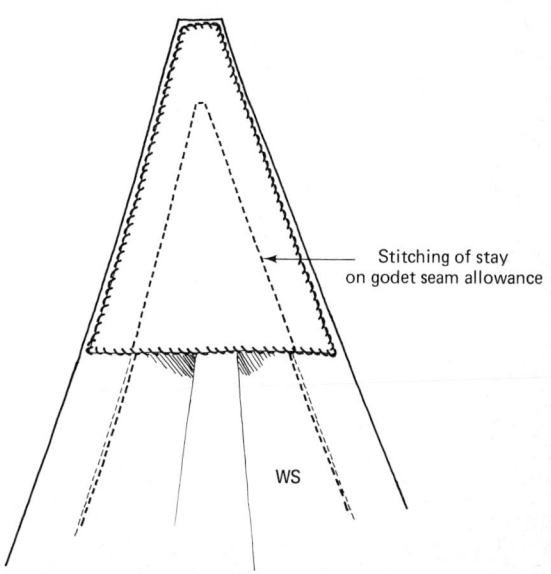

Stitching of stay on godet seam allowance

WS

6 The other layers

An interfaced garment will retain the freshness and crispness of its detail much longer than its non-interfaced counterpart. The mechanical functions of interfacing are: to strengthen areas, and to prevent the edges of the garment from stretching. Equally important are its aesthetic functions. It gives a crisp, positive quality to any edge, and may be used to stiffen an area so that it behaves in a manner which contrasts with the rest of the garment.

It is sometimes suggested that interfacing should be applied to the facing piece, rather than to the garment, but it is the author's experience that the garment piece should be interfaced whenever this is practical, because this method produces a better result. The shape of the interfaced edges is made more positive, and the extra resilience provided by it helps the seam line at the edge to roll to the faced side of the garment. Because the layer of interfacing is interposed between the garment and the seam allowances, these cannot show through as a shadow, and they are also much less likely to mark the surface of the fabric when the garment is pressed. However, it is safer not to interface the garment fabric when using iron-on interfacing, and when untried woven interfacing is being used on a garment which will be laundered.

Woven interfacings provide the widest range of combinations of weight and stiffness. Before using interfacing on a garment which will be laundered, check that the interfacing will not shrink. If no light-weight interfacing can be purchased when interfacing a summer dress, use a piece of plain material of the same type and weight as the dress fabric, so that both layers will behave in the same way when washed. This may be white, but if it blends in colour with the dress, the interfaced areas will not show as a change in tone. For the same reason, when using a sheer fabric, interface with organdie or organza in a colour which blends with that of the garment.

All woven interfacing must be cut on the same grain as the part of the garment to which it will be applied. The free edge should always be finished by hand, because machine finishing will create a hard edge which can show as a ridge on the RS of the garment.

Non-woven interfacing has a grainless structure which makes it economical to use, because the pieces can be cut with the straight-grain lines pointing in any direction. It does not shrink, stands up well to repeated washing or dry-cleaning, and is available in a range of weights. Its non-fraying qualities make it attractive to the dressmaker, but its usefulness is limited by the fact that it cannot be moulded into shape.

Iron-on interfacing is available in both woven and non-woven forms. Neither type needs to have its edges finished. It should be cut without seam allowances, after being marked by tracing along the seam lines of the pattern piece using a tracing wheel and dressmaker's carbon paper. The position which the interfacing will occupy on the facing should be marked, and the interfacing positioned exactly, because once it and the facing are bonded together it will be difficult to separate them. For the same reason, the facing piece must be completely free from creases and the weave undistorted. If necessary, the facing piece may be pinned out on to an ironing board by its seam allowance, so that it will be held in shape while the interfacing is being applied.

Interfacing must be attached firmly so that it will be held in place during wear and laundering.

When a garment and its facing are cut separately, the interfacing should be basted to the WS of the garment piece. The facing and the garment piece are then placed with their RS together in the usual way, and the three layers basted and stitched together along the seam line. The interfacing seam allowance is trimmed away close to the stitching before the facing is turned to the WS. When the edge is formed of several sections, the interfacing should be basted to each piece individually before they are joined. If the edge to be interfaced needs to be stay stitched, the interfacing may be attached at the same time.

When the garment and facing are cut as one piece the interfacing can always be attached to the fold with catch stitches.
Stage 1   Cut out the interfacing. No seam allowance is required on the edge which will be placed in the fold. When using woven interfacing hand-finish this edge.
Stage 2   Pin the interfacing to the WS of the fabric (normally the garment piece) with its edge 1 mm ($\frac{1}{16}$ in.) short of the fold line, so that when the fabric is folded it will not buckle the edge of the interfacing.
Stage 3   Catch-stitch the interfacing to the fabric just on the facing side of the fold line. Each stitch should only pick up one or two threads in the facing so that the stitches hardly show on the RS.

When the interfaced area is finished with top stitching, baste the interfacing into place after following stages 1 and 2 only.

In cases where the facing will not show, the interfacing may be attached to the fold by machine.
Stage 1   Cut out the interfacing, allowing a 1 cm ($\frac{3}{8}$ in.) seam allowance on the fold-line edge.
Stage 2   Position the interfacing on the WS of the fabric, (normally the garment piece), overlapping the fold line by 1 cm ($\frac{3}{8}$ in.). Pin and baste.
Stage 3   Stitch the interfacing 1 to 2 mm ($\frac{1}{16}$ in.) on the facing side of the fold line. Trim away the interfacing seam allowance close to this line of stitching.

A facing can be applied to any free edge of a garment so that the inside of the edge is neatly finished. It is always turned to one side of the garment, usually the WS, but it may still show as it does in the case of lapels. The facing can be cut in one with the garment piece only if the junction between them is straight. An applied facing can be used on either straight or curved edges, and provides not only a positive edge, but one which is

firm and will keep its shape during wear and laundering.

An applied facing should always be cut on the same grain as the part of the garment to which it will be attached. Before applying it, any seams or openings which run into the edge should be completed, and any bias sections of the garment edge should be stay stitched to prevent them from stretching. When stitching past a corner, or towards a fold or edge, shorten the machine stitch to 1 to 1·5 mm (18 to 22 stitches per inch) to prevent the seam allowances from pulling out, and finish off the stitching by reversing, or by sewing in the thread ends.

Trim the corners of the garment and facing seam allowance so that they do not cause a bulge by being forced together when the facing is turned RS out, but leave 2 mm ($\frac{1}{16}$ in.) between the stitching and the cut edge at the point.

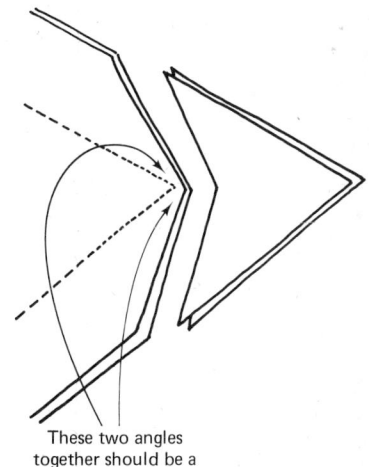

These two angles together should be a little less than the angle enclosed by the stitching

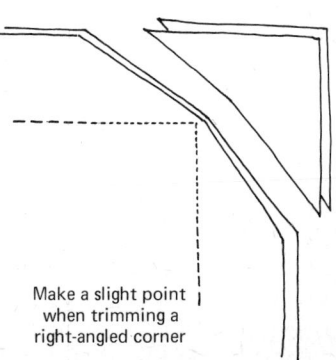

Make a slight point when trimming a right-angled corner

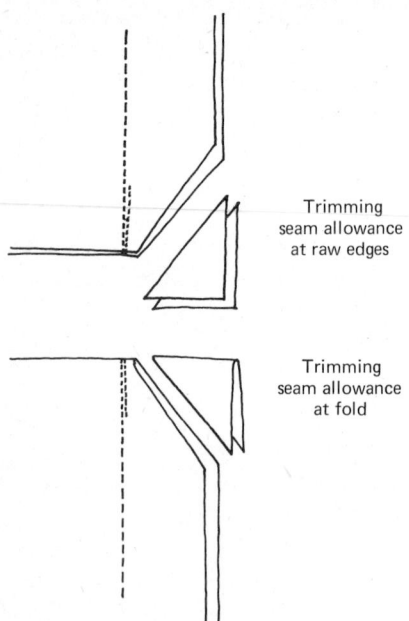

Trimming
seam allowance
at raw edges

Trimming
seam allowance
at fold

Understitching is used to ensure that a facing which has been cut separately will stay rolled to the WS. After the facing has been pressed so that it lies across the seam allowances, or the part of the garment has been turned RS out, put in the line of understitching through the facing and both seam allowances from the facing side. Use a normal stitch length for the fabric, a matching thread, and place the stitching 1, or at the most 2 mm ($\frac{1}{16}$ in.), from the seam line. To prevent the seam allowances from pleating up where they have had to be clipped, baste them to the facing before understitching. In small enclosed shapes such as pocket flaps, which are difficult to understitch by machine, small running stitches with a backstitch every centimetre ($\frac{3}{8}$ in.) or so may be used instead.

A strip cut on the true bias provides a neat finish for sheer fabrics where the shadow of a wider shaped facing would be distracting. It can also be used in place of a shaped facing, at the neck and armholes of a dress for instance, when it is necessary to economise on material. When using a bias strip to face an edge which is curved, the finished width of the strip should not exceed 1·2 cm ($\frac{1}{2}$ in.), but any convenient width can be used on a straight edge.

Applying a bias-strip facing to a curved edge

Stage 1   Stay-stitch the edge of the garment.
Stage 2   Make and join a sufficient number of strips cut on the true bias to form the necessary length. Crease the seam allowance along each edge, and if the facing is to be applied to a sharp curve, such as an armhole, pre-shape it by pulling it into a curve while pressing.
Stage 3   Place the facing and garment with their RS together with the stitching crease of the facing on the seam or hem line of the garment. Cross-pin and baste. Ease the strip on a concave edge, and stretch it on a convex one, taking care not to distort the edge of the garment by pulling the binding too tight.

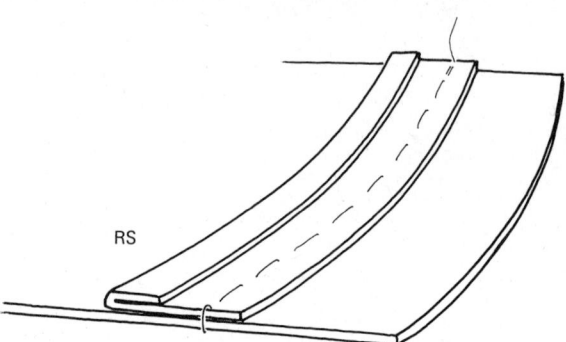

RS

Stage 4   Stitch the facing to the garment along the crease, and remove the basting thread. Trim the garment seam allowance so that it is slightly narrower than the width of the finished facing. Clip or notch the seam allowance almost to the stay stitching to enable it to lie smoothly when folded over.
Stage 5   Fold the facing so that it lies across the raw edge of the garment seam allowance, and understitch it close to the fold to ensure that it will roll completely to the WS.

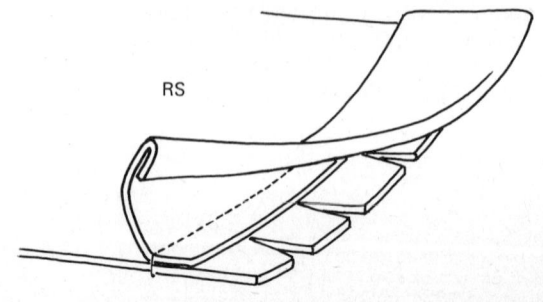

RS

Stage 6　Turn the whole of the facing to the WS along the line of stitching and press this fold. Cross-pin, baste, and either hem or slip-hem the facing into place. When slip-hemming, the facing may be hemmed to any seam allowances it crosses for greater firmness.

Stage 3　Fold the facing and garment piece RS together along the fold line. Pin, baste and stitch the facing and garment together at both ends of the fold.

Stage 4　Remove the basting. Grade and clip or notch the seam allowance, and turn the faced section RS out.

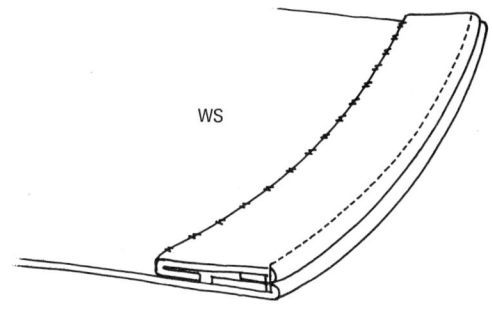

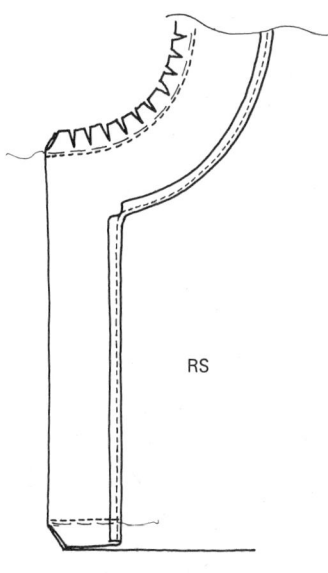

A facing cut in one with the garment piece can only be used on edges which are, at least in part, straight: examples include band cuffs, bias roll collars and the opening front edges of blouses.

Stage 1　Baste-mark the fold line and interface the garment piece if this is desired.

Stage 2　Finish the raw edge of the facing if it will remain free, to prevent it from fraying.

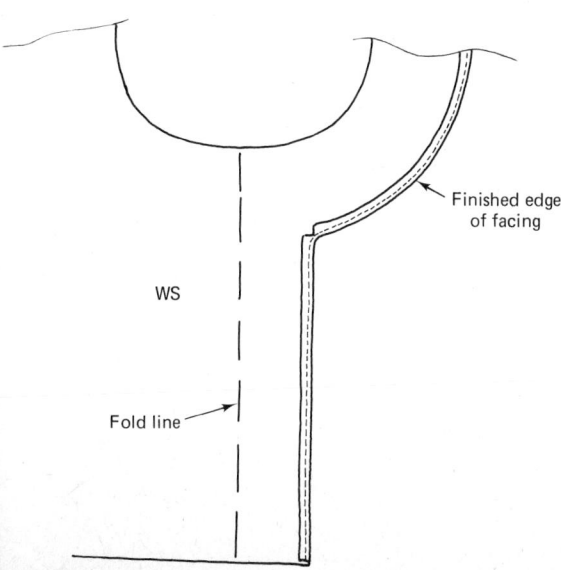

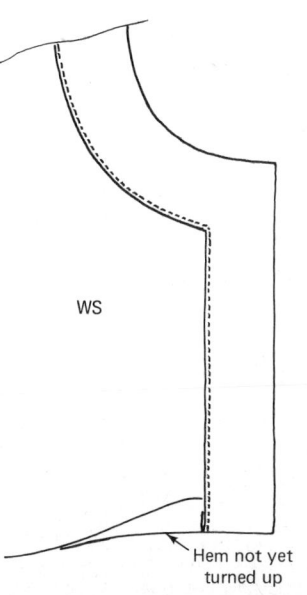

77

A separate facing must be used on sharply curved and angled edges and may be used on straight ones. It can be made whatever width is required and will still lie perfectly flat. If any alterations which cross an edge to be faced are made to the pattern, the same alterations must also be made to the facing.

A simple modification of a pattern, for instance the omission of sleeves in a dress, may result in it becoming necessary to face an edge. In such a case a pattern for the shaped facing can be made in the following way.

Stage 1   Pin tracing paper on to the pattern pieces so that it covers the part which needs to be faced, and transfer all the markings from the pieces on to the tracing paper. Draw grain lines which are parallel with the grain lines printed on the main pattern pieces.

Stage 2   The facing pattern must be even in width. Make a cardboard gauge the same width as the finished facing, and using it at right angles to the stitching line, mark the inner cutting line of the facing.

Stage 3   Using these new pattern pieces, cut out and mark the facing in the usual way.

Attaching a separate shaped facing

Stage 1   Stay-stitch the bias sections of the garment edge, interface the garment pieces if necessary, and stitch the seams which run into the edge to be faced.

Stage 2   Stitch and press open any seams in the facing, and finish any raw edge which will remain free.

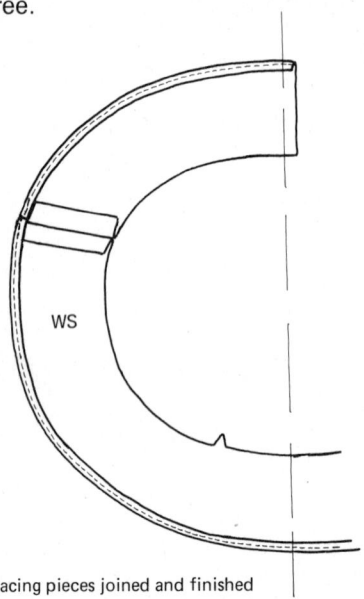

Facing pieces joined and finished

Stage 3   Place the RS of the facing and garment together, matching tailor tacks and balance marks. Cross-pin and baste. Stitch the facing to the garment along the seam line. Remove the basting.

Stage 4   Grade and clip or notch the seam allowances to allow them to set correctly when the facing is turned in.

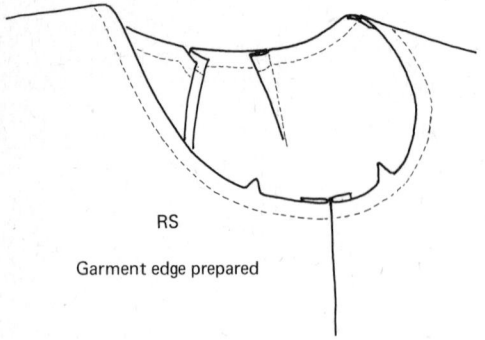

Garment edge prepared

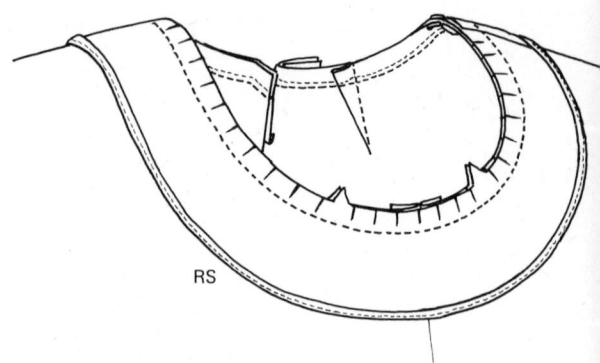

Stage 5   When the shape of the facing permits, press the facing over the seam allowances, so that the stitching line is brought right to the fold. Baste the facing and seam allowances together to prevent them from pleating up during stitching, and

understitch them close to the fold either by hand or machine. Remove the basting and cut off the balance marks.

Stage 6   Turn the facing to the WS and rolling the seam line so that it will lie just behind the garment edge, press the edge to set it.

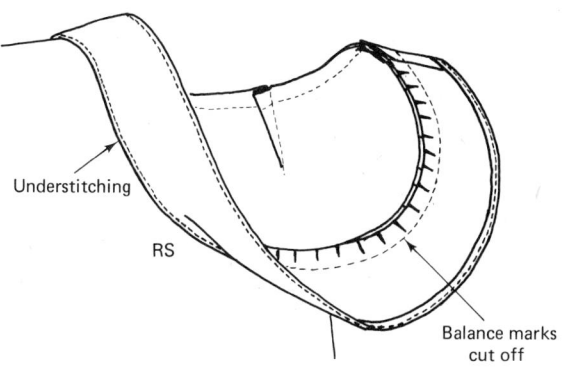

Understitching

RS

Balance marks cut off

A combination facing – that is one in which the neck and armholes are cut in one piece – is used on dresses and blouses which are both sleeveless and collarless. It is the only variety of neck or armhole facing which is attached before the shoulder seams are joined.

Stage 1   Mark with tailor tacks the points on both the garment and the facing pieces where the shoulder seams will intersect with the neckline and with the armhole seams.

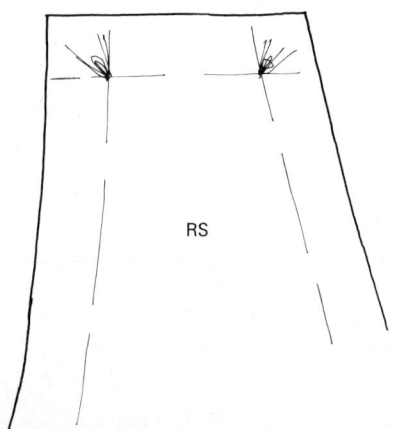

RS

Stage 2   Interface the garment pieces if desired, and stay-stitch the curved sections of the garment edge. Join and press open the underarm seams of both garment and facing, and finish the raw edges of the facing which will remain free.

Stage 3   Make a diagonal fold through each of the tailor tacks put in at stage 1, so that a small triangle is turned to the WS. Pin and baste these folds into place.

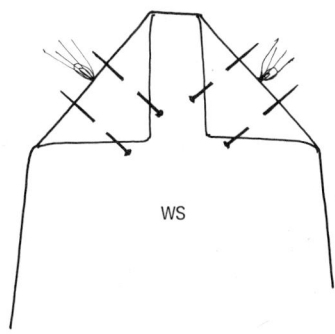

WS

Stage 4   Cutting parallel with the fold, trim away about half the depth of each turned-in triangle.

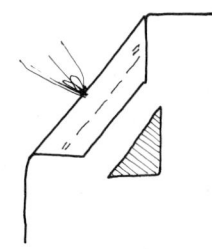

Stage 5   Fold the shoulder seam allowance of each facing piece to the WS. Baste.

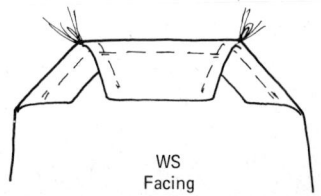

WS
Facing

Stage 6 Pin and baste the facing and garment pieces RS together around the armholes and neckline, carefully matching balance marks and tailor tacks. Stitch along these seam lines and stop at each diagonally folded corner. Sew in the thread ends. Remove the basting from these edges and that which is holding the corner folds.

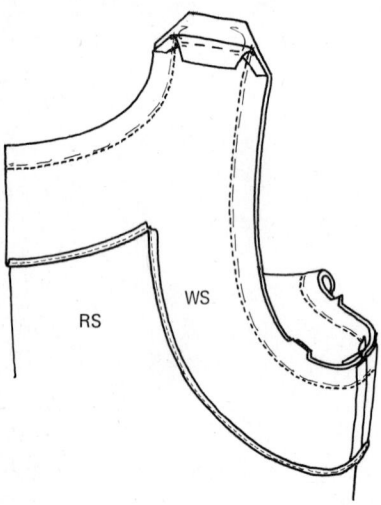

Stage 7 Grade and clip the seam allowances. Turn each shoulder section right through between its facing and the garment to bring the facing to the WS. The shoulder seam allowance of the garment will now be sticking out, and the facing seam allowance will be turned inside. Work the stitching right to the fold around the armholes and neckline. Baste to hold it in place and press. Remove the basting.

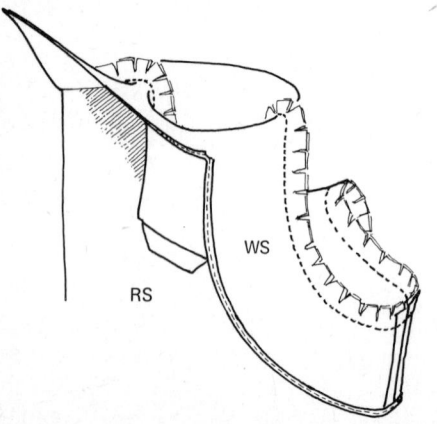

Stage 8 Turn the garment WS out. Place the RS of each pair of shoulder seam allowances together, being careful to line up the neck and armhole edges of the back and front. Pin and baste. Machine stitch or backstitch the garment shoulder seams together, taking care not to catch the folded edge of the facing. (When working in bulky fabric this process is made easier if a zip foot is used.)

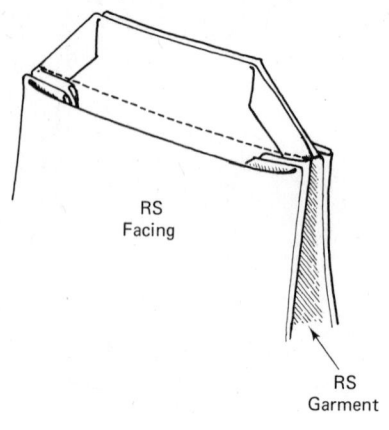

Stage 9 Remove the remainder of the basting. Press the shoulder seam open over a seam roll, tuck each garment seam allowance under its own facing and slip stitch the facing folds together. Press.

The join in a bias-faced edge should be made in exactly the same way as the join in a bias-bound edge. Faced edges may end at an opening which has its facing either cut in one with the garment or applied. In the case of a facing meeting a hem, at the front of a coat for example, the end of the hem should be enclosed by the vertical faced edge. When the faced edge ends against a zip opening, the facing may be attached either before, or after the zip is inserted.

When a zip is applied before the facing
Stage 1 Make the facing the total length of
the edge including the seam allowances of the
opening. Apply the facing in the usual way
continuing the stitching and understitching
across the turned-in garment seam allowance.

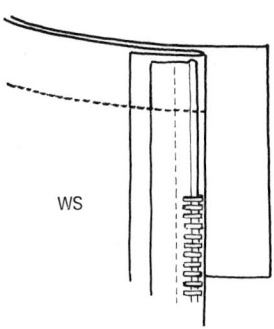

Stage 2 Press the facing so that it lies
across the raw edge, and fold its end to the
WS enclosing the zip tape.

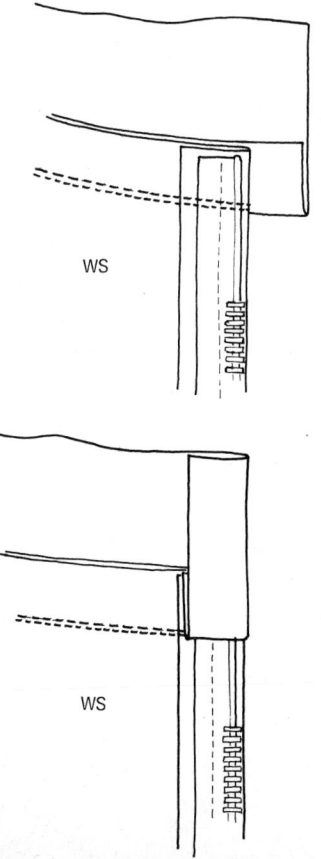

Stage 3 Turn the facing to the WS. Arrange
the fold at the end to slope slightly to clear
the teeth of the zip, and hem it to the back of
the zip tape.

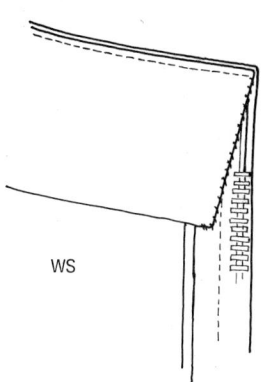

When the facing is applied before the zip

Stage 1 Apply the facing by stitching and understitching the garment and facing together, right to the edge of the seam allowance of the opening.

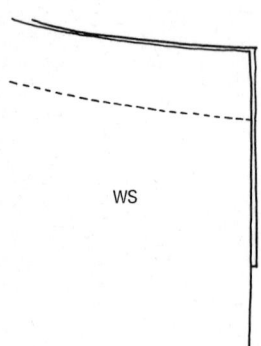

WS

Stage 2 Notch the neckline seam allowance on the seam line of the opening to remove bulk in the fold. Turn the seam allowance of the opening to the ws, and continue the fold across the free ends of the facing.

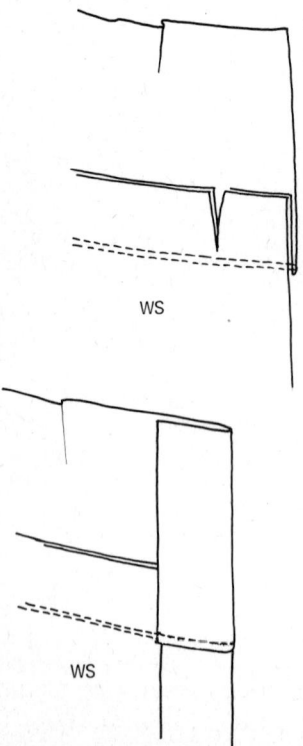

WS

WS

Stage 3 Fit the zip, and arranging the fold in the end of the facing to slope slightly to clear the teeth of the zip, hem this fold to the back of the zip tape.

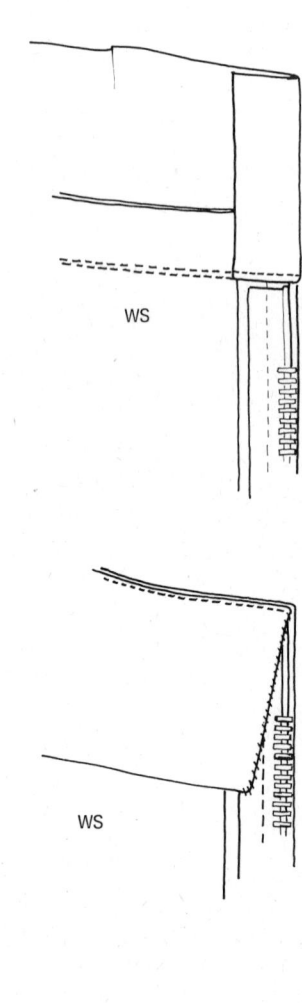

WS

WS

A lining is made from a slippery firmly woven fabric. All linings can be dry-cleaned, but if the garment will be laundered, a washable lining material must be chosen. A lining will help the garment to keep its shape, prevent it from riding up, protect the skin from a rough-surfaced fabric and provide a neat finish. It may be made up using the main garment pattern pieces, but for suits and coats separate pattern pieces are usually provided. However, the garment pattern pieces cannot be used in the case of a pleated skirt, and the lining for this must be cut to a flared shape. Any adjustments which are made to the garment must also be made to the lining. The body of the lining should be cut out and marked, and the darts and seams joined in the same order as they were when the garment was assembled. Where decorative tucks occur, they should be folded and pinned in the pattern pieces so that the lining can be cut to the finished size. After the lining has been basted into place, try the garment on to check that fitting the lining had not affected the set of the garment.

When lining a skirt or trousers, baste the lining to the waist seam of the garment before the waist band or facing has been applied, so that the upper edge of the lining will be enclosed when the waistline is completed. Similarly, a dress lining should be fitted before the neck facing or collar is applied, and, if the dress is sleeveless, before the armhole facings are fitted as well. Link the lining to the side seams of the dress at waist level with chain tacks to prevent it from twisting. If the opening is in the form of a zip, the edges of the lining should be turned in and slip-hemmed to the zip tape. When the opening is faced, the lining may either be machine stitched or slip-hemmed to the edge of the facing. The hem of the lining of a skirt, dress or trousers should hang free, level with the upper edge of the hem.

The lining for the body part of a short coat or jacket should be made up and fitted after the facings have been applied. A small vertical pleat is usually made in the CB of the lining to allow for movement and this should be folded and basted at the level of the neck, waist and hem before the lining is applied. If the edge of the lining which will be fitted to the neck and front opening is stay stitched,

the stitching can be used as a guide when the free edge of the facing is lapped to the lining. The lining should be loosely sewn to the armhole seam allowances and also down the side seams from the underarm to the waist. The long seam of the sleeve lining is joined, and the sleeve head adjusted to the correct length with a single row of ease stitching. The sleeve lining is then slipped inside the jacket sleeve and slip-hemmed to the body side of the armhole.

When attaching the hems of sleeve and body, place the garment on a dress form or put the garment on, and get someone else to help. Pin and baste the lining to the garment about 10 cm (4 in.) above the upper edge of the hem line in both the sleeves and the body. Be careful to match the seams.

Turn the jacket WS out, and pin a 6 mm ($\frac{1}{4}$ in.) tuck in the lining between the basting and the hem. These tucks will allow for movement so that there is no danger of the lining splitting. Turn in the edge of the lining so that the fold just covers the upper edge of the garment hem, and slip-hem the lining into place. Remove the pins from the tuck. A full length coat lining is treated in the same way as a jacket, but the hem is finished separately and left to hang free.

Mounting or underlining is a technique in which a second layer of fabric is used to support a material which would be difficult to use on its own, or to provide a foundation on which a draped style can be constructed. Openwork fabrics such as lace are always mounted, and they can be thrown into interesting relief by the use of a contrasting colour. Soft, loosely-woven fabrics will keep their shape better when this technique is used. Garments made in sheer fabrics are shown off to greater advantage if they are mounted on an opaque material which conceals the conflicting lines of underwear, seam allowances and facings.

The fabric used for mounting should be firmly woven, and of good quality because, unlike a lining, it cannot be taken out and replaced. If the garment will be laundered, both show, and mounting fabrics should be similar in their washing requirements, and ironing temperature, and may need to be shrunk before they are made up.

When the garment fabric is thin, it may be placed on the mounting fabric, and the two cut out as one. If the garment fabric is thick, cut out the two sets of pieces separately. Sandwich each pair of mounting pieces, placed with their RS together, between the matching garment pieces which should have their RS facing outwards. Replace the pattern pieces and mark through all layers.

After taking off the pattern and separating the pairs of pieces, the garment may be interfaced by inserting interfacing between the show and mounting fabrics. However, if the interfacing would show through, it can be attached to either the RS of the mounting piece, or the facing. Connect each pair of mounting and garment pieces with uneven basting placed close beside the seam line, taking care that left- and right-hand halves are created. Baste the layers together along the centre lines of any darts. From this point the two layers may be made up as if they were one. When finishing the garment, trim the mounting fabric so that it ends just short of any hem fold. Stitch the hem to the mounting fabric only.

7 Openings

Before making an opening, consider the type of fastening which will be used to close it, because in many cases at least part of the fastening has to be worked before the opening is completed.

All openings are constructed so that their edges are strengthened with extra layers of fabric and rows of stitching. Structurally, openings fall into two groups: those which meet edge to edge, and those in which one edge is placed on top of the other for fastening. The first group includes faced and bound slashes, and slot-seam zips (details of fitting zips will be found in the section on fastenings). The second group consists of lapped openings which are of two types; those in which the garment fabric itself extends beyond the centre line, for example faced, lapped openings in blouses and jackets, and those in which strips of fabric are applied to extend one or both edges of the opening, eg a front band.

The direction of lap is a matter of convention, and when considered from the wearer's point of view, front openings in men's garments lap left over right: in women's garments, both CF and CB openings lap right side over left. A side-seam opening always laps front over back, and in a cuff the edge of the opening nearest to the underarm seam, forms the underlap.

A faced slash opening has no overlap, and its facing is cut from a single piece of fabric. It may be used at the neckline or sleeve end of a garment.

Stage 1   Mark the centre line of the opening on the garment with a basting thread.
Stage 2   Cut a piece of fabric on the same grain as the opening. (If the garment fabric is bulky, a facing piece of thinner fabric may be used.) Its length should be $1\frac{1}{2}$ times the length of the finished opening, plus one seam allowance. The width of the facing piece will depend upon the size and position of the opening, but on a sleeve as little as 2·5 cm (1 in.) may be allowed between the stitching line and the edge of the facing. In a neck opening it should be made the normal facing width. Finish the raw edges of the facing which will remain unattached.

Stage 3   Mark the centre line of the facing piece with basting, and place it on the garment with their RS together. Line up the two centre lines, and also the raw edges of the fabric at the open end.

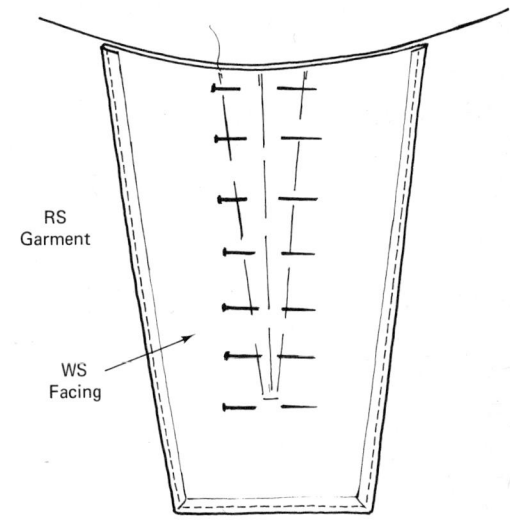

RS
Garment

WS
Facing

Stage 4   Stitch the facing to the garment, beginning at the raw edge 6 mm ($\frac{1}{4}$ in.) to one side of the marked slash line. The line of stitching should converge with the slash line so that they are between 1 and 2 mm ($\frac{1}{16}$ in.) apart at the point. Turn, taking one or two stitches across the point, and return along the other side. Shorten the stitch to 1 mm (20 stitches per inch) for 2 cm ($\frac{3}{4}$ in.) on each side of the point.

Stage 5   Cut the garment and facing along the centre line of the opening, stopping, 1 mm ($\frac{1}{16}$ in.) short of the stitching at the point. Remove the basting.

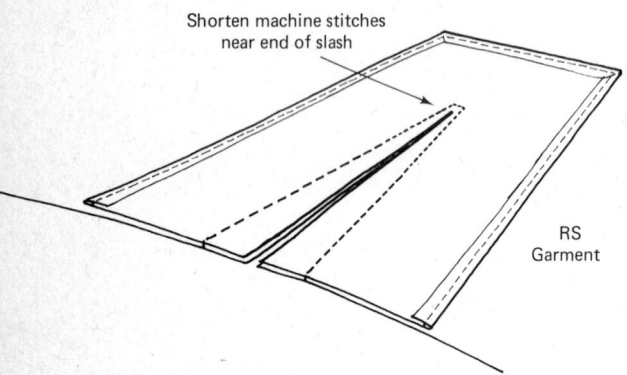

Shorten machine stitches
near end of slash

RS
Garment

Stage 6   Working from the RS, press the facing over the raw edges of the seam allowances so that the stitching line is brought right against the fold.

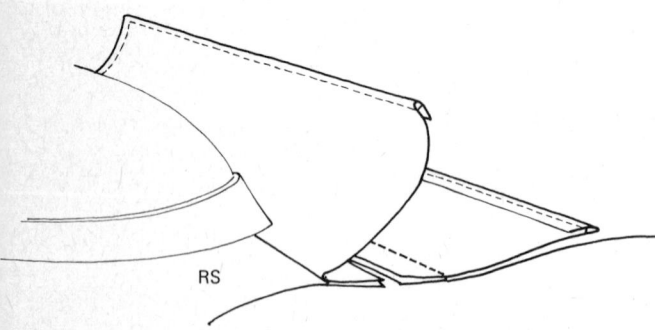

RS

Stage 7   Turn the facing to the WS, easing it through at the point, and gently pulling it into shape until it lies flat. Understitch

through the facing and both seam allowances 1 mm ($\frac{1}{16}$ in.) from the seam line. Press.

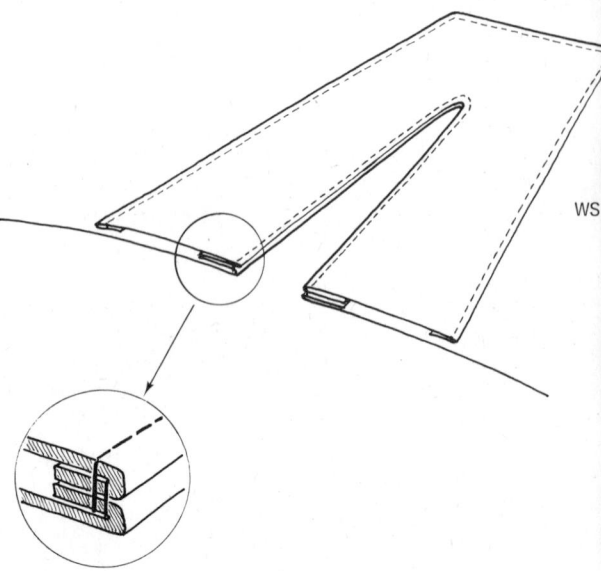

WS

In a simple lapped opening the garment piece extends beyond the centre line of the opening, so that no extra strip of show fabric needs to be added. Such openings may be faced either with a facing cut in one with the garment or with one which is applied. The centre lines of the opening should always be marked with basting. They are placed over one another when fitting the garment, and are also used as a guide when positioning fastenings.

It is quite easy to convert a pattern with a CF fold or seam to a lapped opening. Take the front pattern piece and pin or tape it to a piece of tissue which is the same length as the front edge and 15 cm (6 in.) wide, so that the pattern overlaps the edge of the tissue. The original place-to-fold line, or seam line, will now be the CF line of the garment and enough allowance must be made beyond this to form the lap plus a seam allowance.

Use the modified pattern to cut the garment and facing pieces. If there is to be a collar which may be worn open, be careful to make each facing piece wide enough at this part so that its free edge will not show. Mark the CF line with basting, and the new corner positions with tailor tacks.

A continous strip opening, which is often made in the sleeve ends of garments made from light-weight fabric, is stronger than a faced slash and will withstand machine washing. It takes the form of a small slit which may be either a slash, or the open end of a seam, bound with a single strip of fabric which is pressed to one side.

A continous strip applied to a slash
Stage 1 Baste-mark the centre line of the slash, which must be on the straight grain of the fabric. Stay-stitch beside the seamline to form a guide when stitching the strip. The distance of the stay stitching from the centre line should be 6 mm ($\frac{1}{4}$ in.) at the open end, tapering to 1 to 2 mm ($\frac{1}{16}$ in.) at the point. As the point cannot be a perfect one, take one or two stitches across its end.
Stage 2 Cut a piece of garment fabric on the straight grain, which is twice the length of the finished slash plus two seam allowances, by twice the finished width of the strip plus 1·2 cm ($\frac{1}{2}$ in.) for seam allowances.

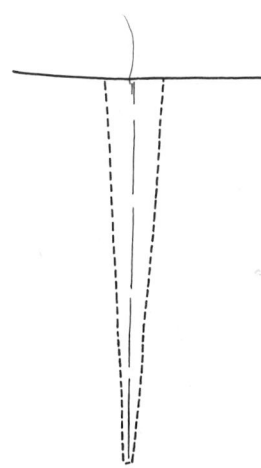

Stage 3 Cut along the centre line of the slash stopping at the stay stitching and pull the slash open so that the stay stitching forms a straight line. Cross-pin the RS of the strip and garment together, so that the stay stitching is 6 mm ($\frac{1}{4}$ in.) from one edge of the strip all the way along. Baste.
Stage 4 With the WS of the garment uppermost, stitch 1 mm ($\frac{1}{16}$ in.) on the garment side of the stay stitching, taking care not to catch in the pleats at the point of the

slash. Shorten the stitch to 1 mm (20 stitches per inch) for 2 cm ($\frac{3}{4}$ in.) on each side of the point. If the fabric tends to fray, oversew the garment seam allowance to the strip along the length of the shortened machine stitches.

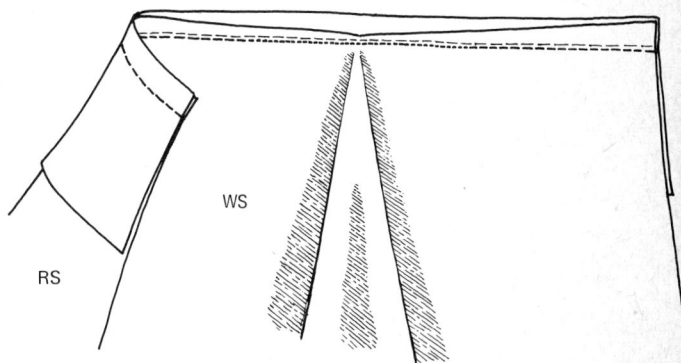

Stage 5 Press the strip over the raw edges of the seam allowances. Turn the work WS up and press 6 mm ($\frac{1}{4}$ in.) of the free edge of the strip to the WS. Cross-pin this fold against the line of stitching on the WS, and hem the fold to the machine stitches.

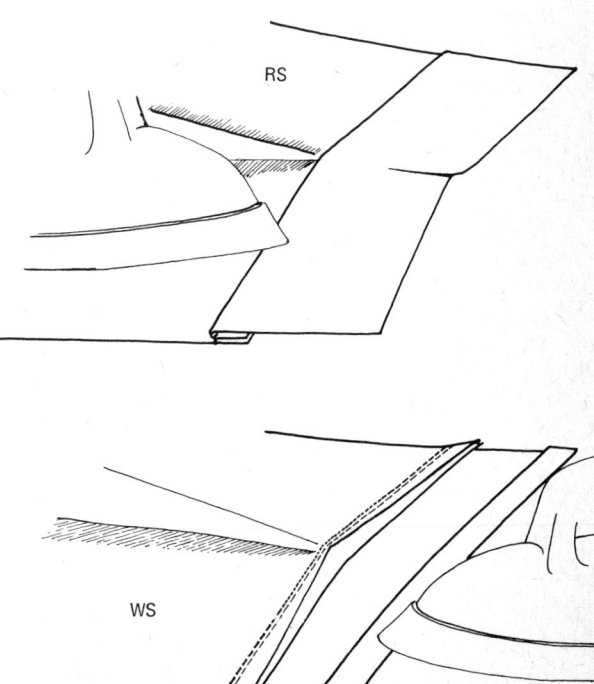

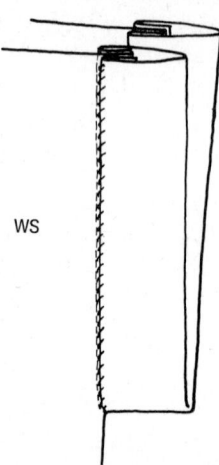

WS

A continuous strip applied to the open end of a seam is similar to a continuous strip applied to a slash. The garment seam should have been stitched as far as the opening and the thread ends finished off.

Stage 1   Snip the seam allowances almost to the stitching line level with the point where the stitching ends. An open seam should be pressed open, and the seam allowances which will be enclosed by the strip should be reduced to 6 mm ($\frac{1}{4}$ in.). The cut ends which will not be enclosed by the strip, should be finished with overcasting or loop stitch. A french seam should be pressed to one side and its end finished similarly.

Stage 6   Allow the slash to resume its normal shape, with the projecting strip on the ws of the garment, and press the folded strip to one side. Make a row of back stitches through the four layers of the strip, 3 mm ($\frac{1}{8}$ in.) from the fold at the bottom of the slash, so that the strip cannot come through to the RS inadvertently.

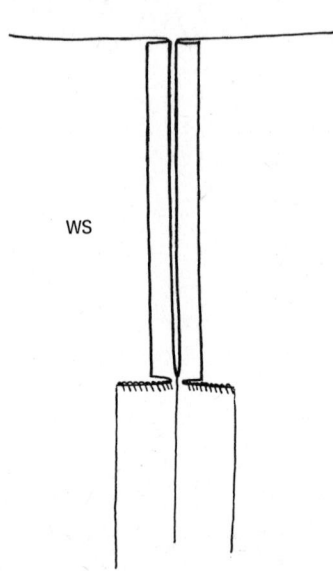

WS

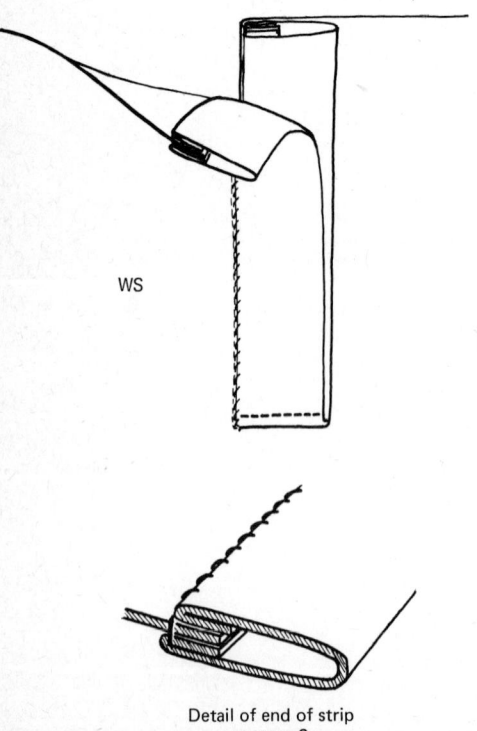

WS

Detail of end of strip
at stage 6

Stage 2   Cut a piece of fabric on the straight grain, which is twice the length of the finished slash plus two seam allowances, and in width is twice the finished width of the strip plus 1·2 cm ($\frac{1}{2}$ in.) for seam allowances.

Stage 3   Pull the edges of the opening apart so that the trimmed seam allowances form a straight line. Cross-pin and baste the RS of the strip and garment together with their raw edges level.

Stage 4   With the WS of the garment uppermost, stitch along the seamline taking care not to catch the pleats at the point of the slash, but the line of stitching must pass through the final stitch of the garment seam.

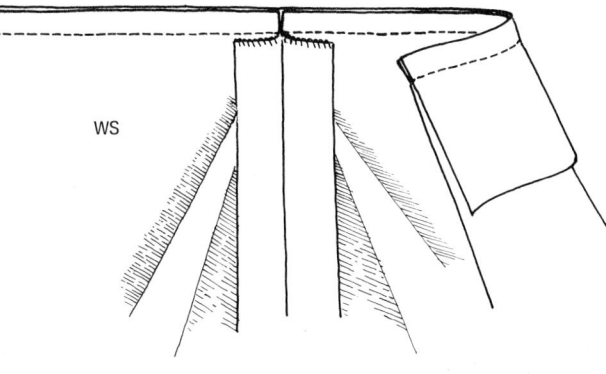

For stages 5 and 6 see a continuous strip applied to a slash.

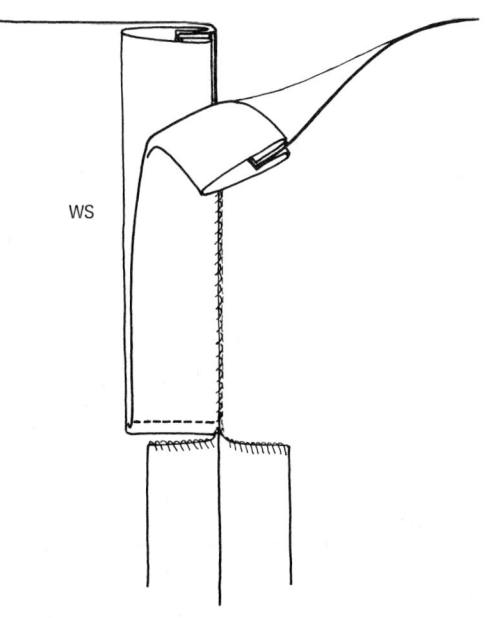

A placket opening, also known as **a wrap and facing opening**, is useful on garments where a zip would be too stiff for the fabric. It tends to gape if it is used in closely fitting garments where it would come under lateral strain, but is perfectly satisfactory used in the side of a full skirt, in the underarm seam of semi-fitted dresses, and at the back neck of blouses and children's dresses. It is closed with hooks and eyes and snap fasteners, and is made by adding two pieces of fabric to the seam allowances, an underlap on one edge, and a facing piece to strengthen the overlap, on the other. It can be made where there is no seam, but in this case a pleat must be formed at the base of the opening to provide seam allowances to which the underlap and facing pieces can be attached.

Stage 1   Stitch the garment seam to the point where the opening begins, and finish off the thread ends. Press open the seam allowances of the seam and opening.

Stage 2   Clip the seam allowance of the underlap edge 6 mm ($\frac{1}{4}$ in.) beyond the end of the placket opening, stopping 1 to 2 mm ($\frac{1}{16}$ in.) from the stitching line. This will enable the underlap to be turned forward, while the seam allowances beyond the end of the placket remain pressed open. Finish the cut end of the underlap seam allowance which will not be enclosed by the underlap piece.

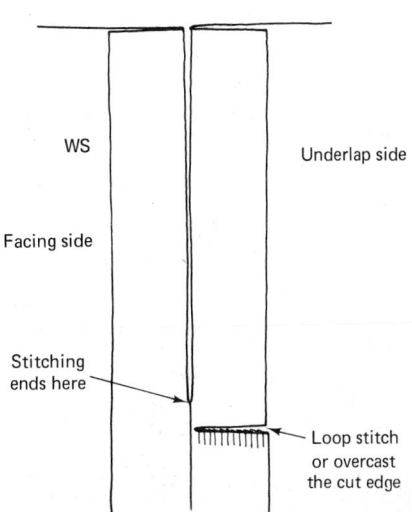

Stage 3 Cut an underlap piece on the true bias; in width it should be 3 cm ($1\frac{1}{4}$ in.) plus two 6 mm ($\frac{1}{4}$ in.) seam allowances. Its length should be equal to that of the finished opening plus two normal seam allowances. The facing piece is cut, either to the curve of the part of the garment being faced, or on the true bias, and is made 1·5 cm ($\frac{5}{8}$ in.) plus two 6 mm ($\frac{1}{4}$ in.) seam allowances wide, its length is the same as the underlap piece.

Stage 4 Turn and crease a 6 mm ($\frac{1}{4}$ in.) seam allowance to the WS along each long edge of both the facing and underlap pieces. Fold the underlap piece in half lengthwise and press.

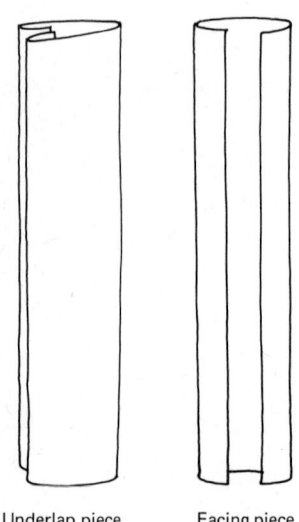

Underlap piece   Facing piece

Stage 5 Place the RS of one seam allowance of the underlap piece on the RS of the underlap seam allowance of the garment with the stitching creases together. If the placket is open at one end, the ends of the underlap piece and the opening should be level. If the opening occurs in the middle of a seam, the underlap piece should extend beyond the opening by an equal amount at each end. Trim the garment seam allowance to 6 mm ($\frac{1}{4}$ in.). Enclose the trimmed seam allowance

within the underlap piece, and hem its fold to the line of machine stitches.

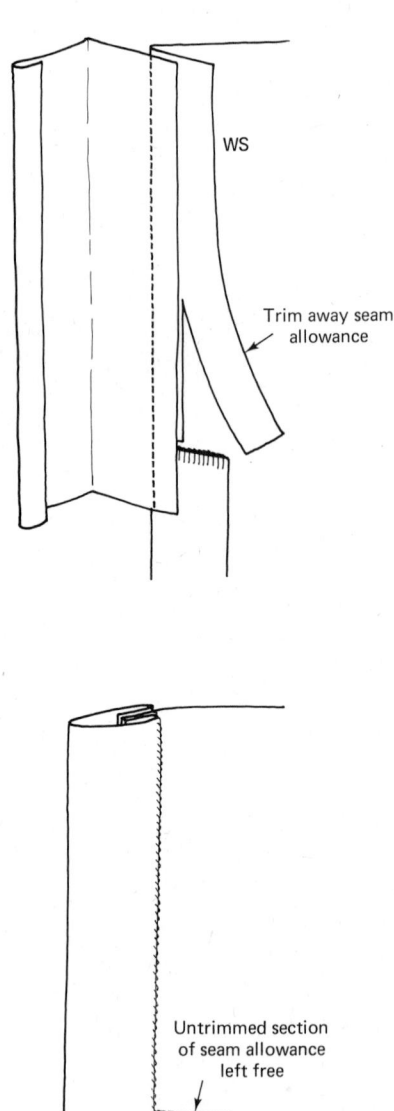

WS

Trim away seam allowance

Untrimmed section of seam allowance left free

Stage 6 Attach the facing piece by placing one of its seam allowances RS together with the other garment seam allowance, lining up their stitching creases, and with the ends of the underlap and facing pieces level. Pin, baste and stitch it to the garment seam line. Trim the garment seam allowance to 6 mm ($\frac{1}{4}$ in.), stopping 6 mm ($\frac{1}{4}$ in.) beyond the end of the opening. Hem or slip-hem the folded edge of the facing to the WS of the garment, as unobtrusively as possible.

Stage 7   Press the underlap piece forward, so that it lies on the facing, and pin the placket closed. Working from the RS, stab-stitch across the placket, level with the end of the opening. To finish: overcast or loopstitch the ends of the underlap and facing pieces to the seam allowance.

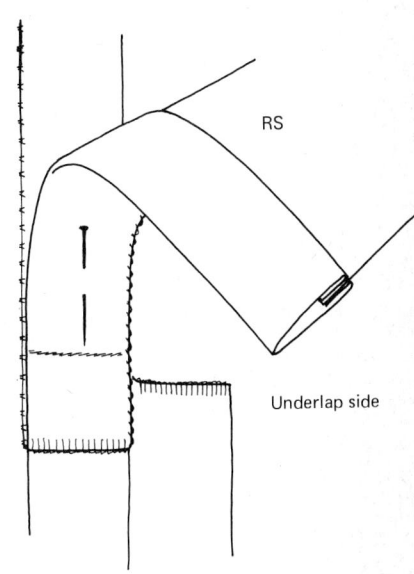

WS
facing side

RS

Underlap side

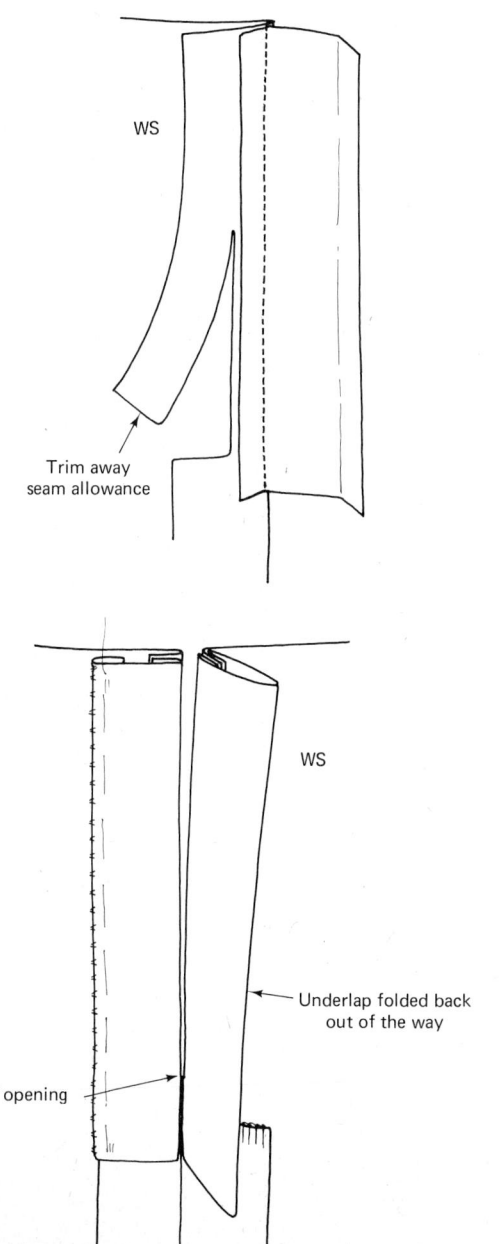

WS

Trim away
seam allowance

WS

Underlap folded back
out of the way

End of opening

A band opening is similar to a placket in its general construction, but in this case, the applied pieces are intended to show. Each band may be thought of as consisting of two halves: a show half, and a facing half which is cut in one with it. They may be cut on the true bias for a decorative effect, or made in a fabric which is different from the rest of the garment, but the weight and handle of contrasting and garment fabrics should be similar. A band may be attached to the overlap side only (the underlap edge being finished with a facing), or one may be attached to each edge of the opening, in which case the second band is made and attached in the same way as the first. A band is always buttoned: it may end in a seam, or in the middle of a skirt panel, or continue right through to the hem. A band is normally used at the CF, and the CF line of the garment should come in the middle of the finished band.

Before attaching a band to an edge, all seams running into it must be joined, pressed, and their edges finished. Check that the two sides of the opening are the same length. Stay-stitch around the lower end of any band opening which does not run through to the hem. Clip diagonally into each corner, cutting up to, but not through the stay stitching. If a band is to end at a pleat, this must have been formed and basted into place before the lower end of the band opening is stay stitched.

Preparing a band and attaching it to an edge

Stage 1   Cut out the band making it twice the finished width plus two seam allowances. It should be as long as the finished opening plus two seam allowances.

Stage 2   Baste-mark or crease the line of the fold along the centre of the band piece. Mark with tailor tacks the CF points at the upper end of the band, the points at the corners where the stitching lines will intersect, and the button or buttonhole positions.

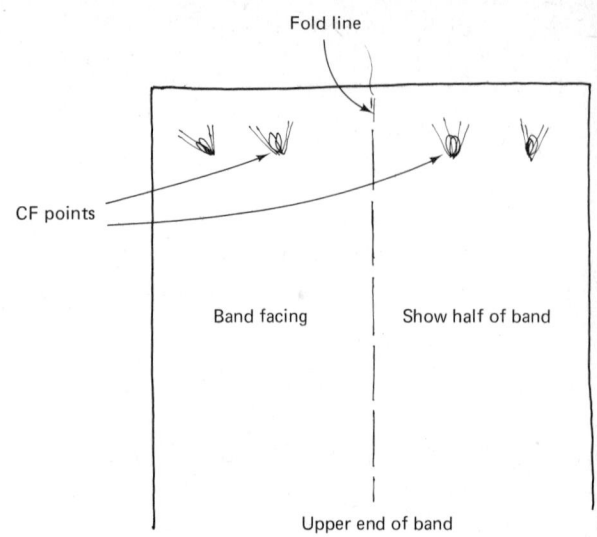

Fold line

CF points

Band facing   Show half of band

Upper end of band

Stage 3   Interface the band, taking care to apply the interfacing to the WS of the show half of the band (for the method see page 75), but when forming the corner at the top of the band, fold the upper end of the band in half RS together, and machine stitch on the neck-edge seam line from the fold as far as the tailor tack which marks the CF of the band. Do not stitch across the lower end of the band at this stage.

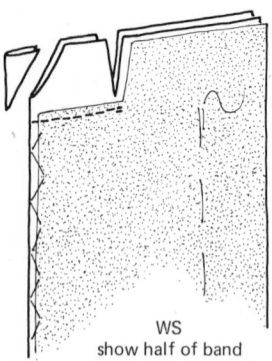

WS
show half of band

Stage 4 Finish off the thread ends firmly. Trim off the seam allowance at the corner, and snip the seam allowance of the top edge at the point where the stitching ends, stopping 1 to 2 mm ($\frac{1}{16}$ in.) from it. Turn the band right side out, taking care to make the stitched corner square. Pull up the seam allowances of the unstitched portion of the top edge. They will provide attachment for the collar after the band is finished.

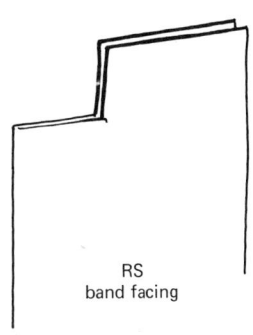

RS
band facing

Stage 5 Place the show half of the band and the edge of the garment opening with their RS together, and with the raw edges level. Fold the facing half out of the way, and cross-pin, baste and machine stitch the whole length of the band to the garment. Grade the garment and interfacing seam allowances.

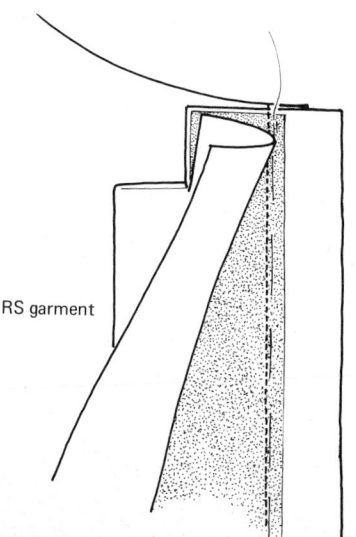

RS garment

Stage 6 Remove the basting stitches, and working from the RS press the band so that it covers the seam allowances, and a crease is formed against the line of stitching. Turn the work over and crease the seam allowance of the facing half to the WS. Baste the fold to hold it in place.

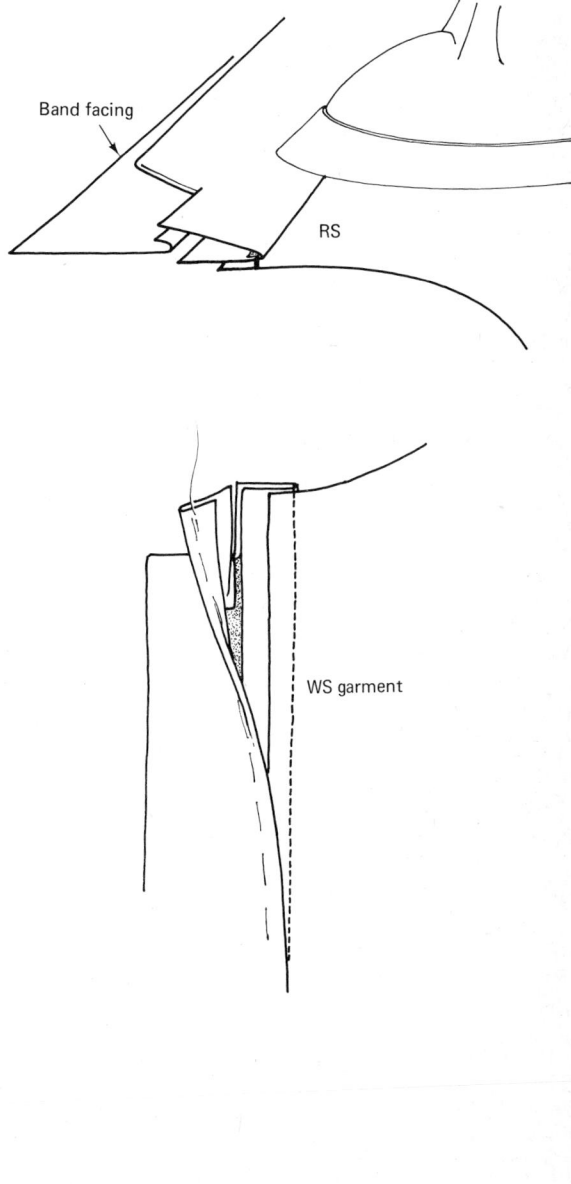

Band facing

RS

WS garment

When the band runs through to the hem, mark the hem fold, then fold the lower end of the band in half RS together and machine stitch across it at the level of the hem fold.

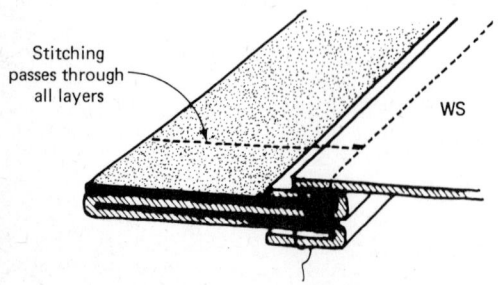

Stitching passes through all layers

WS

Trim the corner and grade the seam allowance. Turn the band RS out and press. Finally slip-hem the edge fold of the facing half into place, picking up the machine stitches on the WS.

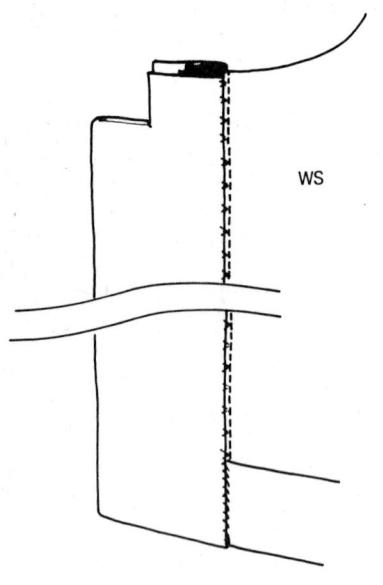

WS

When the band ends at a seam or pleat or in a plain panel

Stage 7   Slip-hem the long edge of the facing half of the overlap to the row of machine stitches on the WS. Keeping the facing half of the underlap band out of the way, baste 10 to 15 cm (4 to 6 ins.) of the lower end of the completed overlap band to the show half of the underlap band to keep them correctly registered.

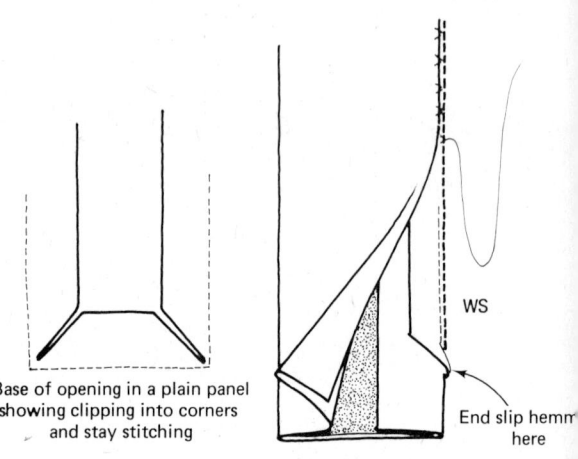

WS

Base of opening in a plain panel showing clipping into corners and stay stitching

End slip hemm here

Overlap band

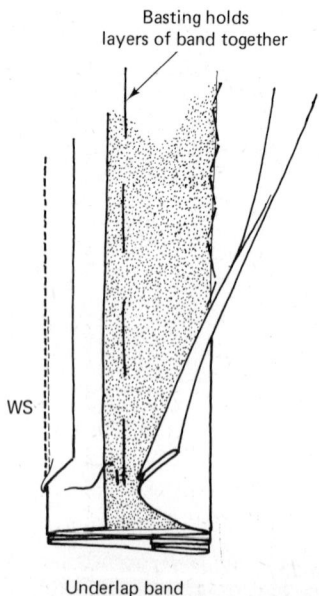

Basting holds layers of band together

WS

Underlap band laid on overlap band

Stage 8   Lay the garment piece on a flat surface RS up and bring its hem back over the band until the crosswise fold is level with the seam line which crosses the lower end of the band. Arrange the garment seam allowance at the bottom end of the band so that it lies RS down on the band seam allowance. Cross-pin, and baste it on the stitching line through all layers except the underlap band facing which must be kept free.

Stage 9   Check from the RS that no puckers or holes are apparent at the bottom corners of the band.

Stage 10   With the band and garment arranged as it was in stage 8, stitch across the lower end of the band close to the stay stitching, and finish off the thread ends firmly. Remove the basting and tailor tacks. Trim and grade all the seam allowances at the bottom of the band, and press them up into the band.

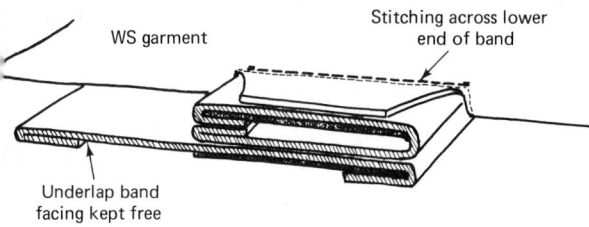

WS garment

Stitching across lower end of band

Underlap band facing kept free

Stage 11   Trim the corners of the facing half of the underlap band to remove bulk, fold its seam allowances in and hem it to the bottom of the band. Continue sewing up the long edge with slip hemming.

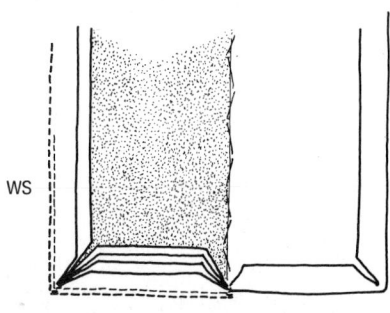

WS

Underlap band and facing seam allowances trimmed and turned in

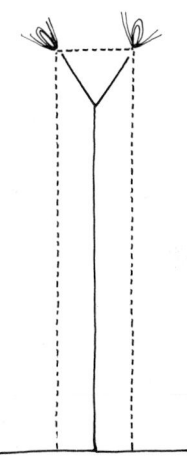

WS   WS

Completed lower end of band viewed from inside of garment

A shirt sleeve opening, which is sometimes called a shirt sleeve placket opening, is another opening formed from two applied strips of fabric. It is not only used for sleeves, but may also be used as a short opening in the front of a blouse or dress.

Stage 1   Prepare the garment piece by marking the centre line of the opening with a basting thread, and the lower corners of the opening with tailor tacks. Stay-stitch around the opening parallel with the centre line, and passing through the inner corners of the tailor tacks. The stay stitching should extend the length of the opening and include the seam allowances at the open end.

Stage 2   Cut along the centre line of the opening, stopping 1 cm ($\frac{3}{8}$ in.) from the end, and snip into the corners.

Stage 3   Cut an overlap piece, 5 cm (2 in.) wide plus two 6 mm ($\frac{1}{4}$ in.) seam allowances, by the length of the stay-stitched section plus

3 cm ($1\frac{1}{4}$ in.). The underlap should be the length of the stay-stitched section plus a 6 mm ($\frac{1}{4}$ in.) seam allowance, by 4·5 cm ($1\frac{3}{4}$ in.) wide.

Stage 4   Crease the overlap piece in half lengthwise WS together. Turn and crease a 6 mm ($\frac{1}{4}$ in.) seam allowance to the WS along each long edge of both the overlap and underlap pieces.

Stage 5   Position the RS of one edge of the underlap piece on the WS of the underlap half of the opening with its crease over the stay stitching. Cross-pin, and stitch in the crease, stopping level with the stay stitching at the end of the opening. Remove the pins and press the underlap piece over the opening. Turn it through to the RS, enclosing the raw edge of the underlap, and position the fold of its free edge so that it just covers the stay stitching. Press it into place, and edge-stitch the full length of the fold.

Stage 6   Place the RS of one edge of the overlap piece to the WS of the overlap side of the opening, matching the crease to the stay stitching. Cross-pin, and stitch in the crease as far as the stay stitching at the end of the opening. Remove the pins, press the overlap piece over the opening, and bring it through to the RS.

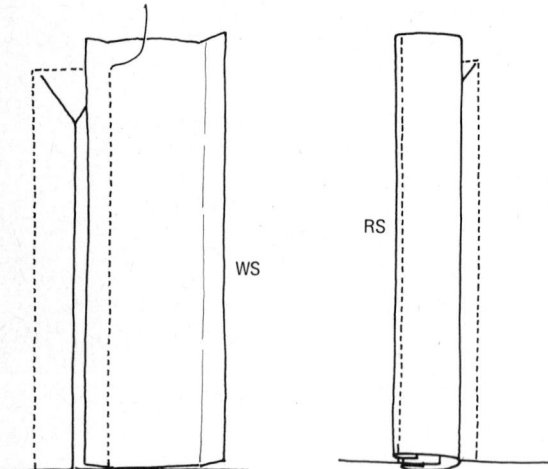

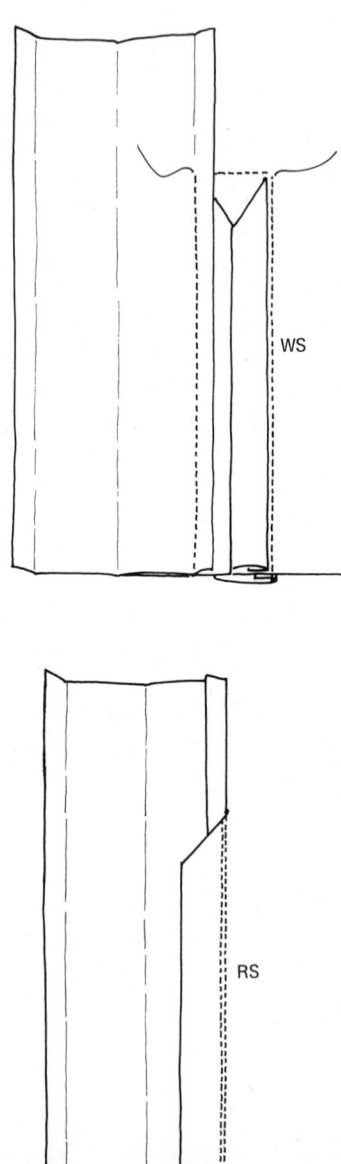

Stage 7   With the pieces as shown in the previous diagram pin the underlap and overlap pieces together, being careful to keep the edges of the opening parallel. Turn the work ws up, and folding the upper part of the sleeve back, arrange the triangle at the end of the slash to lie on the two strips. Stitch along the line of stay stitching, being careful not to catch the fold of garment fabric.

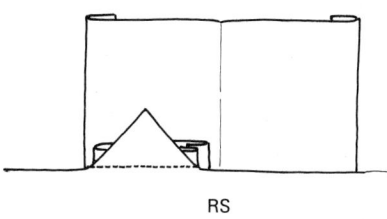

RS

Stage 8   Trim away part of the overlap piece above the stitching, as shown in the diagram, leaving a 6 mm ($\frac{1}{4}$ in.) seam allowance beside the crease.

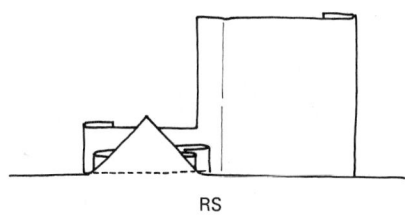

RS

Stage 9   Crease the top corners of the overlap piece to mitre them.

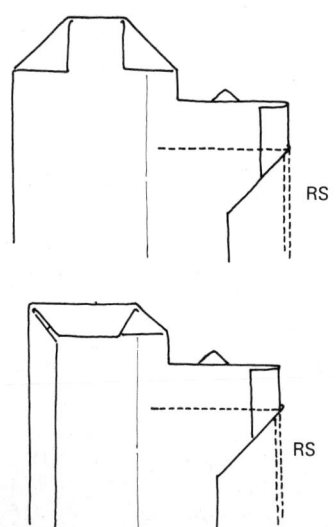

RS

RS

Stage 10   Fold over the free half of the overlap piece so that it lies on the opening and covers the lines of stitching. Baste it into place and stitch as shown in the diagram. Remove the basting and press.

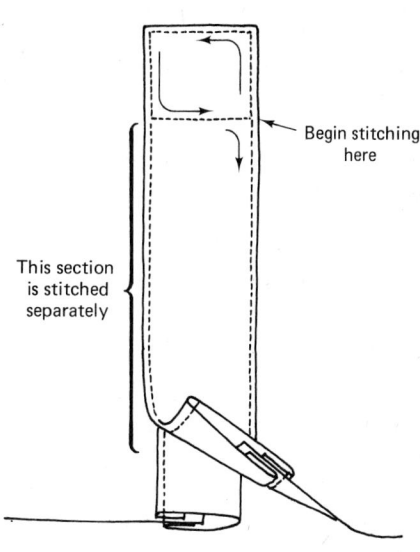

Begin stitching here

This section is stitched separately

A button fly front opening is a type of lapped opening in which the buttons are concealed. It occurs frequently on clothes used for work where it is important that the buttons cannot catch, and it is found on fashion garments as well. Essentially, it consists of three parts: an underlap carrying the buttons, a fly in which the buttonholes are made, and an overlap which conceals the fastening. It can be made in several versions, only one of which is described in detail, but other forms are shown in diagrams at the end of the section.

When making an opening of this type which includes part of the neck facing, it is usual to join the garment shoulder seams and attach the back-neck facing after stage 2, and to attach the collar after stage 6. These processes have been omitted for the sake of clarity.

Stage 1　Cut out the pieces and mark the CF points on the neck edge of the garment and facing with tailor tacks. Mark with even basting the fold lines of the overlap and fly,

and also the single fold line on the underlap. Mark the button holes on the fly piece, and the button positions on the underlap.

Stage 2　Interface the WS of the facing sections of the underlap and the fly, catch-stitch the interfacing to the fold in each case. The interfacing is applied to the facing so that it supports the buttonholes in the fly section, and so that both fronts of the garment present the same appearance when finished. Finish the free edges of the facing.

Stage 3　Fold and pin the fabric RS together along the length of the overlap fold line. Repeat for the fold line of the fly, and also for the underlap.

Stage 4　Stitch along the neck-edge seam line from the fold of the underlap to the tailor tack which marks the CF. Repeat for both the overlap and fly sections. Finish off the thread ends firmly. Trim the corners, and clip the neck-edge seam allowances at the points where the stitching ends.

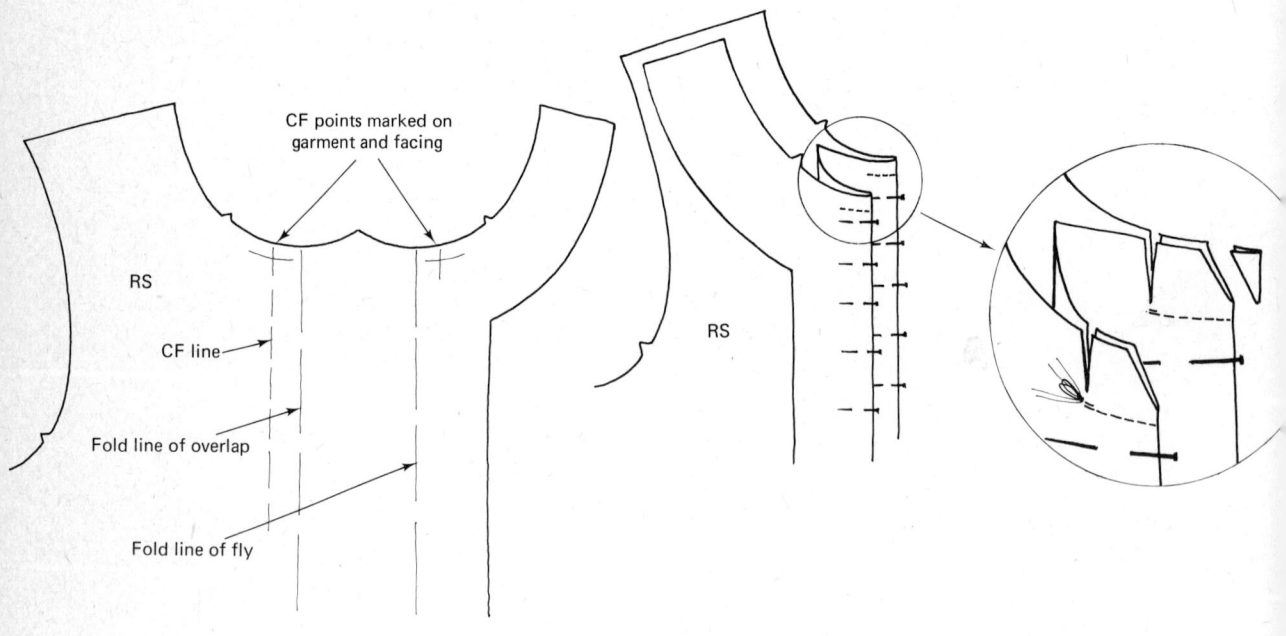

CF points marked on garment and facing

RS

CF line

Fold line of overlap

Fold line of fly

RS

Stage 5   While the pieces are still folded RS together, baste and stitch the underlap piece across the width of the facing at the level of the hem. Stitch the overlap and fly sections to their respective facings, only stitching as far as the inner fold. Trim the seam allowances at the corners.

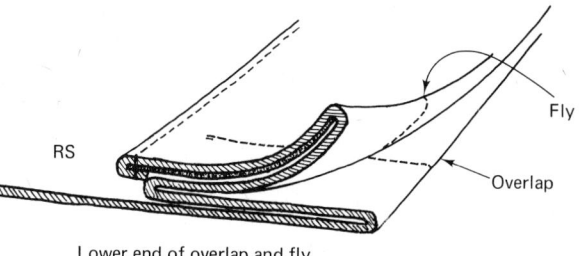

Lower end of overlap and fly

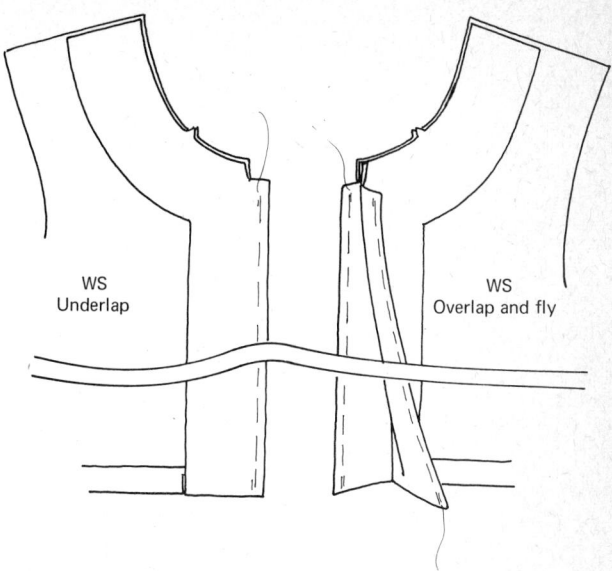

Stage 6   Turn the sections RS out, and press the seam lines at the neck and hem edges, taking care to bring the stitching line to the fold in each case. At the top end, pull out the seam allowances of the unstitched portion of the neck edge.

Stage 8   Slip-stitch the neck edge of the overlap and fly together from the fold to the CF point, and similarly slip-stitch the overlap and fly together at the hem. Catch the edge folds of the two layers together between each buttonhole.

Stage 9   Baste the overlap and fly together firmly, and working from the RS stitch through all layers, parallel with the edge and just catching the inner fold.

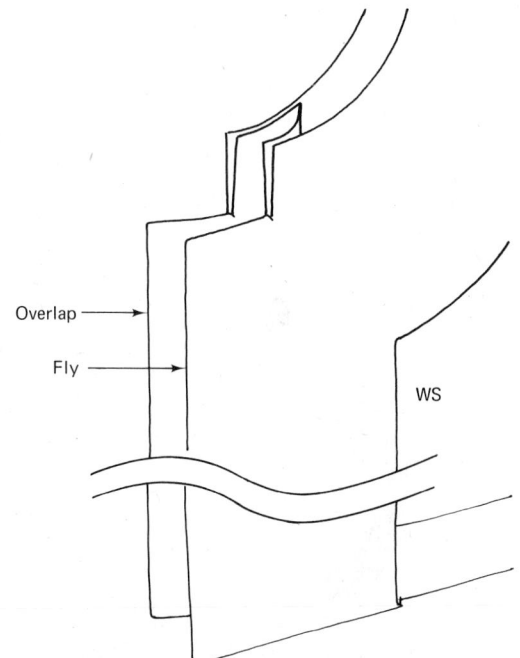

Stage 7   Baste each outer fold to hold it in place, and press it. Work the buttonholes in the fly by hand or machine.

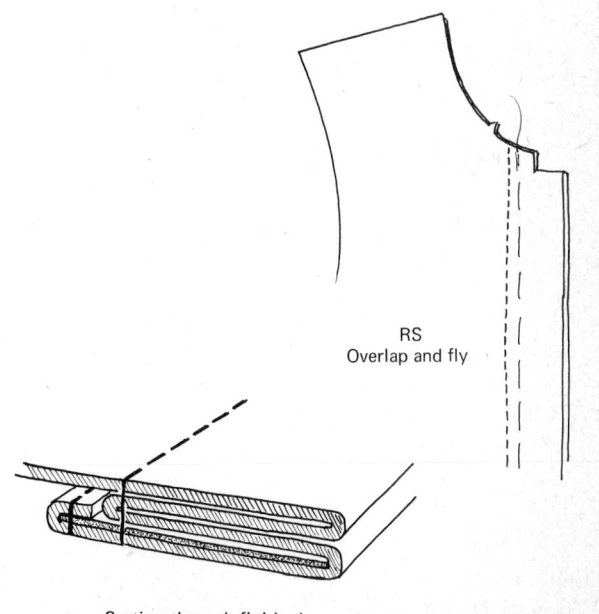

Section through finished overlap and fly

Alternative methods of making fly openings

RS

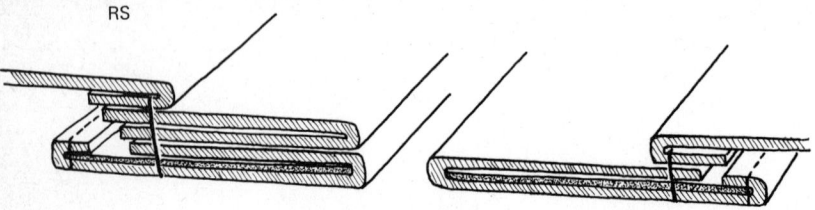

Fly front opening made
with applied bands

RS

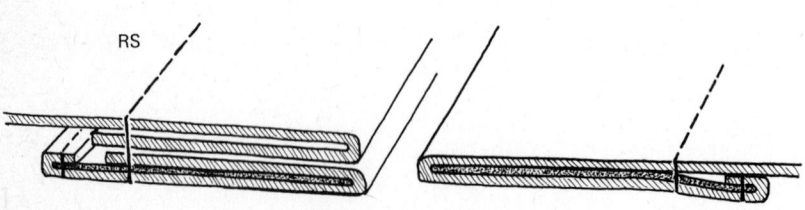

Fly and its facing
cut separately from
the garment

Although a zip fly front opening is called a 'fly front', its construction is quite different from that of a button fly front opening, and much nearer to the lapped method of concealing a zip in a seam.

Stage 1 Cut out the pieces including those for the zip guard, and mark them with tailor tacks. Baste-mark the placement line on the RS of the underlap piece, and the final stitching line on the RS of the overlap.

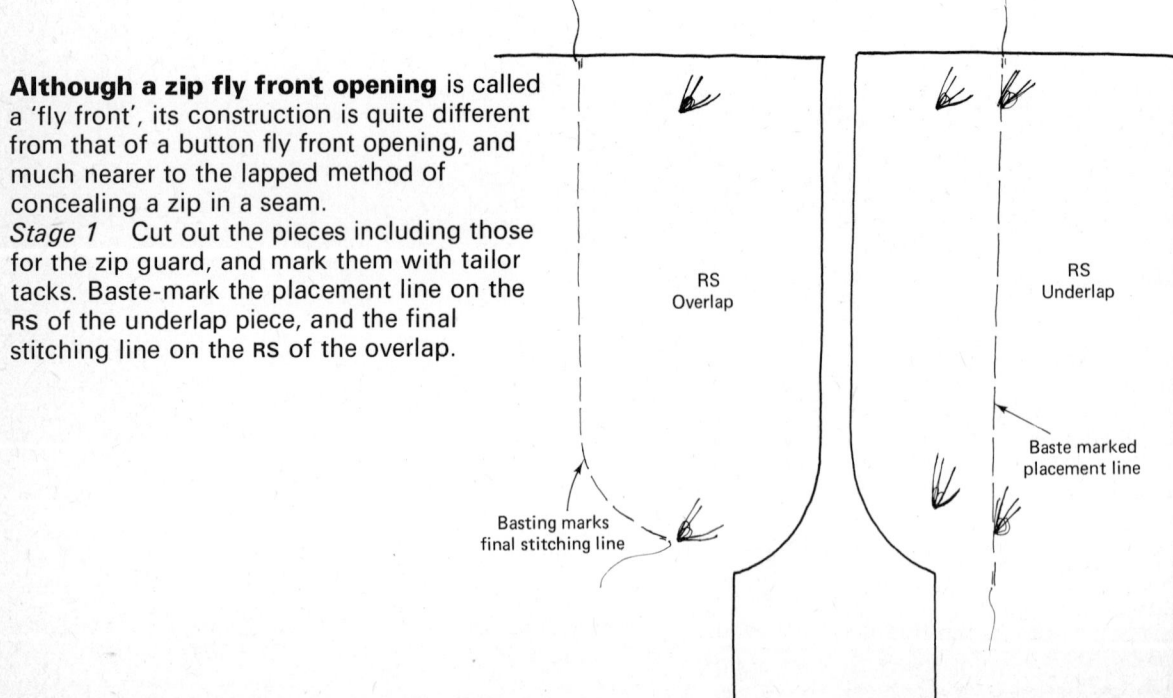

RS
Overlap

RS
Underlap

Baste marked
placement line

Basting marks
final stitching line

Stage 2   Close the seam which runs into the opening. Press the seam allowances open and continue up the overlap side of the opening creasing the foldline.

Stage 3   Clip the seam allowance at the base of the underlap, almost to the stitching line. Press the underlap to the WS along its fold line.

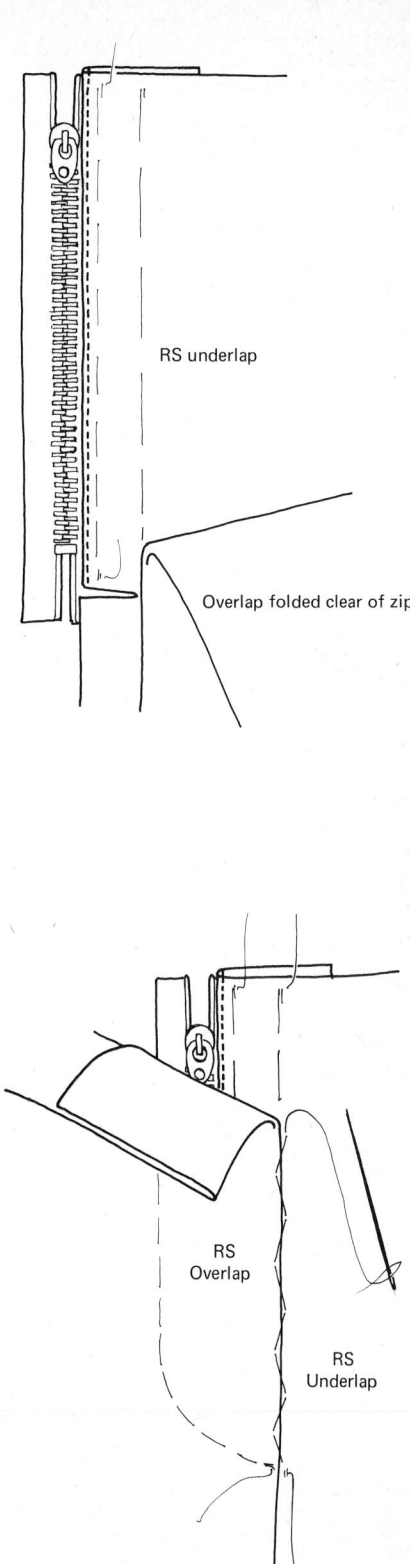

RS underlap

Overlap folded clear of zip

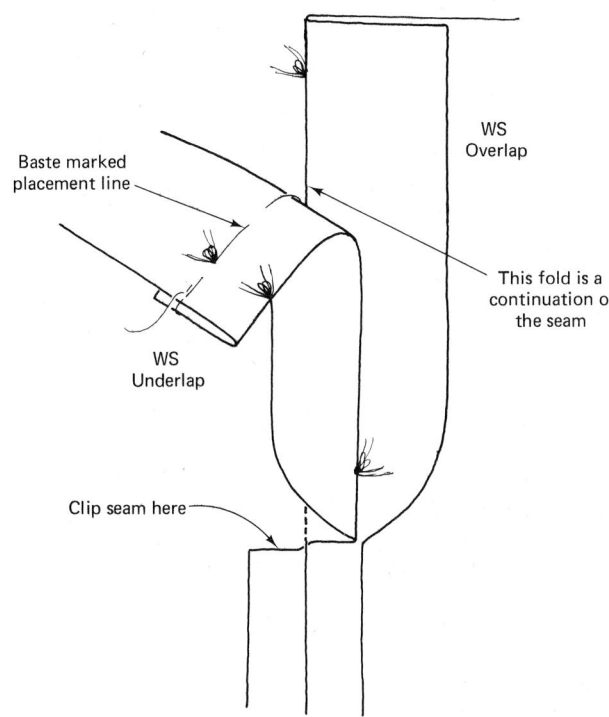

Baste marked placement line

WS Overlap

This fold is a continuation of the seam

WS Underlap

Clip seam here

RS Overlap

RS Underlap

Stage 4   Turn the work RS up, and place the tape of the closed zip beneath the underlap side, with the edge of its chain close to the fold. Baste and edge-stitch the fold to the zip tape, keeping the overlap side out of the way.

Stage 5   Place the folded edge of the overlap against the fitting line of the underlap, and temporarily catch-stitch them together.

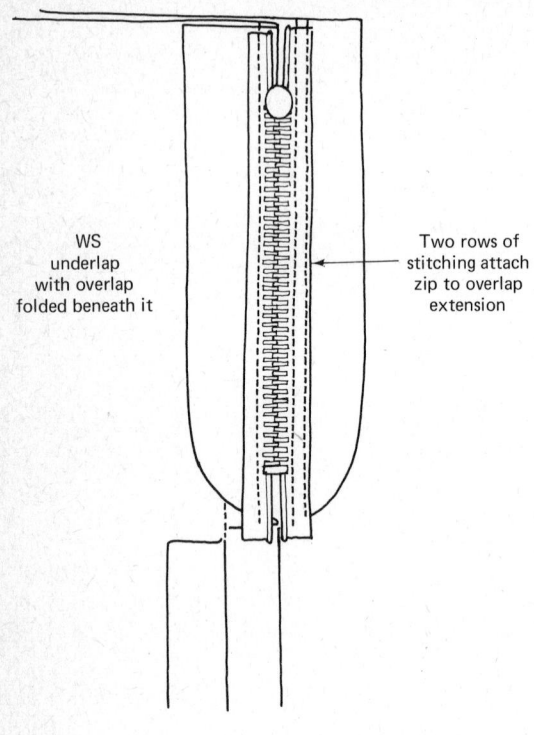

WS underlap with overlap folded beneath it

Two rows of stitching attach zip to overlap extension

Stage 6   Fold the overlap side RS together with the underlap, exposing the overlap extension. Turn the work over. With the WS of the zip uppermost, baste its free half to the extension and stitch twice, once close to the chain, and once near the outer edge of the tape. Remove the basting.

Stage 7   Place the RS of the zip guard and its lining together. With the guard uppermost, pin, baste, and stitch along the seam line of the longer edge. Trim the seam allowance to 6 mm ($\frac{1}{4}$ in.), and notch it around the curve. Turn the guard RS out and press it.

Stage 8   Baste the guard and its lining together along the remaining long edge. Then place the guard, lining side up, on the WS of the underlap extension. Baste the raw edges of the guard and underlap extension together, and stitch, keeping the remainder of the garment clear.

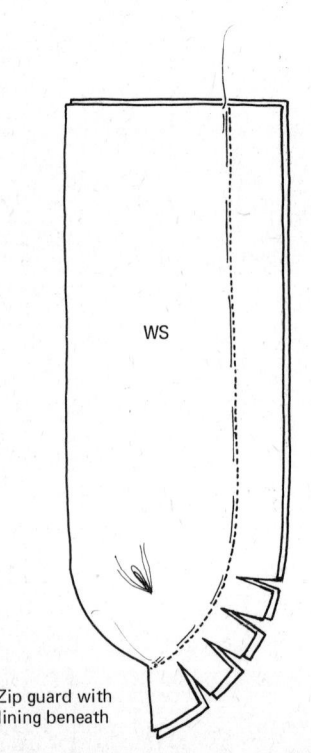

WS

Zip guard with lining beneath

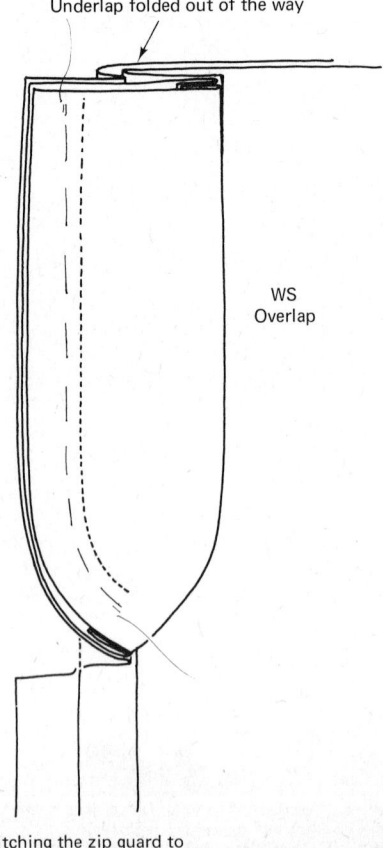

Underlap folded out of the way

WS Overlap

Stitching the zip guard to the underlap extension

Stage 9   Open the zip, and working from the RS, stitch through all layers along the line of stitching which holds the underlap side of the zip in place.

Stage 10   Working from the RS, and keeping the zip guard out of the way, top-stitch through the overlap and its extension along the line of basting put in at stage 1. Remove all the basting and press.

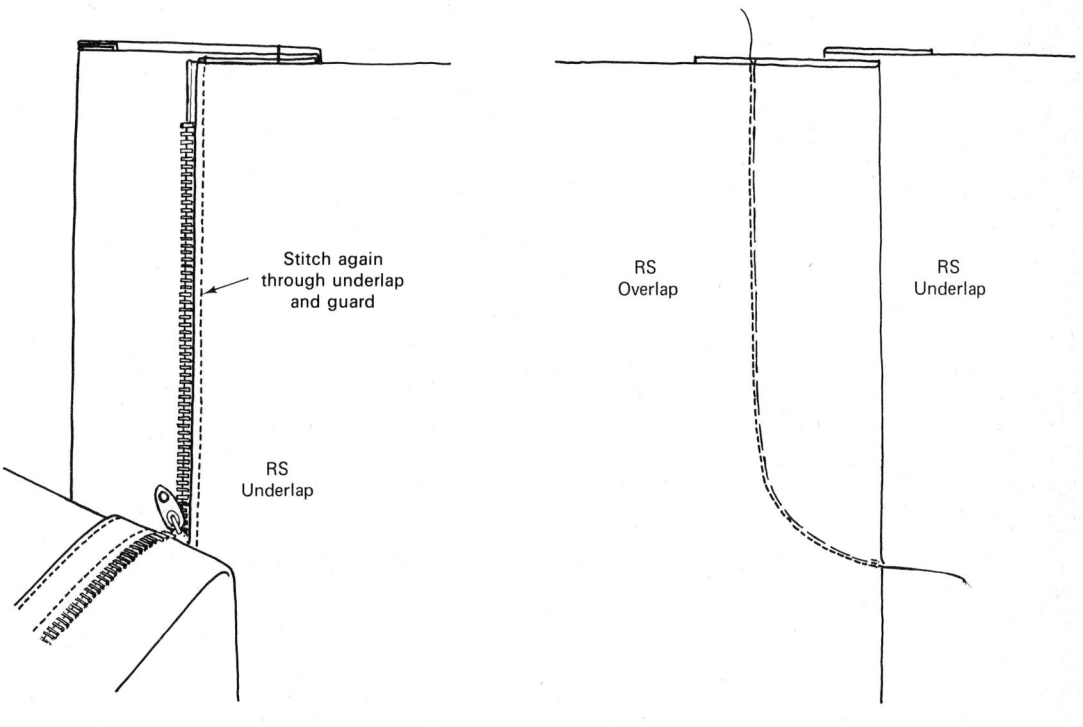

Stitch again through underlap and guard

RS Underlap

RS Overlap

RS Underlap

8 Fastenings

Buttons

Buttons may be functional or purely decorative, conspicuous or hidden. If they play an important part in the design of a garment, their colour, texture, number, size and position must be carefully considered. Remember that their size should not be so great that they overlap the edge, and that if a pattern has to be altered the position of the buttons may have to be changed as well.

It is necessary to strengthen the fabric at the point where functional buttons are sewn on. The interfacing used in the edge of an opening usually provides sufficient support, but for garments which have to withstand hard wear, the button position should, in addition, be reinforced with a 2·5 cm (1 in.) square of self fabric inserted between the facing and the interfacing. Alternatively, the button may be backed with a small button on the inside of the garment, and the two sewn on simultaneously.

Buttons should be sewn on using sewing thread or twist, either of which may be used double if the weight of the work warrants it. Except on sheer and light-weight materials, always sew over a spacer such as a bodkin or matchstick, so that a shank is formed. The thicker the material the longer the shank must be. Before ending off, remove the spacer and wind the thread tightly round the shank six to twelve times to protect it. Bring the thread through to the WS of the garment and finish it off with three or four backstitches. For a neat finish, loop-stitch over the bar of threads formed on the back of the material.

Very large buttons, knotted leather ones for instance, are attached most satisfactorily with tape. Use a stiletto to pierce a hole at the button position. Cut a piece of narrow straight tape, 3 to 4 cm (1½ in.) long, and thread it through the hole in the cloth, and the shank of the button. Take up all the slack, pin the ends of the tape to the WS, turn the cut ends under, and hem around the edges of the tape.

Bachelor's buttons, also called removable shank buttons, are designed to be removed for laundering, and are normally used on garments such as overalls. Pierce a hole with a stiletto where the button will be attached, and work buttonhole stitch around the edge of the hole to keep it open and to protect it from the wear of the metal shank.

Link buttons are sometimes used to close cuffs or edge-to-edge openings. Sew the two buttons back to back, forming a bridge of thread equal in length to the diameter of one button. Loop-stitch over the threads between the buttons, and pass the needle inside the threads to finish off. Another method is to use a very narrow ribbon or tape: thread it through the buttonholes and oversew the selvages of the ribbon together.

A buttonhole must be large enough to allow the button to pass through it without straining the fabric. The length of the buttonhole should be one-eighth longer than the diameter of the button, but when using thick, chunky or domed buttons, whatever their size, add the diameter and thickness of the button together, and make the buttonhole this length.

When a button fastening is liable to come under tension, it is essential that the buttonhole, besides being interfaced, is placed in line with the direction of the strain. Usually this means that the buttonholes will need to be made at right angles to the edge. However, if the garment is loose fitting, buttonholes may be parallel with the edge, as they are in the front band opening of a blouse for example. If the fastening is at the CF, the buttonholes are normally positioned so that when the garment is fastened, the centres of the buttons lie on the CF line. Hand- and machine-made buttonholes are always cut along the line of a thread. Fabric ones, however, may be cut on the bias intentionally (when made in an applied strip which is cut on the bias for decorative effect, for example) and in these cases it is essential that the buttonhole is interfaced to prevent it from stretching.

Hand-worked buttonholes are particularly suitable for garments which will be laundered frequently. They are strong, and therefore can often be made without interfacing, but it may be necessary to use a fine interfacing to give body to a soft fabric, and to prevent the buttonhole stitches from puckering the edge. Hand-worked buttonholes should always be practised on a spare piece of material before they are worked on the garment. A horizontal buttonhole is made with its outer end rounded, and the inner end square. A vertical buttonhole is made with both ends square.

Stage 1　Mark the position of the ends of the buttonhole, and also its centre line, which should follow the line of a single thread of the fabric.

Stage 2　Cut the slit with sharp scissors, beginning at the centre, and cutting towards the ends.

Stage 3　Cut off the correct length of thread or twist — 45 cm (18 in.) will work a 1·5 cm ($\frac{5}{8}$ in.) buttonhole. Use silk for light-weight fabrics, polyester or linen for heavier ones.

Stage 4　Fasten on with a backstitch, and bring the needle out on the RS at the base of the first stitch which should be at the inner end of the buttonhole. To make the stitch, pass the needle through the fabric towards yourself from the WS, and 2 mm ($\frac{1}{16}$ to $\frac{3}{32}$ in.) from the cut edge. Pull the thread through until only a small loop is left. Pass the needle through this loop (which must not be twisted), again towards yourself, and pull up

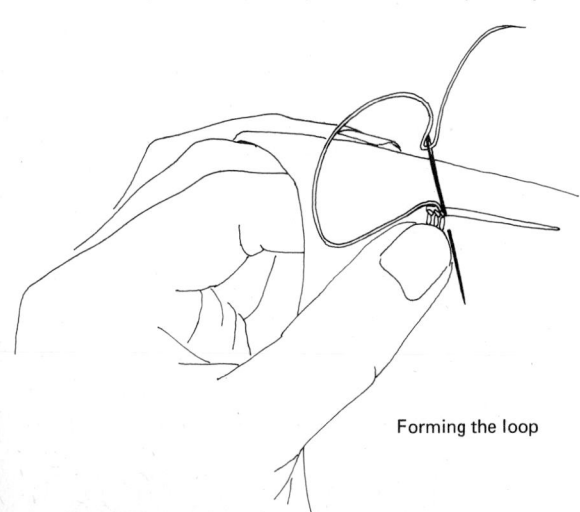

Forming the loop

the knot so that it sits on the edge of the buttonhole. Work the stitches close together so that the knots just touch.

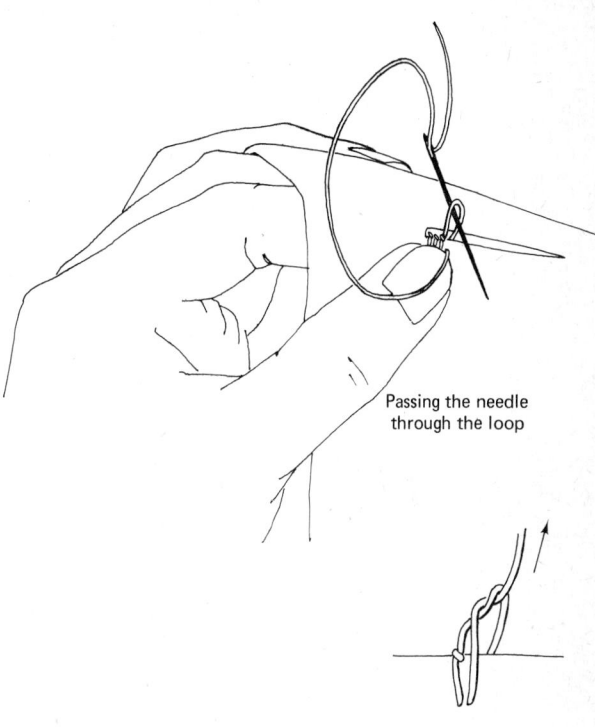

Passing the needle
through the loop

Pull the thread upwards,
away from the edge
to form the knot

Stage 5　The outer end is made semi-circular, and is oversewn with an odd number of stitches (usually five or seven). The last stitch of this section should be a buttonhole stitch in order to bring the thread to the edge of the slit.

Stage 6　Work the second side, and when making the final stitch on this edge pass the needle behind the knot of the first stitch to link the edges together at the inner end.

Stage 7　To finish the inner end, make one backstitch across the full width of the buttonhole. Then work buttonhole stitches over this bar.

Stage 8　Fasten off the thread by taking the needle through to the WS, and slipping it under the stitches.

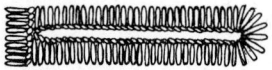

A vertical buttonhole has two square ends. Follow stages 1 to 4. Leave out stage 5. Then, stitching directly across from one long edge to the other, link them as described in stage 6. Link the stitches again at the end of the second side, and work stage 7 at that end. Pass the needle along the length of the buttonhole beneath the stitches and work stages 7 and 8 at the other end.

When making buttonholes in a sheer fabric, take a square of the material, fold it into four, and baste it behind the buttonhole position so that it extends beyond the edges of the buttonhole in all directions. Work the buttonhole through all the layers, and when it is completed cut away the extra fabric of the patch close to the stitching.

Rouleau, or fabric, loops as well as being functional, make an interesting decoration. They can be used to fasten both edge to edge, and lapped openings, and can also be used purely for decoration. Although they may be applied as one continuous strip, the most accurate results are obtained if each loop is cut and applied individually. Find the length of loop needed for a button to slip through by experiment, and add two seam allowances to this to arrive at the total length needed for each button.

Stage 1 Cut a number of strips on the true bias sufficient to make all the loops. The width should be in proportion to the thickness of the fabric, but an average width is 2 cm ($\frac{3}{4}$ in.).

Stage 2 Fold the strip in half lengthwise RS together and baste it.

Stage 3 Stitch along the centre of the folded strip using a short stitch, and stretching the material as it passes through the machine. Alternatively, the strip may be sewn with running stitch.

Stage 4 Thread a bodkin with a length of strong thread which when doubled is equal to the length of the tube. Attach the ends firmly to one end of the tube, slip the bodkin through it, and work the tube RS out by pulling it through itself.

Stage 5 Press lightly, keeping the seam on one edge.

Rouleau loops are attached by seaming their ends between the garment and its facing, or between two garment pieces. If extra strength is required, the ends of the loops may be hemmed to the garment seam allowance before the facing is applied. Before the loops are attached, the seam line should have been baste marked, and the edge of the opening should have been interfaced, so that the ends of the loops will not press through to the RS.

Stage 1 When a number of loops are being applied, it is well worth the trouble of making a card gauge (see diagram) to help position them evenly. Cut the loops, using the gauge to make them equal in length.

This distance equals the space between the same parts of two adjacent loops, and can also be used to mark the button positions

The length equals the total length of a loop and is used as a guide when cutting them

The width equals the distance between the inner faces of the loop

Stage 2   Using the gauge, position the loops on the RS of the garment, with their cut ends level with the raw edge of the seam allowance. The seam of each loop should be arranged to lie on the inside of the curve. Pin each loop and baste it firmly.

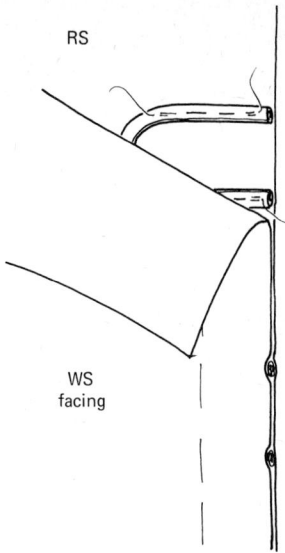

RS

WS
facing

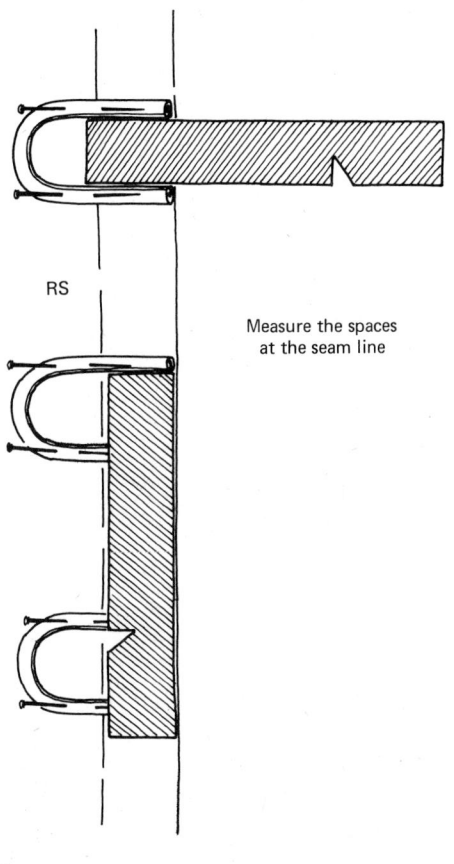

RS

Measure the spaces
at the seam line

Stage 5   Remove the basting. Understitch the edge to set the loops in position (with light-weight fabrics this should be done by hand). Turn the facing to the WS and press. To prevent the ends of the loops from marking the RS of the garment, slide a strip of cardboard between the garment fabric and its seam allowance while pressing.

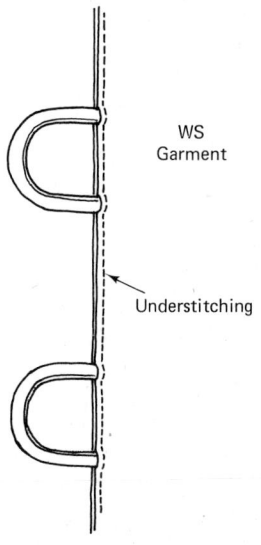

WS
Garment

Understitching

Stage 3   Hem the loops to the seam allowance if desired.

Stage 4   Lay the facing on the garment so that the RS and the raw edges are together, and the loops are covered. Pin and baste the facing into place. Stitch exactly on the seam line.

Stage 6   Grade the seam allowances, and if the loops were not hemmed down, trim about 6 mm ($\frac{1}{4}$ in.) off their ends.

107

Thread loops are sometimes used on babies' dresses, or on very delicate fabrics, where fabric loops would be too heavy in appearance. They are best made in silk thread or twist. The edge of the garment may be strengthened before making the loops, by basting a piece of narrow straight tape to the ws of the seam allowance with its edge against the seam line, and stitching it to the seam allowance close to this edge. Remove the basting, and when forming the loops, catch the tape's selvage with each stitch.

needed in the loop will vary. For very small loops, only two or three threads may be required; a heavier loop will need six to eight. Form the other loops over the same object, using the same number of threads.

Stage 2   When the loop has been formed, loop-stitch over the threads. To avoid dividing the threads, pass the needle through the loop, eye-end first. Keep the row of knots along the outside edge of the loop, and pack the stitches closely together. Finish off with backstitches.

Strengthening an edge for thread loops

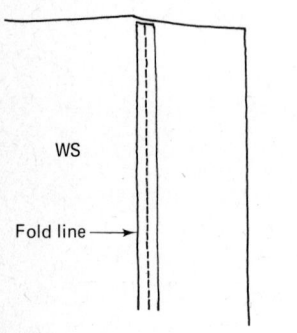
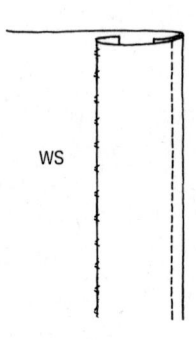

WS

WS

Fold line ⟶

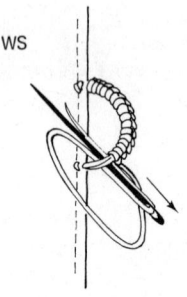

WS

Stage 1   Fasten on the thread at the edge fold, form one loop, and find its right length by passing a button through it. Make a backstitch to prevent the loop from slipping. Once the correct length of loop has been established, it is convenient to stitch to and fro over a cylindrical object of the right size, such as a pencil. The number of threads

Making a thread loop

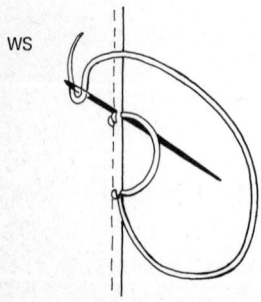

WS

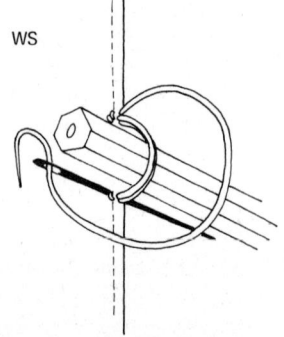

WS

Fabric buttonholes can be made in all weights of fabric except sheers. They are not suitable for use on garments which will be washed frequently, because the small seam allowances are liable to fray and pull out. For convenience in handling, fabric buttonholes are made at a fairly early stage in the construction of the garment.

There are two types of fabric buttonhole, bound, and piped. In the bound version, the seam allowances are left pointing into the slash, and the lips are level with the surface of the garment when the buttonhole is completed. This effect can only be achieved by applying the binding as a single patch. A piped buttonhole is formed when the seam allowances of the opening are pressed away from the buttonhole: from the RS, the lips of the buttonhole appear sunk below the surface of the garment. This type can be made using either a single patch or two folded strips.

The single patch construction is suitable for medium-weight fabrics, but the folds formed at the ends create too much bulk for it to be used in thick materials. The applied strip method may be used when working in either medium-weight or thick fabrics. The organza-patch method combines a faced opening with a piped buttonhole formed from two applied strips, and makes a firm buttonhole for light-weight materials.

Before beginning to make fabric buttonholes, interfacing, if it is to be used, should have been applied to the WS of the opening, and any seams which run into this edge should have been joined. The CF line and the seam or fold line should have been marked with uneven basting.

Bound buttonholes made from a single patch

Stage 1 Join any seam which runs into the edge of the opening and mark the CF and interfacing as one layer, and working from the RS, mark the inner and outer ends of the buttonhole positions on both sides of the fabric. Machine-baste the centre line of each buttonhole.

Stage 2 Cut patches, either on the straight grain, or on the true bias, 5 cm (2 in.) high, by the length of the buttonhole plus two seam allowances. Mark the horizontal centre

line of each patch with basting, or by creasing it with an iron. If the material frays easily finish the raw edges.

Stage 3 Place the RS of the patch and garment together, making sure that the centre line of the patch is exactly over the buttonhole line, and that the patch overlaps the buttonhole position by an equal amount at each end. Pin the patch firmly to the garment.

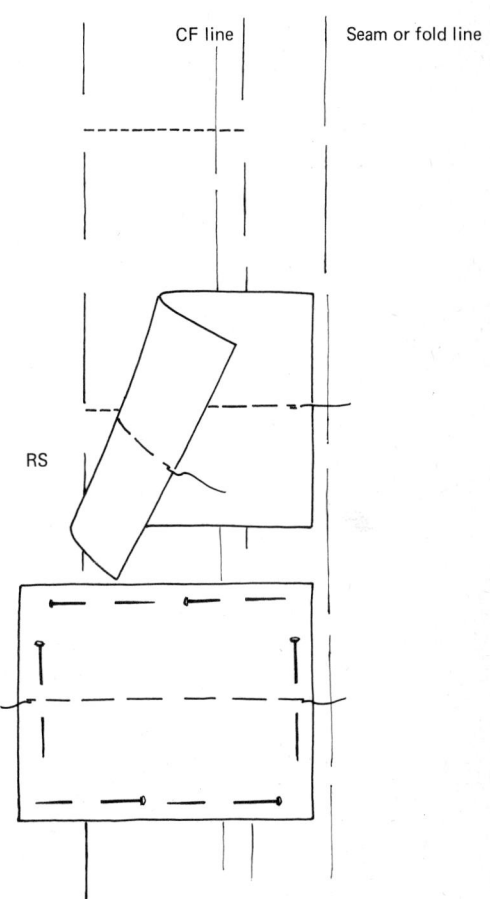

Stage 4 When stitching the buttonhole, the line of stitching on each long side must be the same distance from the centre line (3 to 4 mm ($\frac{1}{8}$ in.) for medium-weight fabric), and parallel with it. The stitching at each end must be at right angles to the long sides, and on the line of basting which marks the end of the buttonhole. Set the machine to a 1·5 mm stitch (18 stitches per inch), and with the garment WS up, stitch round the buttonhole beginning on one of its long sides. Pivot with

the needle down at each corner, and overlap the stitching by about 1 cm ($\frac{3}{8}$ in.). Remove the pins.

Stage 5   Cut along the centre line of the buttonhole, stopping 3 mm ($\frac{1}{8}$ in.) from each end, and from this point snip into the corners, being careful not to cut the stitching.

Stage 7   Turn the patch through the hole, and to hold it while forming an inverted pleat at each end, pin the pleats in line with the buttonhole. Oversew their edges together beyond each end of the opening and remove the pins. Catch-stitch the lips of the buttonhole together lightly from the RS.

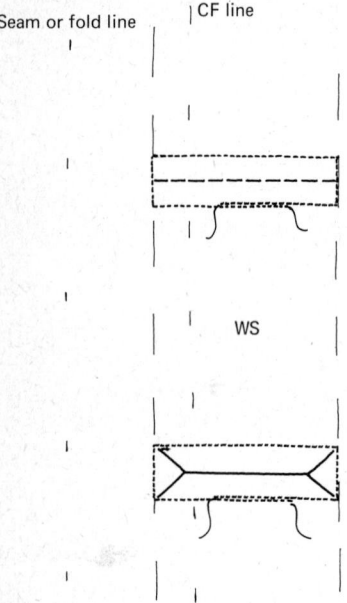

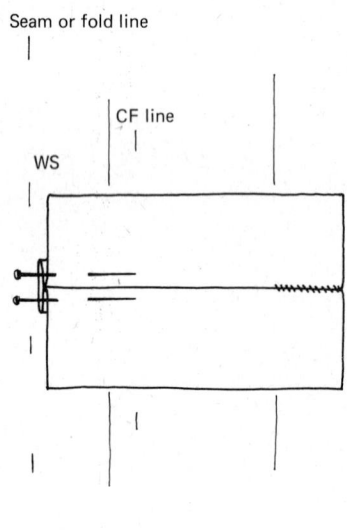

Stage 6   With the garment RS up, slide the toe of an iron under each free edge of the patch, and press the patch over the buttonhole on all four sides.

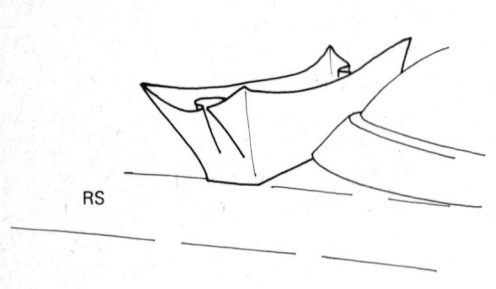

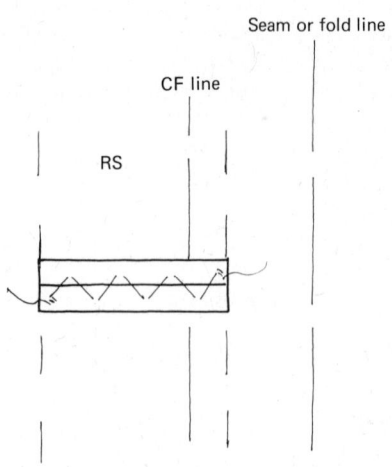

Interfacing is not shown in the diagrams

Stage 8 Turn the work RS up, and fold the garment back exposing the triangle at one end of the buttonhole. Stitch through the triangle and pleat along the line of the previous stitching to strengthen the end of the buttonhole. Repeat at the other end.

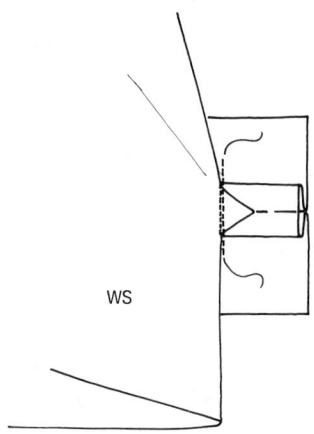

WS

A piped buttonhole made from applied strips

Stage 1 Join any seams which run into the edge of the opening and mark the CF and interfacing as one layer, and working from the RS, mark the inner and outer ends of the buttonhole positions with uneven basting. Machine-baste the centre line of each buttonhole.

Stage 2 Cut, either on the straight grain or on the true bias, a strip of fabric 3 cm (1⅛ in.) wide, and long enough to make all the buttonholes. Each buttonhole will need two strips, each one the length of the buttonhole plus two seam allowances.

Stage 3 Crease the strip in half lengthwise WS together. To form the piping, stitch along the strip (3 mm (⅛ in.) from the fold for light-weight fabrics to 5 mm ($\frac{3}{16}$ in.) for heavy ones). If the buttonhole is to be

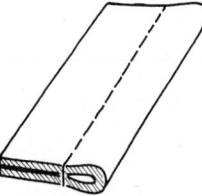

Interfacing not shown in the diagrams

corded, use a cording foot and place a fine piping cord in the crease.

Stage 4 Trim one seam allowance to 1 mm ($\frac{1}{16}$ in.) less than the width of the piping. Cut the strip into lengths.

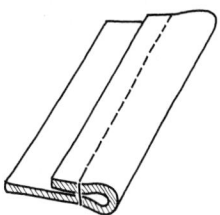

Stage 5 Place the strip on the RS of the garment with its trimmed seam allowances against the centre line of the buttonhole. The ends of the strip should extend by an equal amount beyond each end of the buttonhole. Baste it into place along the piping. Pin the untrimmed seam allowance out of the way, and position the second strip on the opposite side of the buttonhole.

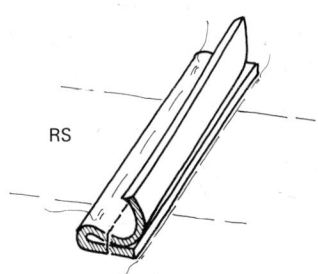

RS

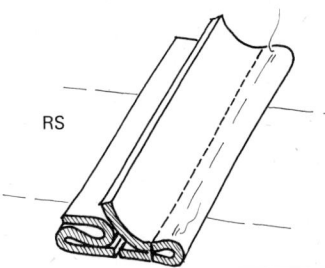

RS

Stage 6 Using a short machine stitch, sew each strip to the garment along the row of stitching put in at stage 3. Begin and end exactly level with the ends of the buttonhole. Sew in the thread ends. Remove the basting.

Stage 7 Turn the garment WS up, and cut along the centre line of the buttonhole, stopping 3 mm ($\frac{1}{8}$ in.) from each end. From this point snip into the corners, being careful not to cut beyond the end of the stitching. Remove the basting stitches.

Stage 8 Turn the strips through the buttonhole to the WS. The edge folds will now lie together to form the lips of the buttonhole. Catch-stitch them together.

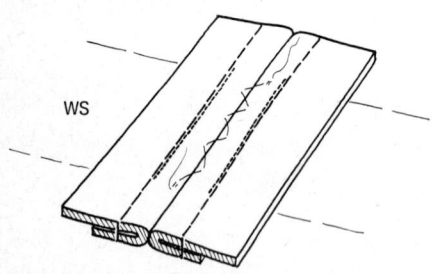

Stage 9 With the garment RS up, fold its edge back to expose the triangle formed by cutting into the corners. Using a short machine stitch, sew the triangle to the strips. Care must be taken that this row of stitching is at right angles to the line of the buttonhole slit, because it forms the end of the buttonhole. Treat the triangle at the other end of the buttonhole in the same way. Press.

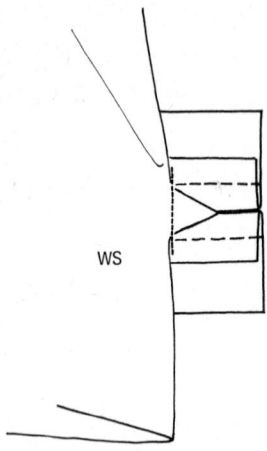

An organza-patch buttonhole. (Diagrams for stages 1 to 4 will be found in the bound buttonhole instructions.)

Stage 1 Join any seams and mark the CF and the seam or fold lines. Mark on both sides of the fabric the positions of the inner and outer ends of the buttonholes. Machine- or hand-baste the centre line of each buttonhole.

Stage 2 Cut patches which blend with the colour of the garment, in organza or organdie. These should be the length of the buttonhole plus two seam allowances, by 5 cm (2 in.) high.

Stage 3 Centre a patch over the buttonhole marking on the RS of the garment, and pin it firmly into place.

Stage 4 When stitching the buttonhole, the line of stitching on each long side must be the same distance from the centre line (2 to 3 mm $\frac{1}{8}$ in.), and parallel with it. The stitching at each end must be at right angles to the long sides, and on the line of the basting which marks the end of the buttonhole. Turn the work WS up, and using a short machine stitch, begin the stitching of the buttonhole on one of its long sides. Pivot with the needle down at each corner, and overlap the stitching by about 1 cm ($\frac{3}{8}$ in.). Remove the pins.

Stage 5 Cut along the centre line of the buttonholes, stopping 3 mm ($\frac{1}{8}$ in.) from each end. From that point snip into the corners being careful not to cut through the stitching. Slip the toe of an iron between the garment and the patch, and press the patch over the buttonhole on all four sides. Turn the patch to the WS, pulling it at the corners to make it set. Press, bringing the stitching line right to the fold, to form a perfectly rectangular hole.

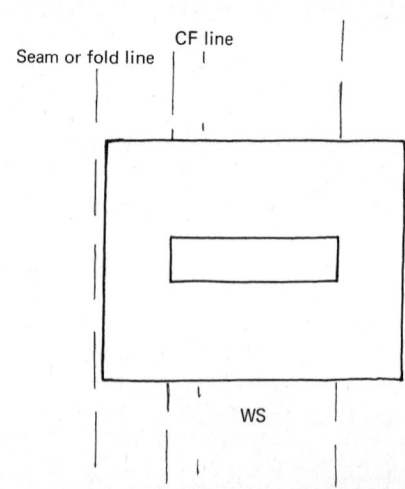

Stage 6   Cut a strip of fabric, either on the straight grain or on the true bias, 3 cm ($1\frac{1}{8}$ in.) wide, and long enough for all the buttonholes. Crease the strip in half lengthwise, and cut it into lengths. A buttonhole will require two strips, each one the length of the buttonhole plus two seam allowances.

Stage 7   Place the two strips with their RS together, and machine-baste them along their creases. Press the seam open.

Stage 9   Keep the garment RS up, and fold it back to expose the buttonhole seam allowances. Using a short machine stitch, sew along each long edge on top of the previous stitching. Overlap the stitching onto the strip at both ends, being careful not to catch the fold of the garment fabric. Remove the pins and repeat across the ends.

Stage 10   Clip off the thread ends and press the buttonhole from the RS. Remove the machine basting from the slit.

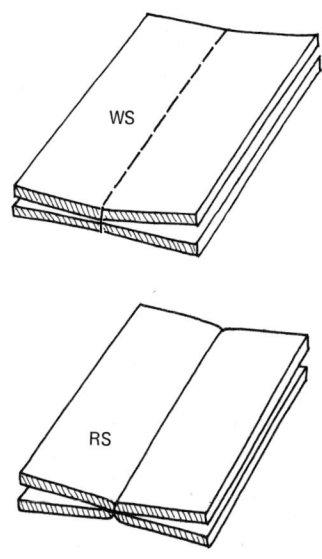

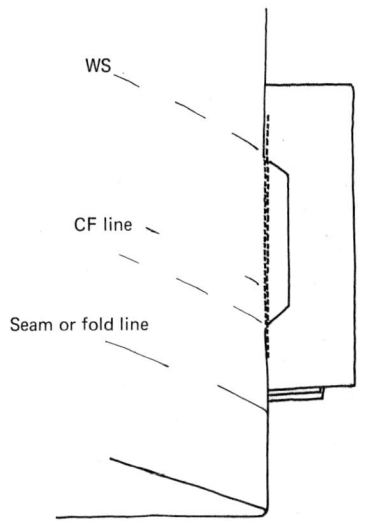

Stage 8   With the garment RS up, place the joined piece beneath the opening with its seam along the centre line of the buttonhole, and an equal amount of overlap at each end. Use one pin at each end, placed in line with the buttonhole slit, to hold the piece to the garment.

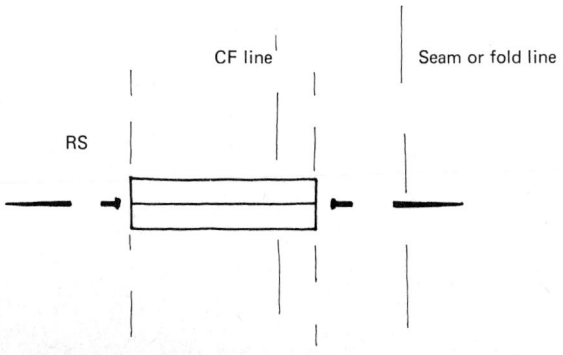

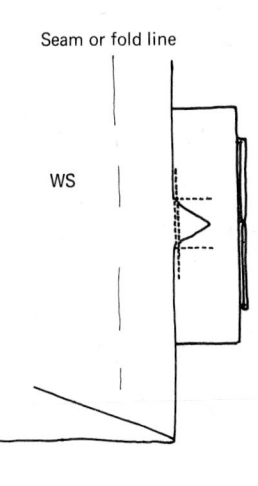

The facing, when making fabric buttonholes, has to be cut to allow the buttons to fasten. The shape of the opening may be either rectangular, or in the form of a boat. If the facing pieces have not already been marked, pin the facing firmly to the garment fabric between each buttonhole. Transfer the positions of the ends of the buttonholes from the RS by stabbing through with two pins.

The boat shape is usually made if the garment will be worn buttoned. Cut the facing along the centre line of the buttonhole, remove the pins, and extend the cut by 3 mm ($\frac{1}{8}$ in.) at each end. Using a needle, turn under 3 mm ($\frac{1}{8}$ in.) of the facing in the centre of each long edge, and hem the fold to the back of the buttonhole with matching thread. Make the seam allowances taper to nothing at each end.

A rectangular opening is normally used when the facing is likely to be seen. It may be made by cutting the facing along the centre line of the buttonhole, snipping into each corner, and turning in and hemming the folded edges to the back of the buttonhole.

A neater finish can be achieved by working stages 1 to 5 of an organza-patch buttonhole in the facing. Transfer the buttonhole markings accurately to the facing and work the rectangles before attaching the facing. The edges of these faced rectangles should be attached to the WS of the buttonholes with slip stitching after the facing is attached and turned to the WS.

Hooks

Hooks, and either eyes or bars are normally used where an opening will be under constant tension. The size of the hook depends on the location of the fastening and the thickness of the fabric. The hook should be sewn to the WS of the overlapping piece, and the bar or eye to the RS of the underlap. Set the hook back from the edge of the fabric far enough to conceal the whole fastening. Hooks and eyes should be attached using oversewing or loop stitch. Sew through the bight of the hook as well to prevent it from pulling away from the fabric.

Edge-to-edge closures which are not under constant tension (eg a cloak fastening or the back neck opening of a blouse), are unlikely to come undone when the hooks are sewn first on one edge and then on the other. In this type of closure a hand-worked bar on the extreme edge of the fabric is less obtrusive than a metal one. (For the method of making a hand-worked bar see 'thread loops', page 108.)

Snap fasteners

Snap fasteners are used where two layers of fabric need to be kept together but where there is very little strain. Sew on the ball half of the fastener with its flat back against the WS of the overlap, and the socket half on the RS of the underlap, making three to five oversewing stitches through each hole.

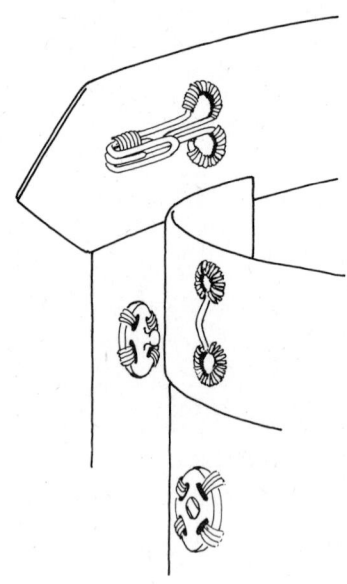

Zip fasteners

Zip fasteners are normally fitted after the seam below the opening has been joined, but while the garment can still be opened out flat. When purchasing a zip, it should be remembered that the nominal length which is on the packet is the length of the zip chain, and does not include the tape at the ends. Therefore, when measuring a garment opening for a zip, do not include the seam allowance, but measure only the distance from the base of the opening to the fitting line at the open end. If one or more hooks are to be fitted above the end of the zip, the length of the zip should be 1 cm ($\frac{3}{8}$ in.) less than the distance between the bottom of the opening and the position of the lowest hook.

When working with velvet, slippery or soft fabrics, the zip should not be stitched by machine, but should be put in by hand using stab stitch. The stitching, whether hand or machine, must not be too close to the chain, because this would impede the movement of the slider, and cause the folded edges of the fabric to be pushed outwards. If the stitching is too far from the chain this too may cause

the chain to show if the zip comes under sideways strain. When pressing, care must be taken not to overheat nylon zips. Invisible zips should only be pressed when closed to avoid distorting the set of the teeth.

Zip concealed in a seam: slot method.
This method can be used for CB and CF openings.
Stage 1   Stitch the seam to the point where the opening begins, and finish off the thread ends.
Stage 2   Press the seam open and crease both the seam allowances of the opening to the WS along their fold lines. Baste the seam allowances to the garment close to the fold.
Stage 3   Place the garment RS up on a flat surface, and position the closed zip so that one side of the opening covers exactly half the width of the chain. Check that the top of the slider comes to the correct place. Pin and baste this side of the opening to the zip tape, being careful not to stretch the folded edge. (If the garment is stretched on to the tape the zip will buckle and spoil the set of the opening.)

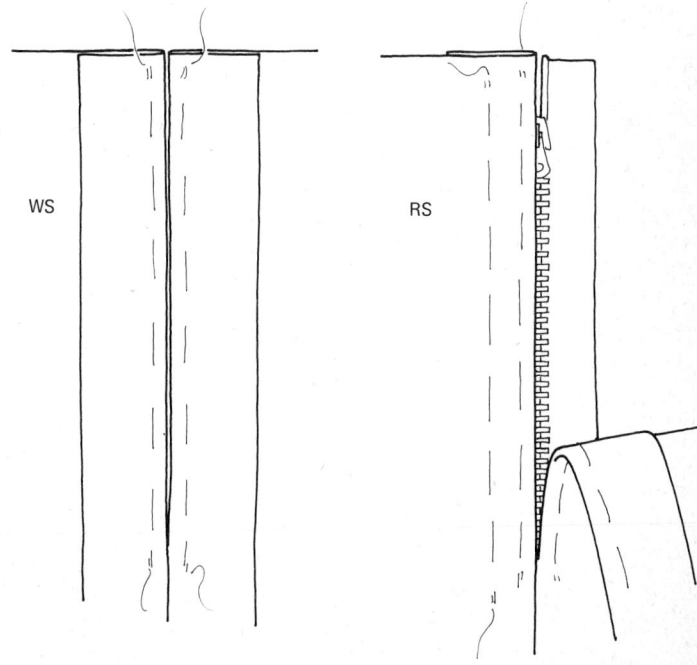

WS

RS

Stage 4   Place the other side of the opening against the first and catch-stitch them temporarily together, so that the two folds are held centrally over the zip.

Stage 5   Baste the second side of the opening to the zip tape. Check that both sides of the opening are exactly the same in length. Remove the basting put in at stage 2.

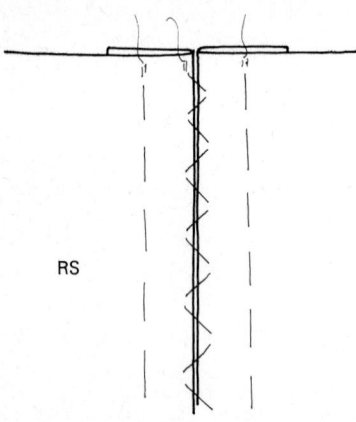

RS

Stage 6   Working from the RS, hand sew, or stitch using a zip foot, parallel with the opening and 3 to 4 mm ($\frac{1}{8}$ in.) from it (this distance depends on the width of the chain). The stitching can usually be put in down one side, across the end, and up the other side, but if the fabric tends to slip it is advisable to stitch each side in the same direction.

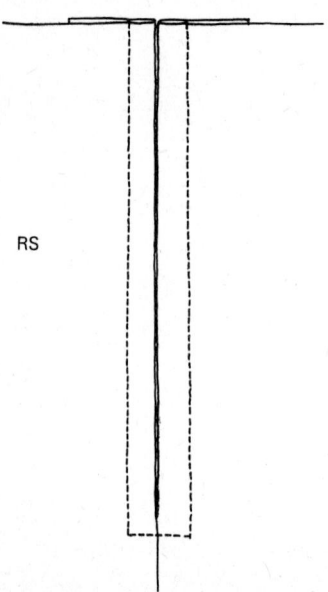

RS

Stage 7   Finishing a zip requires special care because no loose threads must be left which might jam in the slider. Sew the thread ends into the WS of the seam allowances. Remove the basting and catch stitching. Finish the raw edges of the seam allowances beside the zip, and loop-stitch the ends of the tape to the seam allowances at the lower end of the opening. Press.

Zip concealed in a seam: lapped method.
This method is always used when fitting a zip to a side opening and it can also be used with a CB one. The overlap side of the opening should have been cut with an extra 1 cm ($\frac{3}{8}$ in.) added on to the seam allowance as far as the bottom of the zip tape.

Stage 1   Stitch the seam to the point where the opening begins and finish off the thread ends.

Stage 2   Mark the placement line (which is a continuation of the seam line) on the underlap edge of the opening with basting. Clip the underlap seam allowance almost to the stitching line, 2·5 cm (1 in.) below the base of the opening.

Stage 3   With an iron, crease the overlap seam allowance along the fold line (which is also a continuation of the seam line) and baste it to the garment.

Stage 4   Leaving 3 mm ($\frac{1}{8}$ in.) of the underlap seam allowance showing on the RS, turn the remainder to the WS and baste.

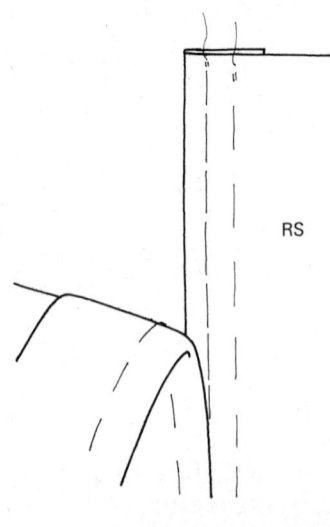

RS

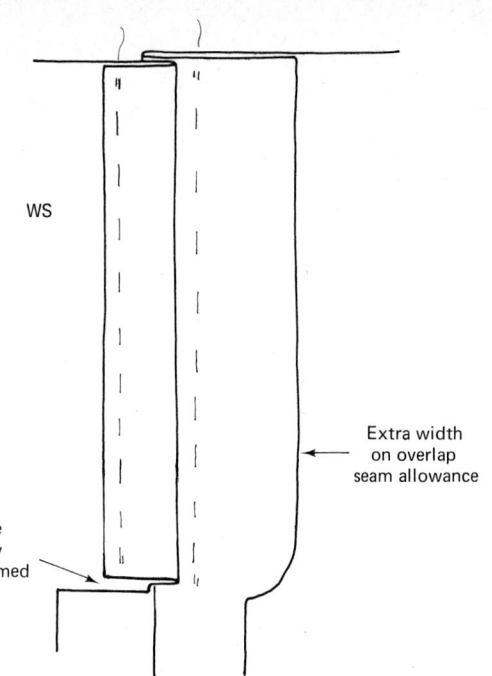

WS

Extra width
on overlap
seam allowance

am allowance
pped to allow
lap to be formed

Stage 5   Place the garment RS up on a flat
surface. Lay the underlap piece on the tape of
the closed zip so that the fold is 2 mm ($\frac{1}{16}$ in.)
from the edge of the zip chain. Check that the
top of the zip comes to the correct place. Pin
and baste the fold to the zip tape, being
careful not to stretch the folded edge. If the
garment is stretched on to the tape, the zip
will buckle and spoil the set of the opening.
Edge-stitch the fold to the zip tape and remove
the basting.

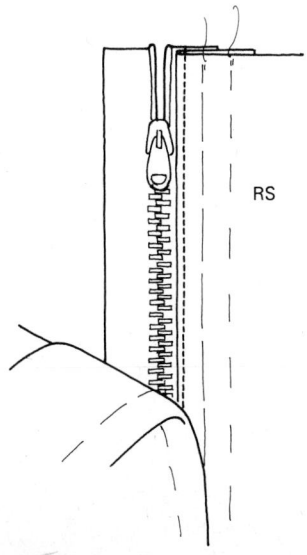

RS

Stage 6   Measure from the placement line to
a point 3 mm ($\frac{1}{8}$ in.) on the far side of the zip
chain and note this distance. Temporarily
catch-stitch the edge fold of the overlap piece
against the placement line of the underlap.
Baste the overlap piece to the zip tape and
check that the upper ends of the opening are
level.

Stage 7   Stitch the overlap to the zip tape
making the distance of the stitching from the
fold the same as the measurement made in
stage 6. Pivot through a right angle at the
bottom of the zip and end the stitching at the
seam. Remove the basting and press.

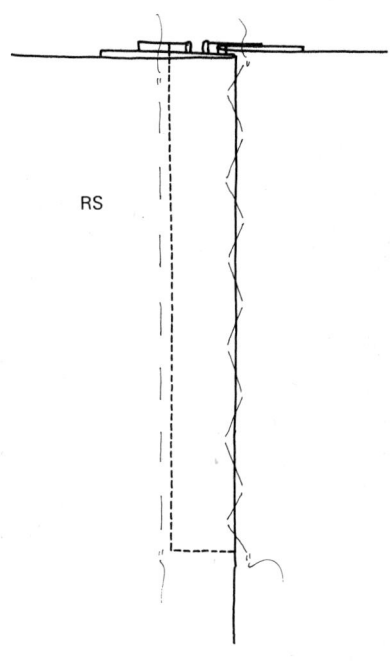

RS

Stage 8   Finishing a zip requires special care,
because no loose threads must be left which
might jam in the slider. Take the thread ends
through to the WS and sew them in. Finish
the raw edges of the seam allowances beside
the zip opening, and loop-stitch the ends of
the tape to the seam allowances at the lower
end of the opening. Press.

When making this opening in a soft fabric it
may be preferable to hem the underlap fold to
the zip tape at stage 5 and stab-stitch the
overlap at stage 7.

117

A conspicuously set zip is often made a feature on sports wear. When this type of zip is to be set into a slash, the opening should be faced, have parallel sides, a square lower end and be 4 mm ($\frac{3}{16}$ in.) wider than the zip chain. Once the facing has been attached, turned and understitched, the zip is centred and basted into the opening and the folded edge of the opening stitched to the zip tape.

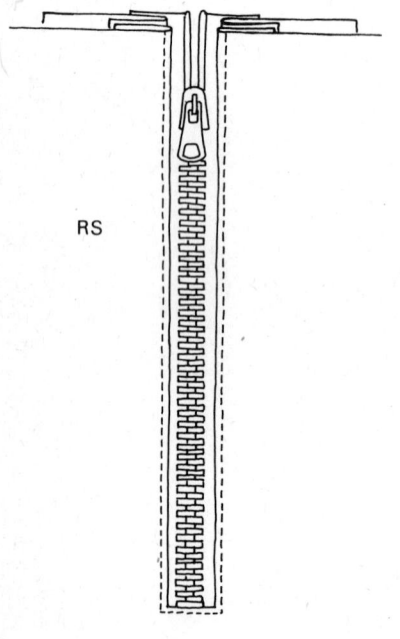

RS

Invisible zips are inserted so that the stitching does not show on the RS. Because the zip tape is sewn to the seam allowance only, the zip is put in from the WS.

Stage 1 Baste the two garment pieces RS together along the whole length of the seam, including the opening. Stitch the seam to the point where the opening begins, and finish off the thread ends. Press the seam allowances of the opening and the seam open.

Stage 2 Take the closed zip and place it, chain uppermost, on the seam allowance. Check that the top of the zip comes to the correct place. Match the 'seam' in the tape to the garment seam, a short length at a time, cross pinning as shown in the diagram. Fold the garment fabric out of the way, and hand-baste, or alternatively use the zip foot and machine-baste, the zip to the seam allowances. Remove the pins.

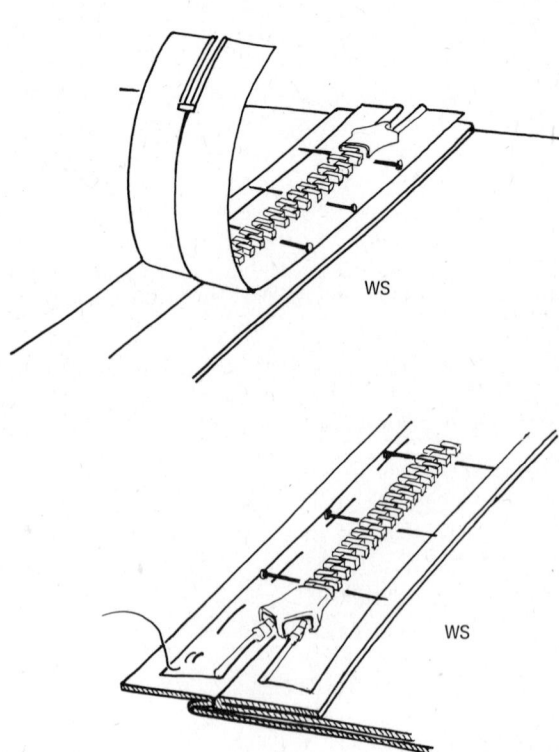

WS

WS

Stage 3 Remove the basting which closes the opening and open the zip fully.

Stage 4 Keeping the body of the garment out of the way, position one of the zip tapes and its seam allowance under the zip foot, with the zip tape uppermost. Make the teeth stand up by pressing them against the side of the zip foot, and stitch each tape to its seam allowance as close to the chain as possible. Do not attempt to stitch the end of the zip where the slider is; this section should be backstitched from the WS of the seam allowance. Sew the thread ends into the WS of the seam allowance. Alternatively the entire zip may be backstitched.

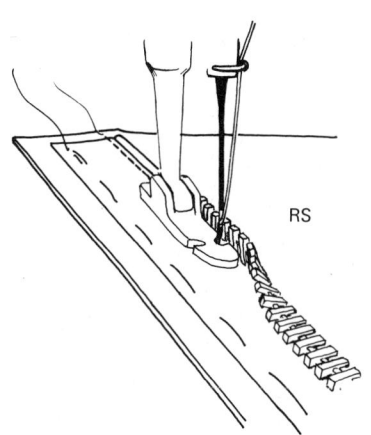

RS

A zip guard should always be fitted behind metal zips if they irritate the skin of the wearer. It will also prevent folds of underwear from being caught in the chain. A guard for a lapped opening in a skirt must be fitted after the zip and before the waistband. The upper end of the guard will then be enclosed when the waistband is applied.

Stage 1 Cut a piece of garment fabric on the straight grain, the length of the opening plus two seam allowances. Make the width 4 cm (1½ in.). If a lined guard is required, cut the lining to the same size as the guard piece, baste them together and treat them as a single layer throughout the remainder of the process.

Stage 2 Cross-pin and baste the RS of the guard and the underlap seam allowances together with their raw edges level. The upper end of the guard should be level with the raw edge at the waistline of the garment.

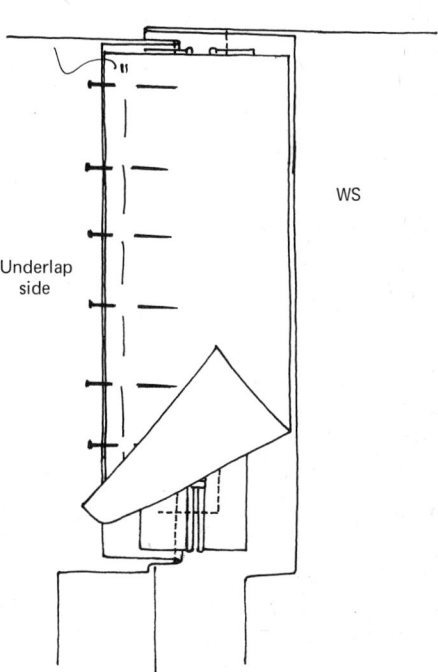

Underlap side

WS

Stage 3 Stitch the guard to the underlap seam allowance 6 mm (¼ in.) from the raw edges.

Stage 4 Loop-stitch the edges of the guard and underlap seam allowance together. Use the same stitch across the base of the opening to hold the guard and seam allowances together, and continue up the free edge of the guard to finish it.

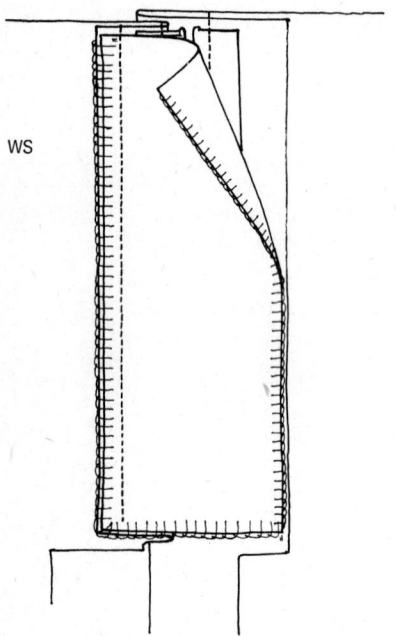

WS

A zip guard for a dress can be adapted from the guard described above. Alternatively, but only if the dress will be dry-cleaned, a guard may be made from matching grosgrain or petersham ribbon. This can be fitted after the garment is completed. The width of the ribbon should be the nearest stock size to the combined width of the two seam allowances of the opening.

Stage 1 If the zip ends at an edge, cut the ribbon to the length of the opening plus 1·5 cm ($\frac{5}{8}$ in.). Make and hem a 6 mm ($\frac{1}{4}$ in.) single fold at one end of the ribbon.

Stage 2 Place this fold against the zip, 6 mm ($\frac{1}{4}$ in.) below the edge of the opening, and pin and baste the ribbon to one seam allowance (the underlap seam allowance if it is a lapped opening).

Stage 3 Beginning at the base of the opening, stitch the ribbon to the seam allowance, 6 mm ($\frac{1}{4}$ in.) from its raw edge, and stop at the free edge of the facing. Hem the top of the ribbon to the facing.

Stage 4 Loop-stitch the lower end of the ribbon to the seam allowances to finish it and hold it in place. Close the zip, and sew a small snap fastener to the free upper corner of the guard to fasten it to the garment.

If the zip is closed at both ends, the ribbon should be cut to the same length as the opening plus 3 cm (1$\frac{1}{4}$ in.). Loop-stitch both raw ends to the seam allowances.

9 Collars

Making collars

Constructionally, collars fall into two categories: that in which part of the collar is cut in one with the garment, and that in which the collar is made independently and then attached. Collars may be regarded also as a graduated series. At one end lie the collars which are cut straight and have a high stand: at the other are the collars which are cut so that the shape of their inner edge almost matches the curve of the neck, and which will therefore lie flat.

Before beginning work on a collar, try on the garment to check that the neckline sets perfectly. Many difficulties experienced in fitting collars arise as a result of a badly fitting neckline. If the length of the neckline edge has been altered, the collar will also need to be modified. Remember when adjusting the collar that it is not the lengths of the raw edges, but the lengths of the seam lines which must be made to correspond.

All collars should be interfaced, and the choice of the interfacing is important. It may need to differ from that used in the rest of the garment, because completely different qualities can be given to similarly cut collars by the use of different interfacing.

Before making an applied collar, one must know whether the seam allowances at the neck edge will be finished by being enclosed in the collar, or whether they will be covered by a facing or bias strip. When they are enclosed, it will make attaching the under collar to the garment easier if the stitching around the edge of the collar does not cross the neck seam allowance.

A collar with a roll line rises from the neck edge before turning over. The group includes roll collars, which are cut on the true bias from a single piece of fabric, as well as the types of roll collar cut from two pieces (an upper and an under collar), which have a high or medium-high roll, and which are used on dresses and jackets. This type of collar should just cover its own neck seam line when it is turned down, but it may be worn turned up, and it is therefore hardly ever finished with a bias strip. To prevent the collar from curling up, extra width must be allowed on the upper collar for the roll. On some collars with a pronounced roll, separate pattern pieces are provided for the upper and under collar pieces, in which case it will not be necessary to trim the under collar at stage 2.

Stage 1   Take the collar interfacing and trim away its seam allowance along the neckline edge. Baste the interfacing to the WS of the upper collar, and catch-stitch the trimmed edge to the neckline seam allowance of the collar piece.

Stage 2   Trim between 3 and 8 mm ($\frac{1}{8}$ to $\frac{3}{8}$ in.) off the neck-edge seam allowance of the under collar. The amount to be trimmed away will depend upon the thickness of the fabric.

Stage 3   Cross-pin, and baste the upper and under collar pieces with their RS together, easing the upper collar on to the under collar at the ends, and distributing the excess width across the roll.

Stage 4   Stitch around the edge, but leave the neck edge open. (If the neck-edge seam allowances will be finished by being enclosed within the collar, begin and end the stitching at the neck seam line.) Shorten the stitch to 1·5 mm (18 stitches per inch) on each side of the corners, and take one or two stitches across the collar points. Trim away the interfacing seam allowance, and (except at the neck edge), half the width of the under collar

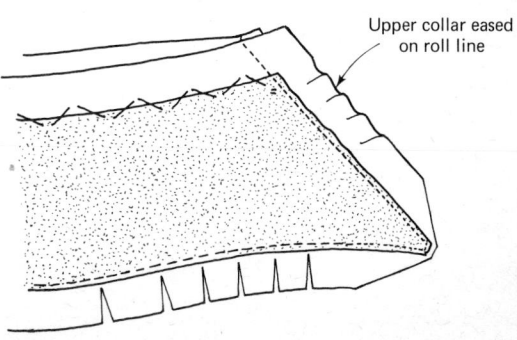

Upper collar eased on roll line

seam allowance. Clip and notch the seam allowances and trim the corners. Press the seam open over the tip of a sleeve board.

Stage 5 Turn the collar RS out, bringing the seam line to the extreme edge and carefully shaping the corners. When working in resilient fabrics it may be necessary to understitch the seam allowances to the under collar, either by machine or hand. Roll the seam line towards the under collar, and baste in order to hold it in place. Press lightly.

Stage 6 Cross-pin the upper and under collar pieces together along the neck seam line, bringing the raw edges exactly together. Turn the collar down along the roll line, and bending it round to resemble its final shape, look to see if there is any tendency for the under collar to bulge at the outer edge. If there is, pass a little more of the under collar into the neck-edge seam allowance and re-pin. When the collar sets smoothly, baste the layers together just on the neck side of the roll line.

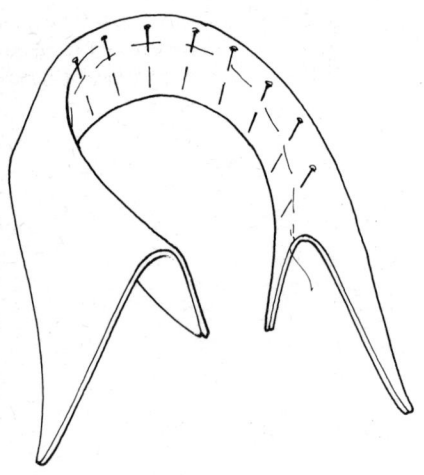

A flat collar, eg a Peter Pan, and one with a very slight roll, eg an Eton collar, can be made either in one piece, or as a two-piece collar with a break both at the back and at the front.

Stage 1 Baste the interfacing to the WS of the upper collar and machine stitch it to the neck-edge seam allowance 2 mm ($\frac{1}{16}$ in.) from the seam line. Trim away the remainder of the interfacing seam allowance along this edge. Remember when interfacing a two-piece collar, to make a right and a left half.

Stage 2 Place the upper and under collar pieces with their RS together, cross-pin and baste.

Stage 3 Stitch around the edge of the collar leaving the neck edge open. If the neck-edge seam allowances are to be finished by being enclosed within the collar, begin and end the stitching at the neck seam line. If the corners are pointed, stitch them using a 1·5 mm stitch (18 stitches per inch), and take one or two stitches across each point.

Stage 4 Trim away the interfacing seam allowance, and also (except along the neck edge) half the width of the under-collar seam allowance. Notch the seam allowances and trim them at the corners. Press the seam open over the tip of a sleeve board.

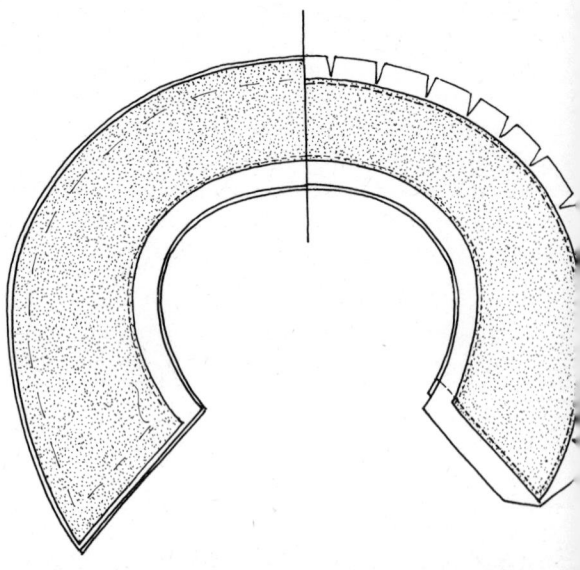

Stage 5 Trim a crescent shaped piece from the under-collar seam allowance. This should

be between 3 and 5 mm ($\frac{1}{8}$ to $\frac{3}{16}$ in.) deep at the centre of the collar piece, depending on the thickness of the fabric, and should taper to nothing at the ends.

Stage 6   Turn the collar RS out bringing the seam line to the extreme edge, and shape the corners carefully. Baste and understitch the seam allowances to the under collar, stitching as far into the corners as possible. Remove the basting. Alternatively, understitch by hand using running stitch.

Stage 7   Rolling the seam line slightly towards the under collar, press the edge lightly. If the collar is in two halves, compare them, and join the ends which will not connect with the garment opening by catch stitching them together at the neck seam line.

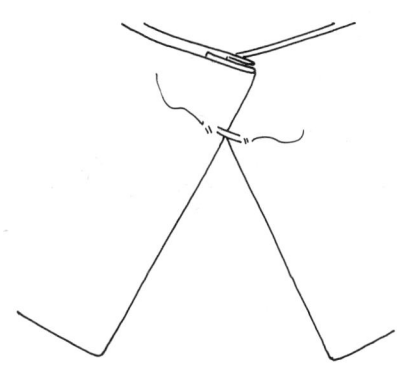

A collar with a stand only may be made from a single strip of fabric cut either on the straight grain or on the true bias (band and turtle collars), or from two pieces which curve slightly in the opposite direction to that of a normal collar so that the collar will lie against the slope of the neck (mandarin or Chinese collar).

Stage 1   Baste the interfacing to the WS of the outer collar. If the collar has been cut to a fold, the interfacing should be cut without a seam allowance on this edge, and catch stitched to the fold.

Stage 2   Cross-pin and baste the RS of the inner and outer collars together. Stitch, leaving the neck edge open. (If the neck-edge seam allowances will be enclosed within the collar, begin and end the stitching at the neck seam line.) Shorten the machine stitch to 1·5

mm (18 stitches per inch) on each side of the corners. Trim away the interfacing seam allowance, and half the width of the inner-collar seam allowance. Trim the corners, and notch the seam allowances if necessary. Press the seams open over the tip of a sleeve board.

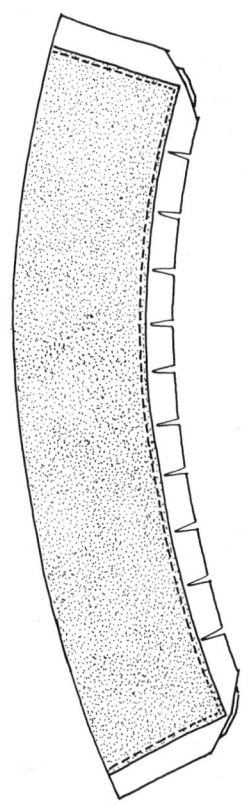

Stage 3   Turn the collar RS out, bringing the seam lines right to the edge. Press, but if a rolled effect is required, only press the ends of the collar.

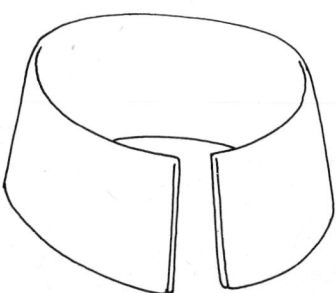

Attaching and finishing collars

Although most collars may be finished by enclosing the seam allowances within the collar, or by covering them with a facing or bias strip, one method will often be easier to carry out than the others, or will give more satisfactory results in a particular context. For example, although a band collar is normally finished by enclosing the seam allowances in the collar, it is simpler to finish a notched band collar with a facing. The way in which the collar seam allowances are finished is also influenced by the garment opening, the type and thickness of the fabric, and the total effect aimed at. For example, if a flat collar were to be applied in association with a front band, it would be finished by enclosing the seam allowances in the collar. However, were the same collar to be applied to a garment with an ordinary lapped opening, the collar could well be finished with a bias strip. A few collars are traditionally made and finished in only one way, or a combination of methods is used, and for these separate instructions are given.

From these remarks it will be seen that if the style of either the collar or the opening, is varied from that given in the pattern, the method of finishing the collar may have to be changed.

To prepare the garment: the seams which run into the neck edge of the garment must be joined, pressed and their raw edges finished. The neckline must be stay stitched, and the opening completed to the right stage for the attachment of the collar. If the collar will be finished with a facing, the neckline may be interfaced, but it is never interfaced when the collar is finished with a bias strip. When the seam allowances are to be enclosed in the collar, the neckline should not be interfaced unless extra support is required for a light-weight fabric, and then a facing must be used as well. In this case the interfacing is applied in the normal way: the facing pieces are joined, and the raw edge which will remain free must be finished. The facing is then basted WS together with the garment, and the layers treated as one when the collar is applied.

When attaching a collar, if its curve and that of the neck edge are very different, it may be necessary to clip the neckline seam allowance of the garment to allow it to straighten while the collar is being fitted. Be careful to match balance marks and tailor tacks, and to line up the ends of the collar with the correct points of the opening.

A collar with a roll line is normally finished with a facing, and the neckline is interfaced to support the weight of the collar. However, bias roll collars may be finished by enclosing the seam allowances within the collar, and this method may be used for other roll collars if they are made in light-weight fabric. When attaching a collar with a roll line its character can be subtly changed: if the collar is stretched slightly as it is stitched on, the roll line will be made more pronounced: if it is eased on to the neckline, the collar will lie flatter.

A flat collar may be finished by any of the three methods, depending on the opening, but if the collar is made in two pieces it must be either finished with a facing or with a bias strip, because the seam allowances cannot be enclosed.

Collars with only a stand must be attached by placing the show side of the collar RS together with the garment. They are usually finished by enclosing the seam allowances within the collar, but if this type of collar were to be attached to a winter dress, for example, a facing would make a flatter finish.

Finishing an attached collar by enclosing the seam allowance within the collar. This method is suitable for garments which are made in light-weight fabric. In thicker materials the seam allowances within the collar become too bulky. It is a good finish to use when the garment will be washed frequently.

Stage 1 Baste and stitch the under collar only to the garment neck edge with their RS together. (In the case of band and mandarin collars, place the show side RS together with the garment and trim off the interfacing seam allowance close to the stitching.)

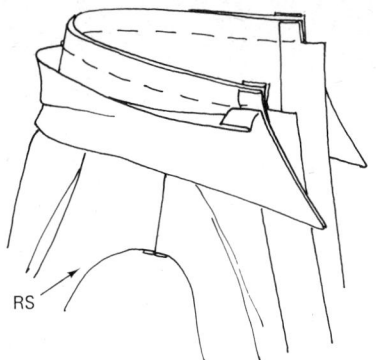

Stage 2   Grade and clip the neck-edge seam allowances and press them into the collar. Check from the RS that no creases have developed along the neck seam line.

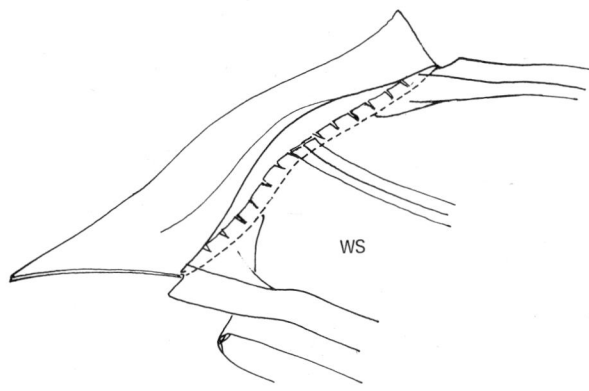

Stage 3   Clip and turn in the seam allowance of the upper collar, (inner collar of band and mandarin), and hem the fold to the neck seam, picking up the machine stitches.

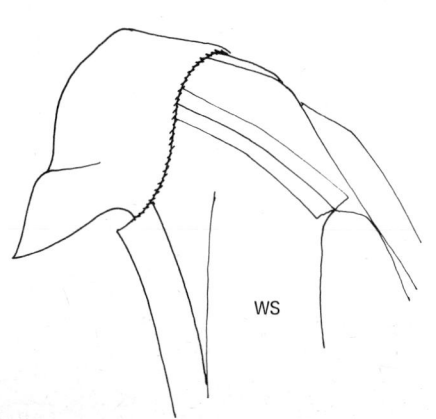

When applying a strip cut on the true bias to finish a collar, remember that the collar must turn down far enough to cover the row of hemming which will show on the RS. It is a good finish to use on garments which need to be frequently laundered.

Stage 1   Place the under collar against the garment with their RS together, and baste both layers of the collar to the garment. If there is a lapped opening, fold the edges of its facing back over the ends of the collar and baste them on the neck seam line.

Stage 2   Cut a strip on the true bias. This may be of self fabric, or of thinner firmly woven fabric in a matching colour if the garment fabric is bulky. The strip should be the same length as the edge to be finished plus 5 cm (2 in.), by 3·5 cm (1⅜ in.) wide.

Stage 3   Find the centre of the length of the strip, and position this point half way along the neckline edge with the RS of the strip on the upper collar, and their raw edges level.

Stage 4   Working from the centre towards the ends of the collar, cross-pin the strip, easing it on to the collar in the process. The easing will ensure that the garment will not be puckered when the strip is turned down and hemmed into place. Lap the ends over the edges of the turned-back facing.

Stage 5   Baste the strip to the collar along the neckline, and fold it downwards to check that its free edge is as long as the part of the garment to which it will be attached. Stitch around the neckline edge. Trim the neck seam allowances to 1 cm (⅜ in.), grade and clip them.

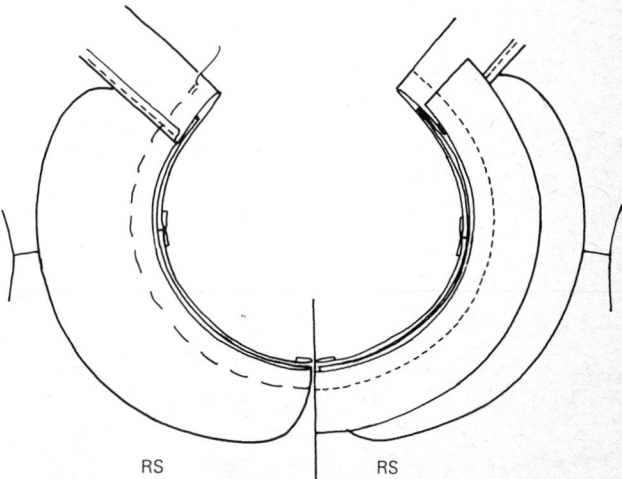

Stage 6 If the opening is a lapped one, the facing should be turned to the WS. Fold the bias strip in half enclosing the seam allowances, and with the garment WS out, pin and hem the fold to the garment parallel with the neck seam. Hem the free edges of the facing to the bias strip.

basting. Grade and clip all the seam allowances. If the material frays readily, finish the raw edges of the neck seam allowances with overcasting or loop stitch.

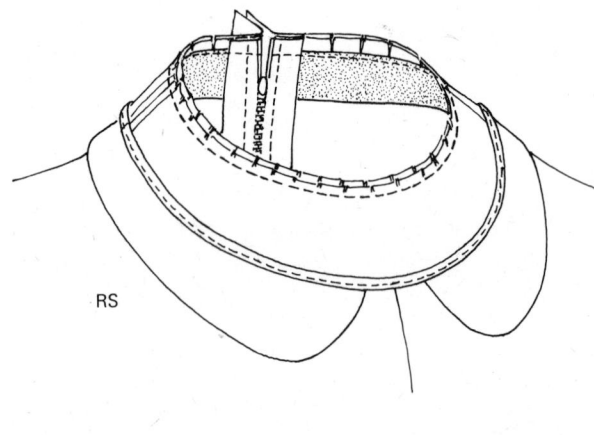

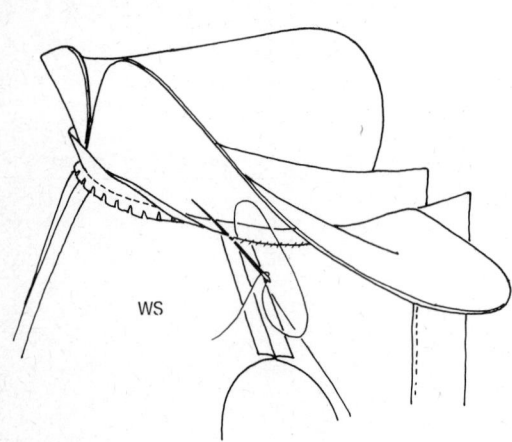

Stage 5 Press the facing over the seam allowances and understitch close to the fold. The understitching will prevent the neck seam line from rolling outwards and showing. At the opening, turn the ends of the facing to the WS.

A facing used to finish a collar is cut in at least two pieces. It is nearly always used when the neckline has no opening, and often when the opening is in the form of a zip or slash. It provides the most satisfactory finish on garments made from bulky fabrics. When the garment has a lapped opening, the facing of the opening often extends as far as the shoulder seams where it will be joined to the back-neck facing pieces.

Stage 1 Place the under collar and the garment with their RS together, and baste both layers of the collar to the garment along the neckline seam allowance.

Stage 2 Join the facing pieces and press the seams open. Finish the raw edge of the facing which will remain free.

Stage 3 Position the RS of the facing against the upper collar, matching balance marks. Cross-pin and baste. When there is a zip opening, leave the seam allowance at each end of the facing free.

Stage 4 Stitch along the neck edge through the facing, collar and garment. Remove the

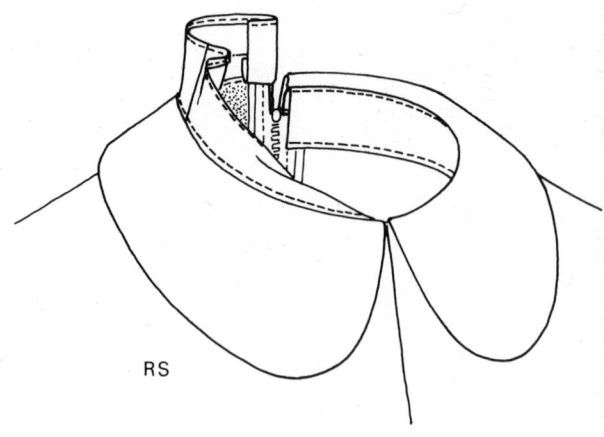

Stage 6 Hem the facing to the shoulder seam allowances where it crosses them. If there is a zip opening, the turned-in ends of the facing should be hemmed to the tape.

When a slashed opening occurs, and its facing extends part of the way round the neck, the collar should be basted to the neckline before the slash is made. The neck and slash facing is then made up and applied as a whole. Stitch around the neck edge including the slash. Cut, turn and understitch the slash and collar following the method given above. Care must be taken to position the collar exactly at the top corners of the slash, and when stitching, to pivot precisely at these points. The ends of the collar must be kept clear of the slash seam while stitching. When the neck seam allowances will be finished by enclosing them in the collar, the slash facing should be applied and turned to the WS before the collar is attached, so that its neckline seam allowance can be enclosed in the collar as well.

When a garment has a double yoke, the collar may be sandwiched between the two yoke layers, which are placed RS together, and one of which is then turned to the WS like a facing. This method is used when applying a flat collar to children's nightdresses. Alternatively, the two layers of the yoke are placed WS together, and the collar is attached and finished by enclosing the seam allowances within the collar. This method is used in a shirt, for example.

Making, attaching and finishing a band collar with ties. This type of band collar is usually cut on the straight grain from a single piece of fabric. Interface the neck section but not the ties. Before attaching the collar, all the seams running into the neck edge must have been joined, pressed and their raw edges finished, and the neckline must have been stay stitched. When this collar is used in conjunction with a faced opening, the facing is turned to the WS before the collar is attached, and its neck-edge seam allowance enclosed within the collar.

Stage 1   Interface the neck section of the strip, catch-stitching the interfacing to the fold.

Stage 2   Place the RS of the interfaced half of the band to the RS of the garment, cross-pin, baste and stitch along the neck edge. Trim off the interfacing seam allowance, grade and clip the seam allowances where necessary.

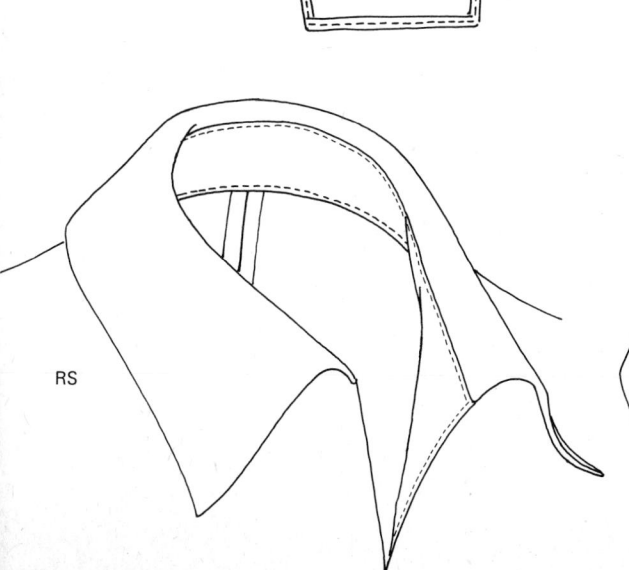

RS

RS

RS

Stage 3 Fold the band lengthwise with its RS together. Cross-pin and baste the tie sections. Stitch across each end and along the edge of the ties, stopping one stitch short of the front edge of the garment. Sew in the thread ends, and trim the corners.

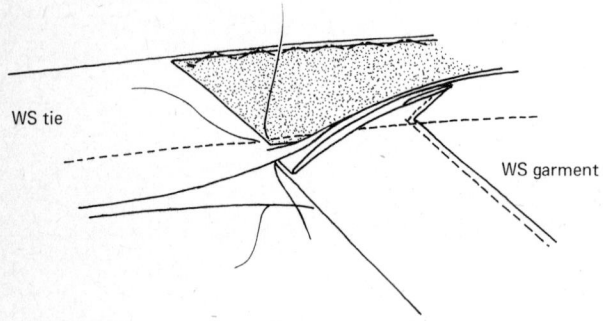

WS tie

WS garment

Stage 4 Press the long seam of the ties open over a seam roll. Turn the ties RS out through the space left in the neckline, and press, bringing the stitching line right to the fold.
Stage 5 Turn in the seam allowance of the free edge of the band, and hem the fold to the machine stitches enclosing the seam allowances in the collar.

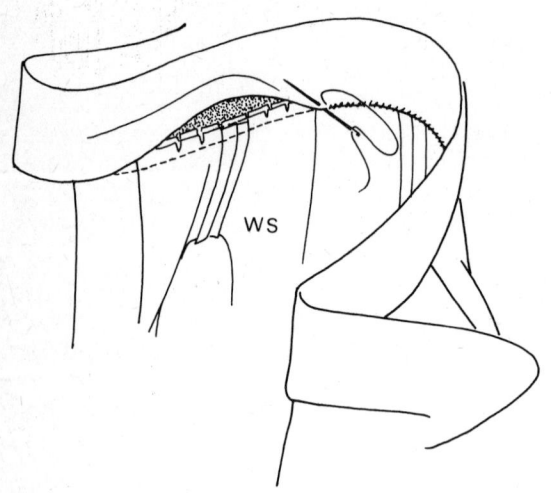

WS

Attaching, and finishing a collar with a separate stand. Straight collars are sometimes constructed with a separate stand. The most familiar example is a shirt collar. The stand piece is always cut on the straight grain. It may be a plain rectangle, or be slightly curved at the ends. It is always cut double and interfaced.
Stage 1 Make up the collar following the instructions for making an attached flat collar (page 122), and top-stitch it if desired.
Stage 2 Interface one of the stand pieces and place its upper edge RS together with the raw edge of the upper collar. Cross-pin. Position the RS of the other half of the stand against the under collar, cross-pin, and baste through all layers. Stitch along the whole length of the stand and across the ends, beginning and ending at the neck seam line.

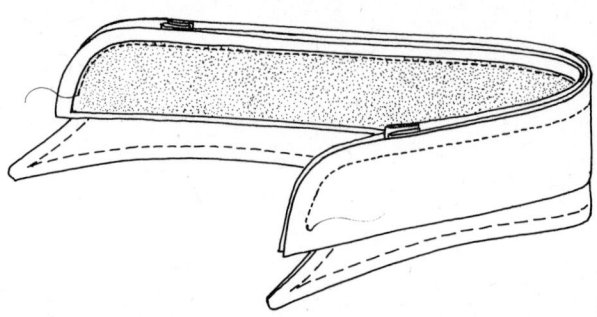

Stage 3 Remove the basting, grade the seam allowances, and clip the curved section of the stand. Turn the stand RS out and press.
Stage 4 Place the RS of the interfaced stand piece to the WS of the garment. Cross-pin, baste and stitch them together. Trim the interfacing seam allowance close to the stitching. Grade and clip the seam allowances, and press the stand over them to bring the stitching line to the fold.

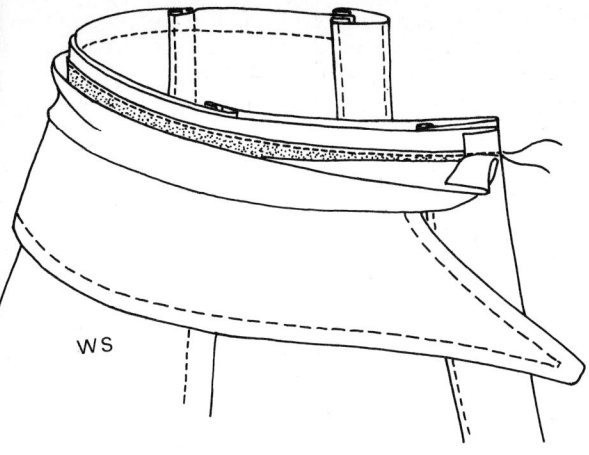

WS

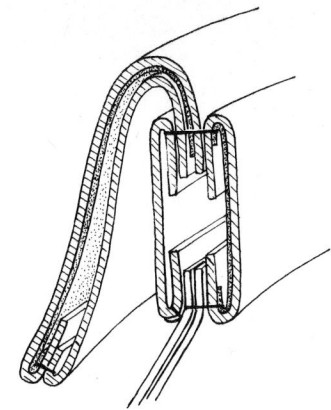

Section through completed collar

Stage 5   On the RS turn in the seam allowance of the free edge of the stand, and hem it to the line of machine stitches. This line of hemming will be covered when the collar is turned down. Top-stitch the stand if desired.

Alternatively, the outer face of the stand may be attached to the garment first and the hemming done on the inside. In this case the interfacing must be stitched to the neckline seam allowance of the stand, and trimmed before the stand is attached at stage 2.

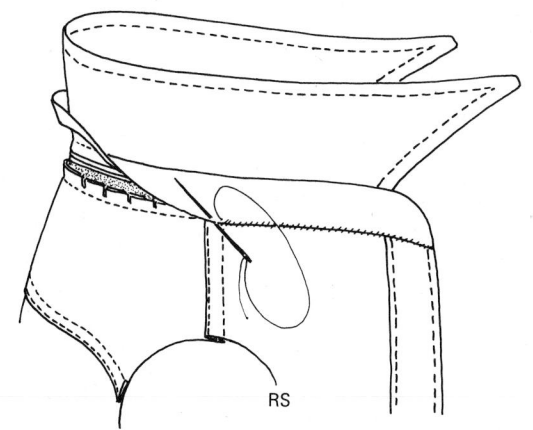

RS

A convertible collar

This type of collar is always combined with a front opening. A notched effect is obtained by making the collar shorter than the edge on to which it is to be set. The front facing, which extends around the neck edge as far as the shoulder seams, may be cut in one with the opening edge, or cut separately, but it must be wide enough for its free edge not to show when the collar is worn open. Make the collar using the method described in 'making a flat collar' (page 122).

Before attaching the collar, all the seams running into the neck edge must have been joined, pressed and their raw edges finished, and the neckline should have been stay stitched. The fold lines of the opening must have been baste marked, and the points on the neck edge, to which the ends of the collar will be matched, marked with tailor tacks.

When a back-neck facing is used, attach it to the front facing at the shoulders, and press the seams open. Finish the raw edge of the facing which will remain free.

Stage 1 Placing the RS of the garment and under collar together, cross-pin and baste the collar to the garment through all three layers.

Stage 2 Turn the facing RS together with the garment by folding it along the fold lines of the opening so that it lies on the collar. Pin and baste the facing to the collar and garment.

To finish a convertible collar with a bias strip, follow the instructions for finishing a collar with a bias strip (page 125).

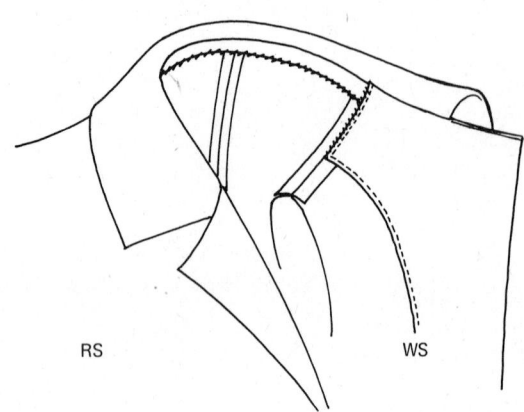

RS   WS

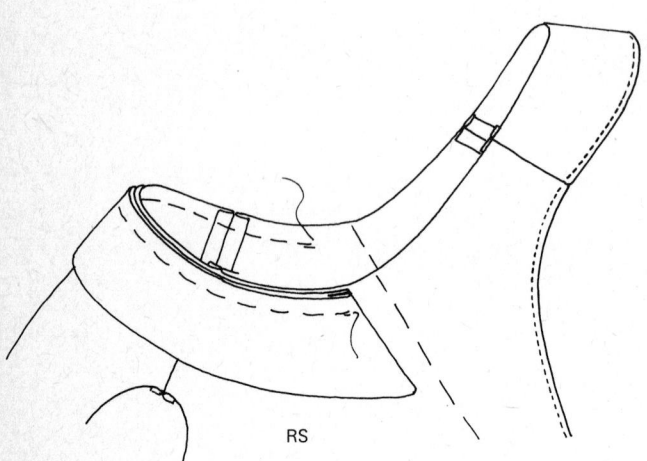

RS

Stage 3 Stitch along the neck seam line. Grade and clip the seam allowances, and trim the front corners. Turn the facing to the WS, and press. Understitch the facing to the seam allowances across the back between the shoulder seams. Hem the edge of the facing to the shoulder seam allowances where it crosses them.

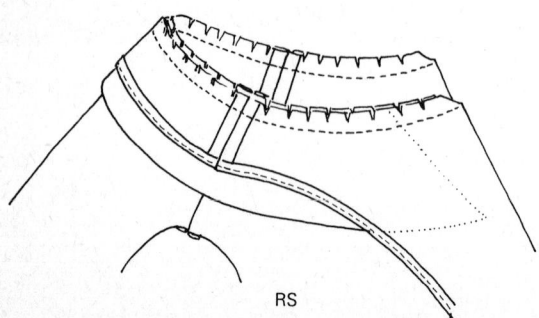

RS

130

Attaching a convertible collar and finishing it by enclosing the back-neck seam allowances in the collar. Stay-stitch the neck edge of the garment, and finish the shoulder-seam ends of the facing and their front edges.

Stage 1   Place the RS of the garment and under collar together. Baste the under collar only to the garment across the back, and stitch this section, beginning and ending exactly at the shoulder seams.

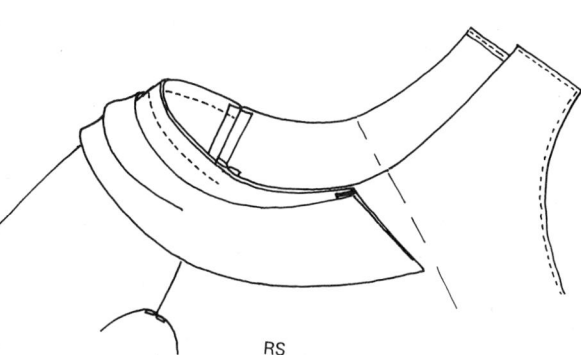

RS

Stage 2   Baste both layers of the collar to the garment from the shoulder seams to the ends of the collar.

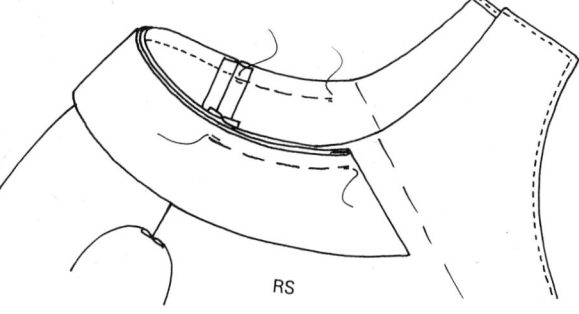

RS

Stage 3   Fold the facing to the RS along the front fold line so that the facing lies on the front part of the collar. Pin, baste and stitch each neckline section from the fold to the shoulder seam. Grade and clip the seam allowances and trim the corners.

Stage 4   Snip both the garment and collar seam allowances exactly at the shoulder seams. Turn the facing to the WS and press.

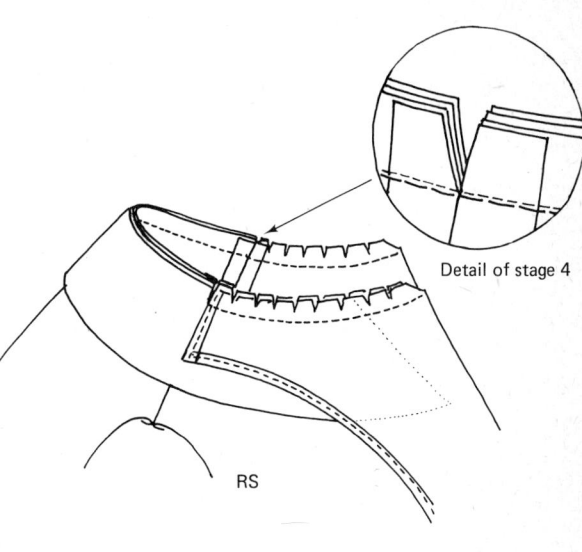

Detail of stage 4

RS

Stage 5   Clip the back-neck seam allowances of the garment and under collar, and press them upwards into the collar. Clip and fold in the seam allowance of the upper collar, and hem it to the back-neck seam line. Hem the ends of the facing to the shoulder seams.

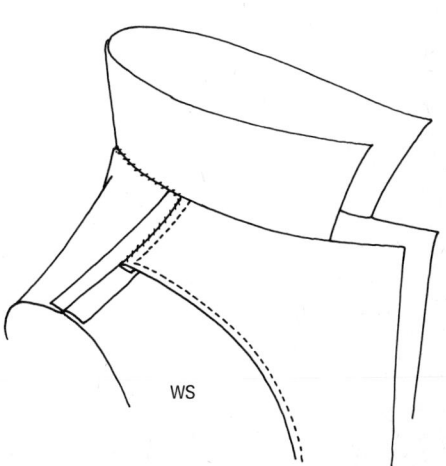

WS

Making and finishing a shawl collar.

This type of collar is always used in conjunction with a front opening. The under-collar pieces are cut in one with the front of the garment, and extend to the CB. The neckline is darted to improve the set of the collar. The upper collar is usually cut with a CB seam, and with extensions on the free edge in front of the shoulder seam to form a facing. Although the seam allowances may be finished by enclosing them in the collar, a facing is the most satisfactory method of finishing the seam allowances at the back of the neck, and it is this method which is described below.

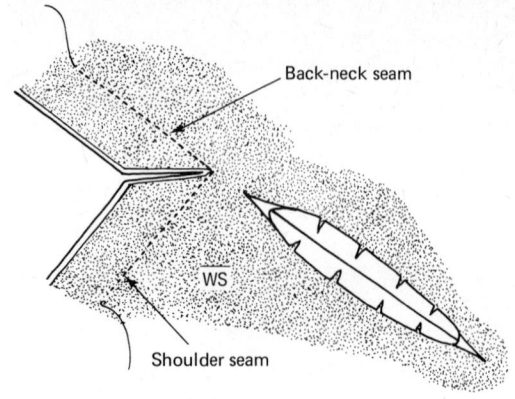

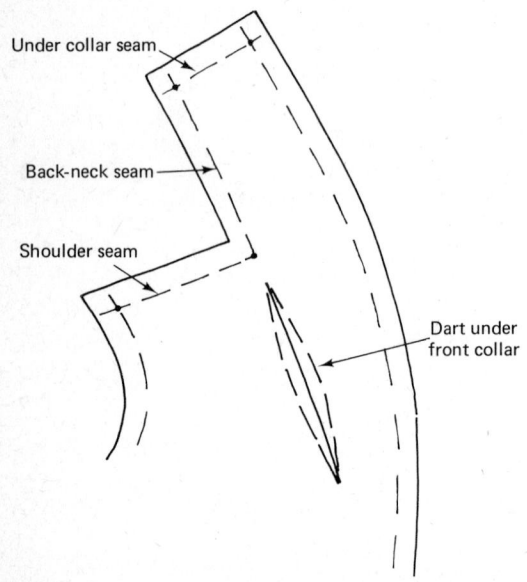

Stage 1 Interface the under-collar pieces and make the darts, taking care to form them by folding the RS of each garment piece together. Clip the dart seam allowances and press them open.
Stage 2 Stay-stitch the angles where the shoulder and back-neck seamlines meet. Snip the seam allowances at the angles, stopping 1 to 2 mm ($\frac{1}{16}$ in.) from the stay stitching. Placing the RS of the under-collar pieces together, join the CB seam. Trim off the interfacing seam allowances, press the seam and finish it.
Stage 3 Interface the neckline section of the two back garment pieces. Join the CB seam and any darts in the back of the garment. Trim off the interfacing seam allowances. Press and finish the seams and darts.

Stage 4 Place the RS of the back and front of the garment together, matching the angles carefully. Cross-pin and baste. (See techniques for making angled seams, page 34.) With the under-collar piece on top, stitch the seam, beginning at the outer end of one shoulder seam and ending at the other. Shorten the machine stitch to 1·5 mm (18–20 stitches per inch) at the angles.
Stage 5 Remove the basting, trim the interfacing, and clip the curved back-neck section. If a back-neck facing will be added to the upper collar, press the seam open. If the seam allowances of the back-neck section are to be enclosed in the collar, press them upwards.

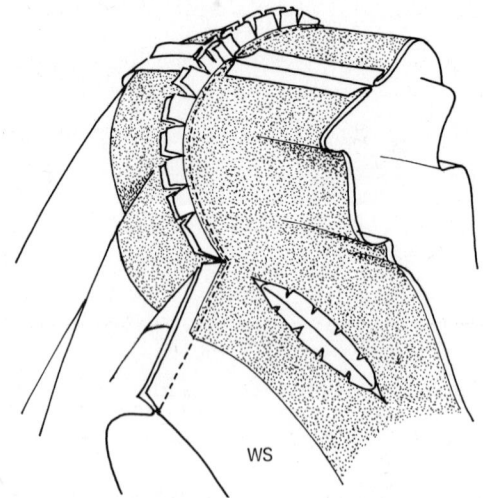

Stage 6 Join the upper-collar pieces at the back-neck seam, press the seam open, and finish its raw edges.
Stage 7 Stay-stitch the angles between the back-neck edge of the upper collar and the

shoulder seams. Snip the seam allowances in the angles almost to the stay stitching.

Stage 8   If a back-neck facing is being used, place it on the neckline edge of the upper collar with their RS together. Cross-pin and baste, matching the angles carefully. With the upper collar on top, stitch, shortening the stitch to 1·5 mm (18 stitches per inch) on each side of the corners. Press the seam open. Finish the edge of the facing which will remain free.

Stage 10   Turn the garment WS out, and folding the back-neck facing out of the way, pin the garment and facing seam allowances together along the neckline between the shoulder seams. Turn the garment RS out to check the roll of the collar. When this is correct, catch-stitch the two neck seam lines together from the inside. Hem the free edges of the facing to the shoulder seams where they cross.

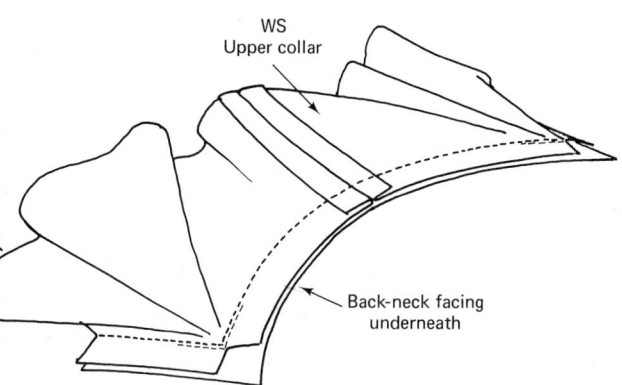

WS
Upper collar

Back-neck facing
underneath

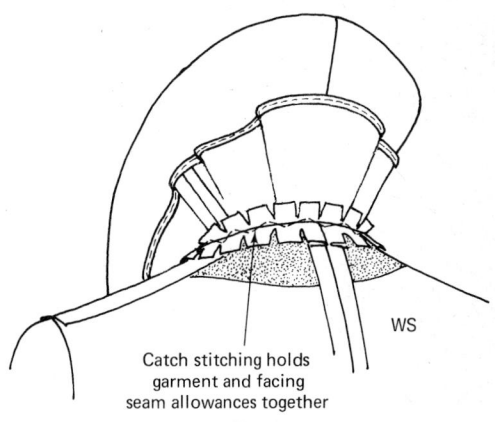

WS

Catch stitching holds
garment and facing
seam allowances together

Stage 9   Place the upper and under collar with their RS together. Cross-pin, baste and stitch them around their outer edge. Remove the basting and trim off the interfacing seam allowance. Grade and notch the seam allowances. Press the seam open, and then turn the collar RS out bringing the seam line to the edge. Press again, rolling the seam line slightly towards the under collar.

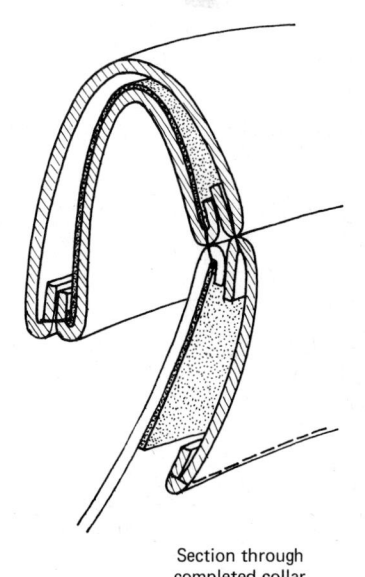

Section through
completed collar

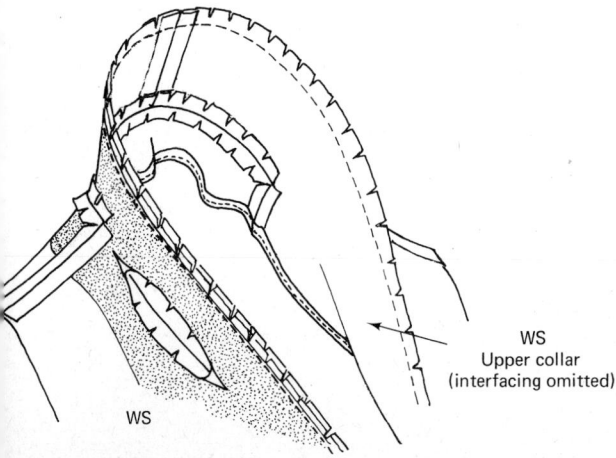

WS

WS
Upper collar
(interfacing omitted)

If a back-neck facing has not been applied, after stage 9, clip and turn in the free edge of the collar along the back-neck section and hem it to the seam line. Turn in the shoulder seam allowance of each facing and hem it to its shoulder seam.

Making and finishing a collar with lapels.

In this collar, which is traditionally used on suit jackets, and blazers, the edges of the opening are extended to form lapels which are worn permanently turned back. The upper and under collar are always cut from separate pattern pieces. The garment must have been joined at the shoulder and back seams before the collar is begun. If bound buttonholes are to be used in the body of the garment, the interfacing should be applied to the WS of the garment, and to the under collar so that the surface of both collar and lapels will present a consistent appearance, and the instructions which follow refer to this version. If, however, the garment fabric is of medium weight or heavier, and is firmly woven, it will be possible to interface the upper collar without the change of quality becoming apparent. If machine- or hand-stitched buttonholes are used, the interfacing can be applied to the WS of the front facing pieces and to the upper collar.

Stage 1   Stay-stitch the neck edge of the garment. Interface the under collar pieces. Join them at the CB, trim off the interfacing seam allowance close to the seam line, press the seam open and finish its raw edges. Interface the garment opening.

Stage 2   Cross-pin the under collar and garment with their RS together, clipping the garment neck edge if necessary. Baste and stitch the seam, beginning and ending level with the seam line at the ends of the collar. Snip the garment neckline to the stay stitching at the places where the stitching begins and ends. Trim off the interfacing seam allowance along the neckline edge. Press the seam open over a seam roll, clipping the seam allowances. Sew in the thread ends.

Stage 3   Join the front- and back-neck facing pieces together at the shoulder seams. Stitch the seams and press them open. Stay-stitch the neck edge of the facing, and finish the edge which will remain free.

Stage 4   Cross-pin the RS of the upper collar and facing together, clipping the facing if necessary. Baste and stitch, beginning and ending level with the seam line at the ends of the collar. Snip the neckline of the facing to the stay stitching at these points. Press the seam open over a seam roll, clipping the seam allowances where necessary.

Stage 5   Cross-pin the RS of the upper and under collars together, beginning at the CB, and being careful to ease the upper collar on to the under collar across the width of the ends. The ends of the upper- and under-collar neck seams must match exactly: stab through with a pin to check that they do so. Continue pinning, easing the facing on to the garment from the points of the lapels inwards. Pin the remainder of the front.

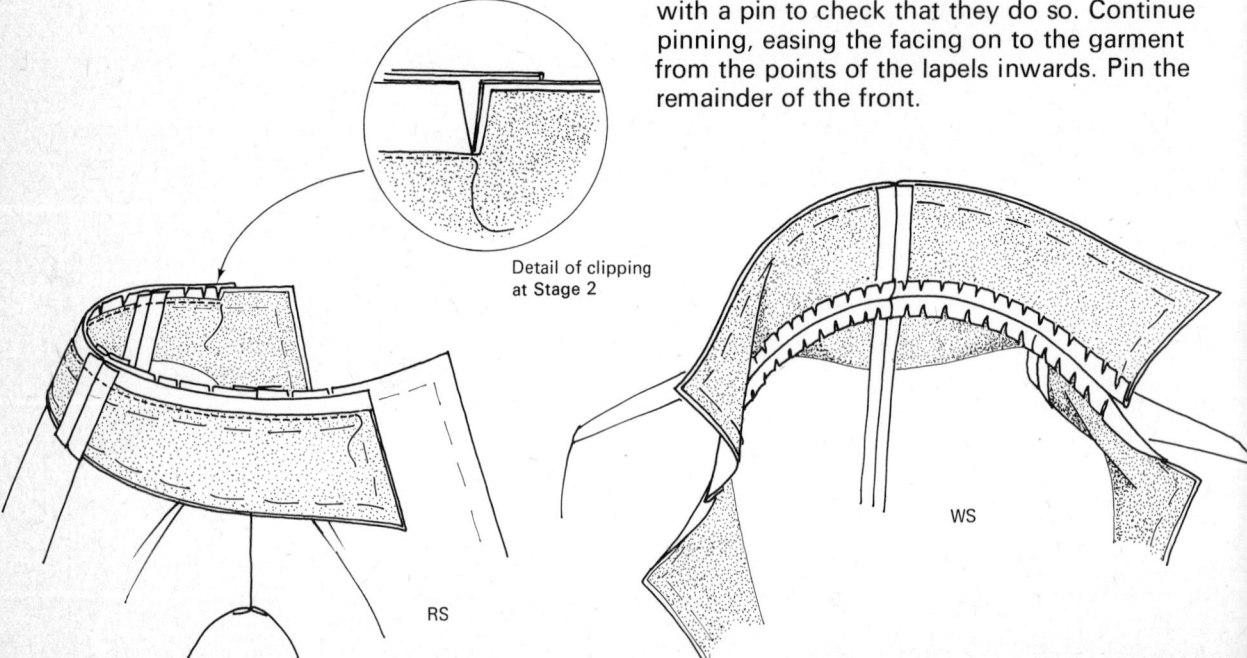

Detail of clipping at Stage 2

RS

WS

Stage 6 Baste firmly, and stitch the entire edge from the hem to the CB neck on each side. The stitching must be very accurately placed at the junctions of the collar and lapel (see diagram), otherwise a hole will appear at this point. Trim off the interfacing seam allowances. Grade and clip the garment seam allowances and trim the corners.

and to the underside from the base of the lapels and around the collar. Press lightly.
Stage 8 Turn the garment WS out, and folding the neck facing out of the way, pin the seam allowances of the garment and facing together along the neckline. Turn the garment RS out and check the set of the collar, adjust if necessary. When it is correct, permanently catch-stitch the two neck seam lines together from the inside.

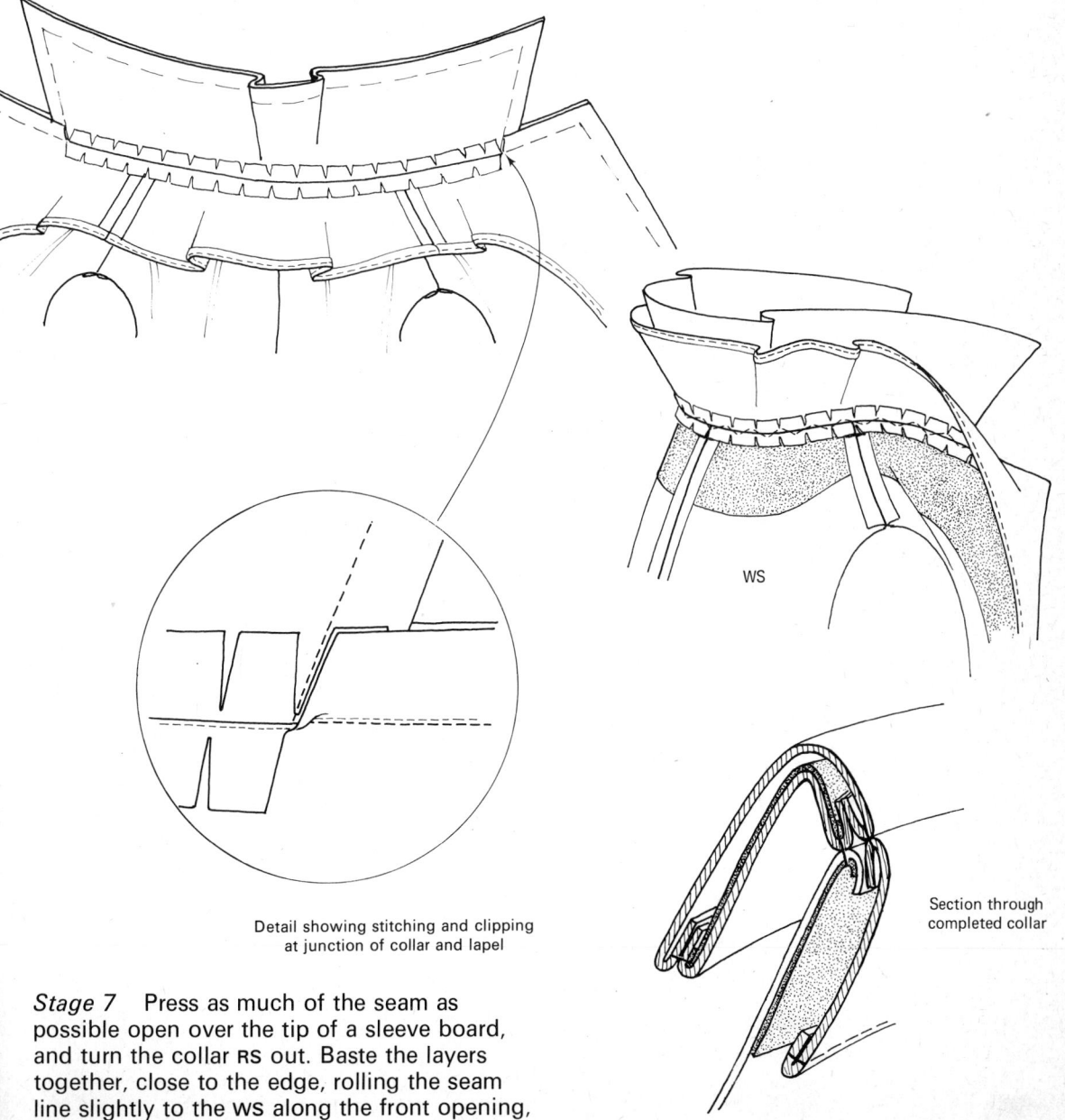

WS

Detail showing stitching and clipping
at junction of collar and lapel

Section through
completed collar

Stage 7 Press as much of the seam as possible open over the tip of a sleeve board, and turn the collar RS out. Baste the layers together, close to the edge, rolling the seam line slightly to the WS along the front opening,

10 Sleeves

Sleeve ends and cuffs

The hem at the end of a sleeve should be worked, or the cuff applied, after the underarm seam has been joined, but before the sleeve is set into the armhole. However, when the cuff has an opening, this should be worked before the underarm seam is joined unless it occurs in this seam. A sleeve, even if it does not end in a cuff, may still be finished in several different ways. The simplest method, which is only suitable for thin fabrics, is to turn in a narrow hem and secure it with slip hemming. A flatter finish is achieved by finishing the edges of the seam allowance with seam binding or a bias strip, and this may be preferable if the garment is made in a medium-weight or thicker fabric. If the sleeve end is slashed or shaped it must be finished with a shaped facing, and the WS of the garment fabric may be interfaced if a crisp effect is desired. Sleeve ends may also be finished with a frill or a ruffle, or a casing made in the hem through which elastic or ribbon is threaded.

A band cuff is cut to a fold and has no opening. It forms an extension to the end of the sleeve, and is attached in the same way as a binding.
Stage 1 If the sleeve is full, put gathering threads into the lower edge of the sleeve. Join and press the underarm seam, and finish its raw edges.
Stage 2 Interface the WS of the show half of the band.
Stage 3 Pin, baste and stitch the RS of the ends of the band together. Trim the interfacing seam allowance close to the stitching. Notch the cuff seam allowance where the fold will come. Press the seam open.
Stage 4 Slide the cuff on to the end of the sleeve so that their RS are together and the interfaced half of the band is at the sleeve end. (If the sleeve is full it will be easier to adjust the gathers if the sleeve and cuff are placed RS together with the sleeve on the outside.) Cross-pin and baste.

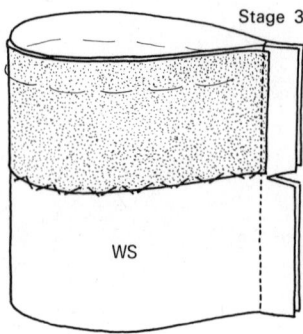

Stage 3

Stage 5 Stitch the band and sleeve together. If the sleeve is very full, put the work under the presser foot sleeve side uppermost, so that the gathers can be controlled more easily. Trim off the interfacing seam allowance close to the stitching. Grade the garment seam allowances, and press the band over them.

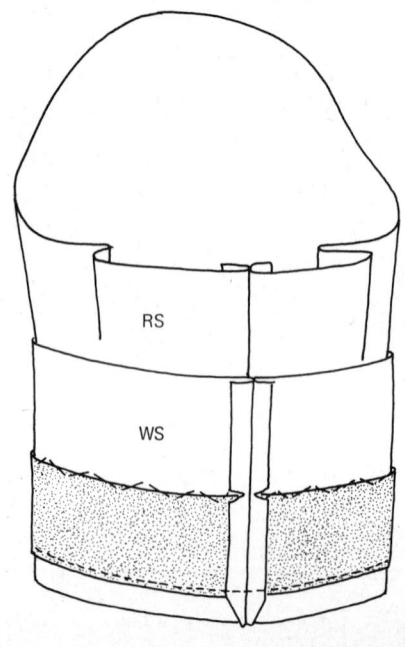

Stage 6   Turn the sleeve and band WS out. Fold the un-interfaced half of the band over the interfacing. Turn in the seam allowance of the free edge of the band, and hem it to the line of machine stitching, enclosing the seam allowances of the sleeve and band. Turn the sleeve RS out and press.

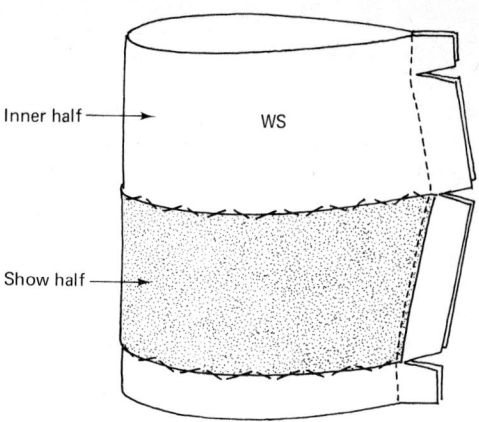

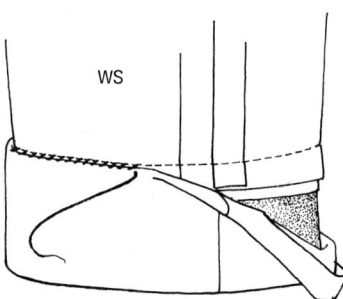

A non-opening turnback cuff may be cut in one with the sleeve, or may be cut separately and applied. To ensure that the cuff will not constrict the sleeve, the fold line of its free edge must be made longer than the circumference of the sleeve at the same level. The depth of the show side of the cuff is made greater by the width of a seam allowance, than the other side, both to allow for the roll, and so that it can be attached well up inside the sleeve.

An applied turnback cuff without an opening is cut in one piece if its free edge fold is straight.
Stage 1   Cut the interfacing to the right width for the show half of the cuff, with seam allowances at the ends, but not on the long edges. Baste the interfacing to the WS of the cuff and catch-stitch it along both long edges.
Stage 2   Placing the RS of the ends of the cuff together, pin and baste along the seam line. Stitch, being careful to change the direction of the stitching at each fold line. Remove the basting, trim off the interfacing seam allowance close to the stitching, and notch the cuff seam allowance at each fold line. Press the seam open over a seam roll.

Stage 3   Slide the cuff on to the end of the sleeve so that their RS are together and the non-interfaced half of the cuff is at the lower end of the sleeve. Cross-pin and baste, matching the seams and also the raw edges of the cuff and sleeve end. Stitch, and trim the seam allowance to 1 cm ($\frac{3}{8}$ in.). Pull the sleeve through the cuff, and press the seam allowances open.

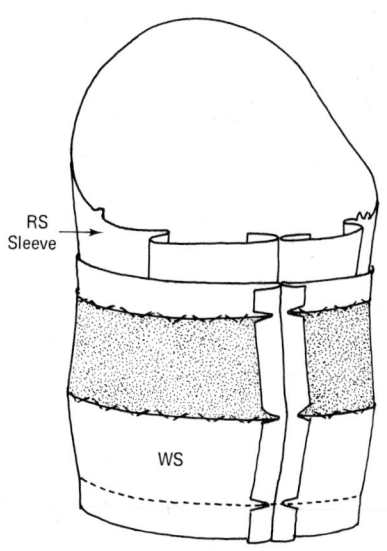

137

Stage 4   Keeping the work WS out, turn the seam allowance of the free edge of the cuff to the WS and baste. Fold the cuff in half WS together, so that the free edge lies over the sleeve end. Leaving a small allowance for the roll line, slip-hem the cuff to the sleeve.

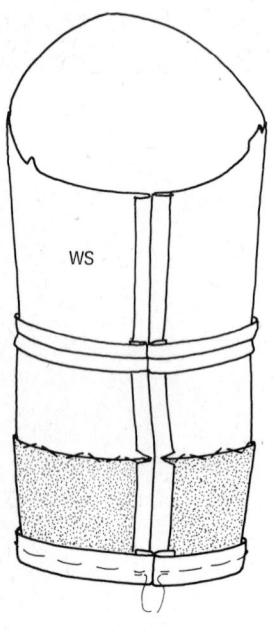

A shaped turnback cuff without an opening must be cut as a cuff piece and separate facing, and is made similarly to a flat collar finished with a bias strip.

Stage 1   Using the cuff pattern, cut out the interfacing, and baste it to the WS of the cuff piece.

Stage 2   Pin and baste the cuff piece and its facing RS together, and stitch around three sides leaving the edge, which will be attached to the sleeve, open.

Stage 3   Remove the basting and trim off the interfacing seam allowance close to the stitching. Grade, clip and notch the seam allowances, and press open as much of the seam as possible.

Stage 4   Turn the cuff RS out and press, bringing the seam line right to the edge. Cut a narrow, crescent-shaped piece from the raw edge of the cuff facing, making it between 3 and 6 mm ($\frac{1}{8}$ to $\frac{1}{4}$ in.) deep in the centre (depending on the thickness of the fabric), and tapering to nothing at the ends. Baste the raw edges together to keep them level.

Stage 5   Place the cuff so that its facing is against the RS of the sleeve, and the raw edges are level. Cross-pin. Make sure that the ends of the cuff just meet, and that they do so in the right place. Baste.

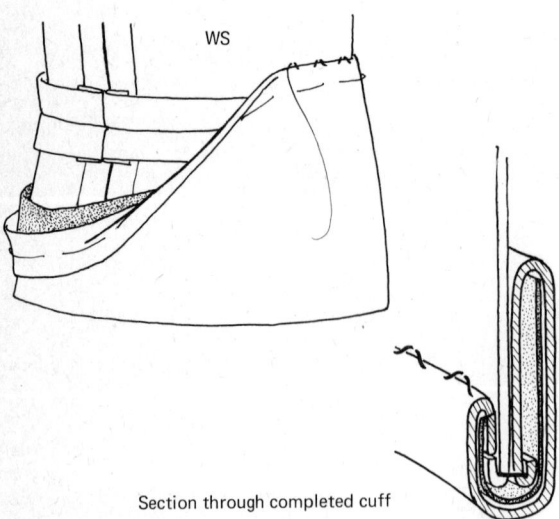

Section through completed cuff

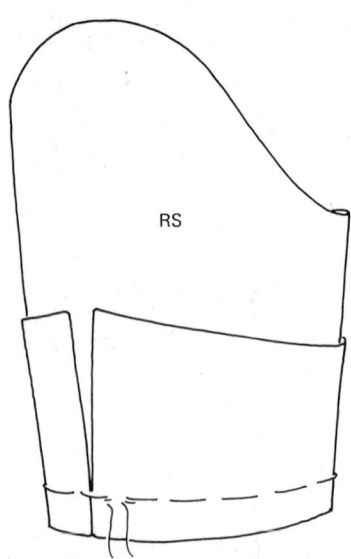

Stage 5   Turn the work RS out, and turn the cuff back so that the seam made at stage 3 lies in the channel at the lower edge of the cuff. Press the cuff carefully.

Stage 6   Cut a strip on the true bias, making its width 3·5 cm (1¾ in.), and its length equal to the distance round the sleeve plus 10 cm (4 in.).

Stage 7   Baste the bias strip to the RS of the cuff, with their raw edges level. Prepare to make a bias-strip join. Stitch through all layers. Trim the seam allowance of the bias strip to 6 mm (¼ in.) and make the join. Remove the basting and grade the seam allowances. Press the binding so that it lies over the seam.

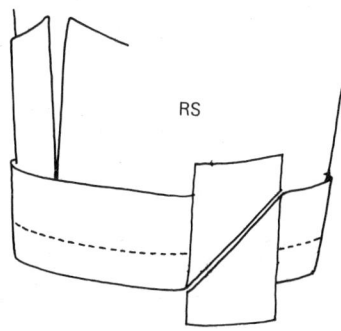

Stage 8   Turn the sleeve WS out and turn the seam allowances and binding to the WS, so that the line of stitching is just on the WS of the sleeve.

Stage 9   Fold in the raw edge of the binding so that it encloses the seam allowances. Slip-hem the fold to the WS of the sleeve, being careful not to catch the cuff facing. Press the roll line of the cuff carefully.

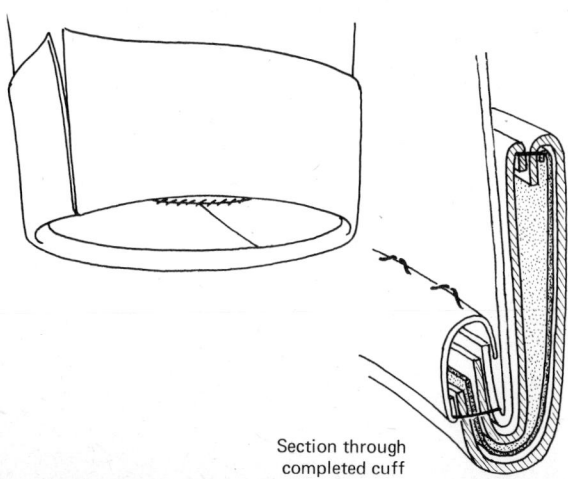

Section through completed cuff

A lapped cuff is usually cut in one piece. The sleeve opening, underarm seam, and gathers must be prepared before the cuff is attached. If the opening is a lapped one, its overlap edge should be turned in and basted to hold it in place while the cuff is applied.

Stage 1   Interface the show half of each cuff, catch-stitching the interfacing to the fold. Take care to make a right and a left cuff.

Stage 2   Fold the cuff and its facing with their RS together along the fold line. Cross-pin, baste and stitch across the overlap end, from the fold to the sleeve seam line. Stitch across the underlap end beginning at the fold, and, pivoting at the corner, continue along the sleeve edge, and end the stitching at the tailor tack which marks the end of the underlap. Clip the sleeve edge seam allowance at this point, so that the seam allowances can still project after the cuff is turned RS out.

Stage 3   Sew in the thread ends. Trim off the interfacing seam allowances close to the stitching. Grade the cuff seam allowances, and trim the corners. Turn the cuff RS out and press.

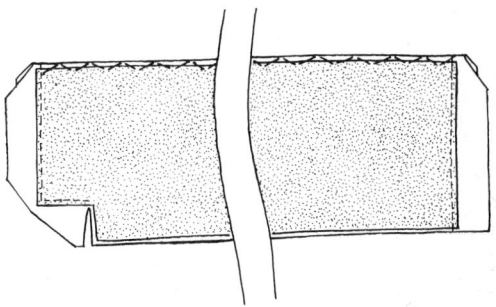

Stage 4   Cross-pin the RS of the interfaced half of the cuff and the sleeve together, and with the raw edges level. The projecting seam allowance at the underlap end of the cuff should be matched to the side of the opening nearest to the underarm seam. The overlap end of the cuff should be level with the other edge of the sleeve opening. Adjust the gathered section to make it the same length as the cuff.

139

Stage 5   Baste the cuff and sleeve together firmly, and stitch, being careful not to catch the cuff facing. Remove the basting, trim off the interfacing seam allowance and grade the garment and cuff seam allowances.

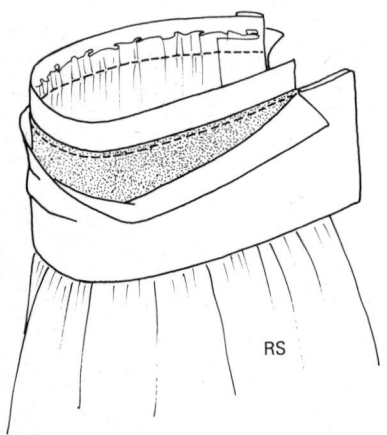

RS

Stage 6   Press the cuff over the seam. Turn in the seam allowance of the cuff facing, and hem the fold to the machine stitches on the WS of the sleeve.

A shirt cuff is cut in two pieces, and is used in conjunction with a shirt sleeve opening. It is decorated with top stitching, and is fastened with a button. The buttonhole is made after the cuff has been applied. Work the sleeve opening, join the underarm seam, and ease-stitch the sleeve end before beginning work on the cuff.

Stage 1   Baste the interfacing to the WS of the cuff piece, and trim away the interfacing seam allowance along the edge which will be attached to the sleeve.

Stage 2   Place the cuff and its facing RS together, and stitch the ends and the edge which will remain free, beginning and ending at the sleeve-edge seam line.

Stage 3   Trim off the interfacing seam allowance, and the corners, and grade the garment seam allowances. Turn the cuff RS out and press.

Stage 4   Turn the sleeve inside out, and place the RS of the cuff facing against the WS of the sleeve end with the raw edges level.

Make sure that the ends of the cuff are level with the edges of the opening.

Stage 5   Cross-pin, baste and stitch the cuff facing to the sleeve. Grade the seam allowances, and press the cuff facing over the seam.

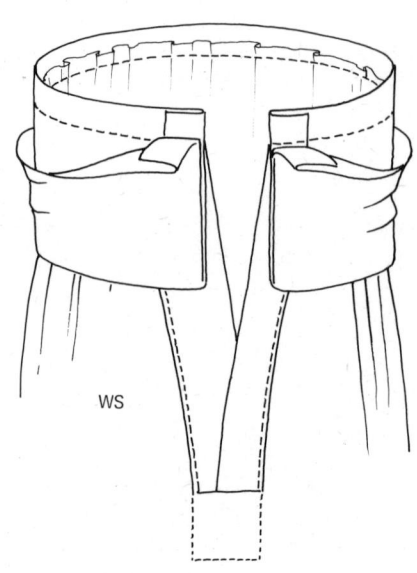

WS

Stage 6   Turn in the free edge of the cuff piece, and baste this fold to the RS of the sleeve end so that it just covers the line of stitches. Edge-stitch this fold to the sleeve, and continue stitching around the edges of the cuff. A decorative line of top stitching should then be put 3 to 5 mm ($\frac{1}{8}$ to $\frac{3}{16}$ in.) inside the edge stitching.

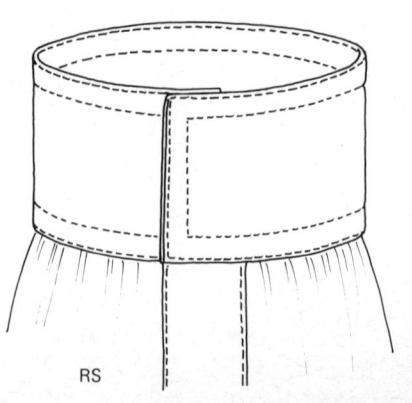

RS

A french cuff is usually cut in two pieces. It is closed with a link fastening. The cuff piece, which is always interfaced, goes against the arm, but shows because the cuff is worn turned back. Prepare the sleeve end and complete the opening, which may be a continuation of the underarm seam, before beginning to attach the cuff. Hand-worked or machine-stitched buttonholes should be made in the cuff after it is attached and finished, and these are always used for the inner half of the cuff. However, when a bound buttonhole is to be made in the show side of the cuff, this must be worked after stage 1, and the facing finished after stage 5.

Stage 1   Baste the interfacing to the WS of the cuff piece, and stitch it to the sleeve-edge seam allowance, 2 mm ($\frac{1}{16}$ in.) from the seam line. Trim away the remainder of the interfacing seam allowance along this edge.

Stage 2   Place the cuff and its facing with their RS together, and stitch the ends and the edge which will remain free, beginning and ending at the sleeve-edge seam line. Trim off the interfacing seam allowance close to the stitching. Grade the seam allowances, and trim the corners. Turn the cuff RS out and press.

Stage 3   Place the RS of the cuff facing and sleeve together, with their raw edges level. Line up the ends of the cuff with the edges of the opening. Cross-pin, baste and stitch the cuff facing to the sleeve.

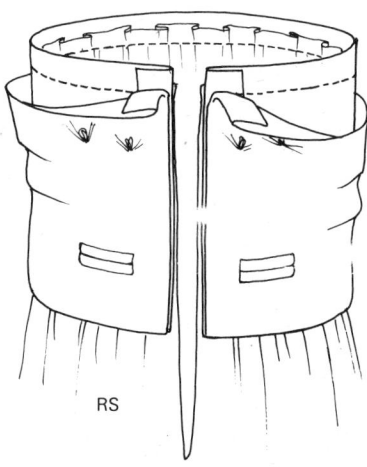

RS

Stage 4   Grade the seam allowances, and press the cuff over them. Turn in the seam allowance of the cuff piece, and hem its fold to the machine stitches on the WS of the sleeve.

Stage 5   Fold the cuff back along its roll line and press lightly.

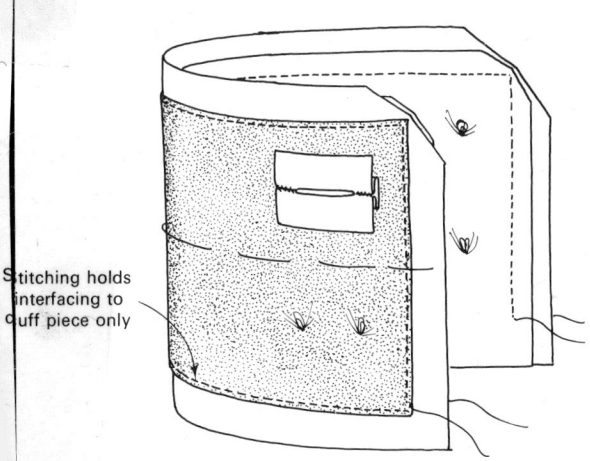

Stitching holds interfacing to cuff piece only

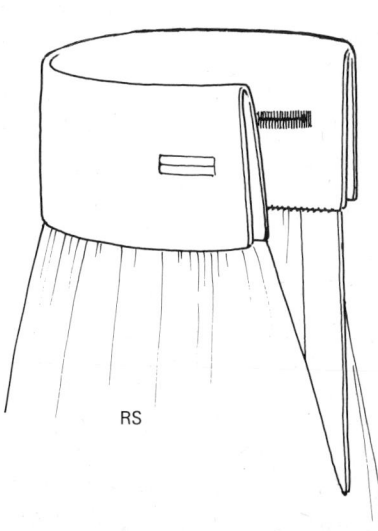

RS

141

Sleeves

Sleeves are of two basic types: those which are cut separately and set into an armhole, and those in which all or part of the sleeve is cut in one with the body of the garment. The set-in variety is usually regarded as the more difficult to fit, but many of the problems arise because the fit of the body at the armhole has not been carefully checked first.

The sleeve itself may be cut in one or more pieces and seams may run around the sleeve as well as down its length. In addition to the shape provided by the seaming, closely fitting sleeves must be eased or darted at the elbow to allow room for the arm to bend. The head of a set-in sleeve is always cut larger than its armhole to allow room for movement, and this extra fullness should be distributed round the upper part of the armhole, usually by easing or gathering, but occasionally in pleats or darts.

Before attaching a set-in sleeve, complete all the seams which run into the armhole. The bodice should fit smoothly round the armhole, and not show any tendency to wrinkle or pull. Very few people have symmetrical shoulders, and occasionally the difference in size is enough to make an adjustment to the garment or sleeve necessary. Stay-stitch the armholes. Make up the sleeves working the darts, cuffs, etc, and making sure that right and left sleeves are formed.

Stage 1 Put two rows of ease stitching over the sleeve head between the balance marks, one row on the seam line and the other 6 mm ($\frac{1}{4}$ in.) from it on the seam allowance.

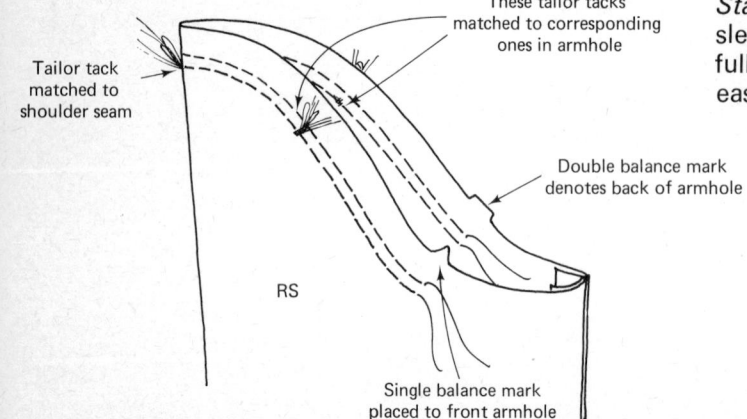

Tailor tack matched to shoulder seam

These tailor tacks matched to corresponding ones in armhole

Double balance mark denotes back of armhole

Single balance mark placed to front armhole

RS

Stage 2 Turn the garment WS out, and slip the sleeve which must be RS out, through the armhole, so that it hangs down inside the garment. Cross-pin and baste the RS of the sleeve and garment together along the underarm section between the single and double balance marks matching the seam at the underarm.

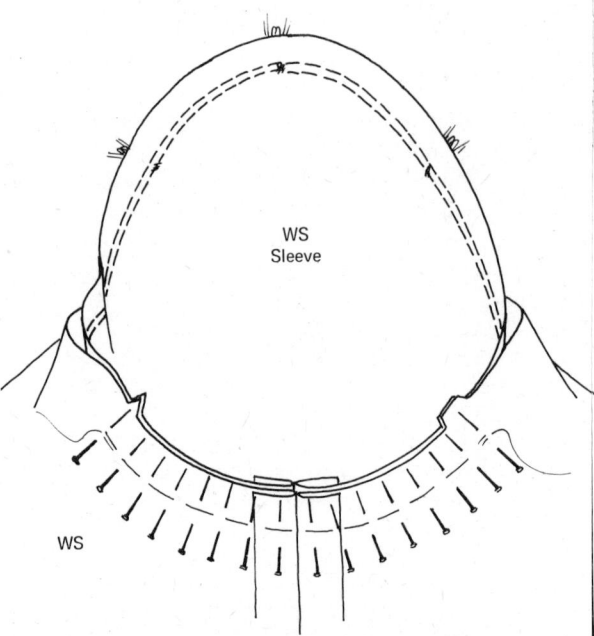

WS
Sleeve

WS

Stage 3 Pin together the tailor tacks in the upper half of the sleeve and armhole. Draw the easing threads up just enough to make the sleeve head the same size as the armhole. Fasten the threads by winding them round a pin.

Stage 4 Cross-pin the upper half of the sleeve and armhole together, distributing the fullness of the sleeve head evenly. Tie off the easing threads, and baste firmly.

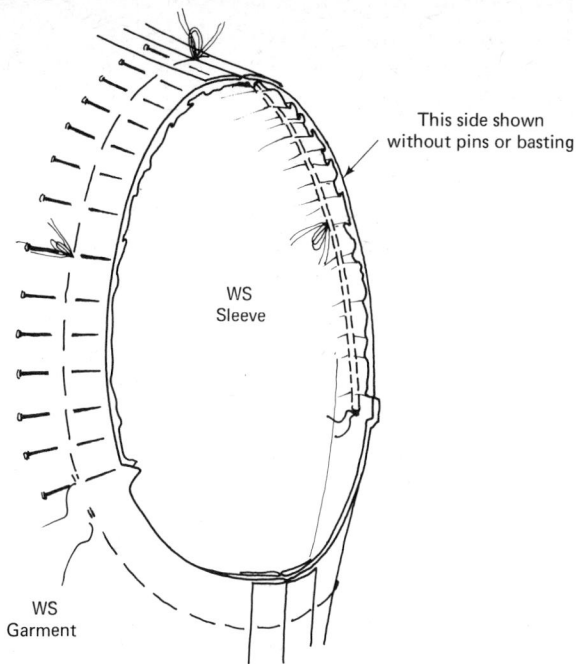

This side shown
without pins or basting

WS
Sleeve

WS
Garment

Stage 5   Fit the other sleeve, and then try the garment on remembering that the untrimmed seam allowances may not allow the sleeves to set perfectly.
Stage 6   Turn the garment WS out, but leave the sleeves inside. With the sleeve side uppermost, stitch the sleeve into the armhole, taking care that no folds of fabric are caught into the stitching. Finish off the thread ends, and remove the basting and easing threads. Do not press the sleeve seam.

Finishing the armhole seam allowance is essential because it will be subjected to a good deal of friction. If it is to be bound, trim both seam allowances to 5 mm ($\frac{3}{16}$ in.), and apply either purchased bias binding or a strip of lining fabric cut on the true bias. The binding should be stitched to the seam allowance on the body side, its free edge turned in and slip-hemmed on the sleeve side. Finish the ends of the binding by making a bias strip join (see page 42), which should not coincide with any other seam in the armhole. In thin fabrics, a strong, neat finish can be made by using one seam allowance to finish the other. Trim the sleeve seam allowance only, to 5 mm ($\frac{3}{16}$ in.). Fold the edge of the seam allowance of the body over

towards the sleeve, and enclose the sleeve seam allowance by hemming this fold to the line of machine stitches. Although this finish is suitable for use on garments which will be washed, if the fabric frays easily, binding should be used. When the fabric does not fray easily and the garment will be dry-cleaned, the seam allowances may be trimmed to 5 mm ($\frac{3}{16}$ in.), and overcast, loop-stitched or zig-zag stitched together.

A raglan sleeve includes part of the shoulder section of the bodice. The seams which join it to the bodice may run diagonally from the underarm straight to the neck edge, or they may be shaped in a variety of ways. Additional shaping is given to the sleeve by a dart or seam on top of the shoulder.
   Prepare the garment by joining any seams which run into the edge to which the sleeve will be attached, and finishing their edges.
Stage 1   Stitch the dart or shoulder seam, press it open and finish its raw edges.
Stage 2   Join the underarm seam. Press and finish it.
Stage 3   Work the cuff or finish the sleeve end.
Stage 4   Turn the garment WS out and slip the sleeve, which should be RS out, inside it. Cross-pin the RS of the sleeve and garment together. Baste. Fit the other sleeve and try the garment on. Stitch the sleeves to the garment and remove the basting.

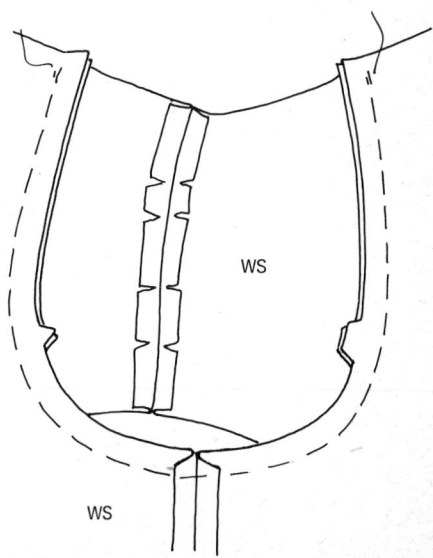

WS

WS

143

Stage 5   To strengthen the underarm section of the sleeve seam, stitch a second time between the balance marks, placing the stitching on the seam allowance 3 mm ($\frac{1}{8}$ in.) from the first row.

Stage 6   Trim the seam allowance close to the second row of stitching, and overcast it.

Stage 7   Clip the seam allowance almost to the stitching line at each end of the second row of stitching. Press the seam allowances open between the balance marks and the ends of the seam, clipping and notching them if this is necessary.

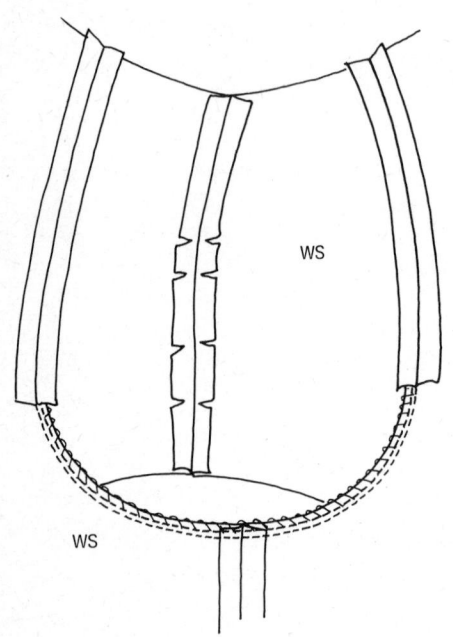

Kimono sleeves are cut in one with the bodice. Some styles allow plenty of room for movement because they are very wide at the underarm. In closer fitting styles, and when the sleeve is short, the underarm seam should be strengthened with tape. When a kimono sleeve is made long and close fitting, extra room must be provided at the underarm by the addition of a one, or two-piece gusset.

Making up a kimono sleeve and taping the underarm seam

Stage 1   Placing the back and front of the body of the garment with their RS together, cross-pin and baste along the upper-arm/ shoulder seam, and also the underarm/side seam.

Stage 2   Baste a piece of stretched bias tape, 10 to 15 cm (4 to 6 in.) long, to the seam line of the underarm/side seam at the armpit.

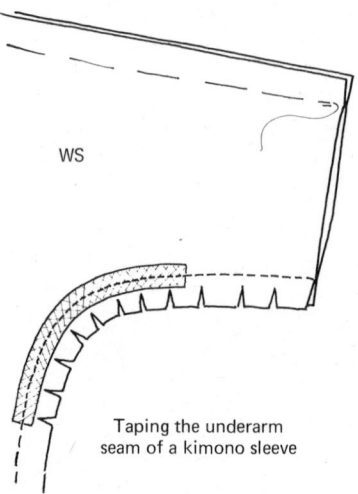

Taping the underarm seam of a kimono sleeve

Stage 3   Stitch the seams, shortening the stitch to 2 mm (12 stitches per inch) for the taped section. Remove the basting, and clip or notch the seam allowances, being careful not to cut the tape. Press the seams open, and finish their raw edges.

When a gusset is to be fitted to the underarm seam of a kimono-sleeved garment, the gusset slash must be faced before the back and front of the garment are joined. The ends of each slash should be marked with tailor tacks.

A one-piece gusset

Stage 1   Cut two facing pieces for each sleeve on the straight grain from garment fabric, or, if this is bulky, from matching thinner fabric. Make each one the length of the slash plus 2·5 cm (1 in.), by 5 cm (2 in.) wide. Hand finish three sides of each piece leaving one 5 cm (2 in.) edge raw.

Stage 2   Place a facing centrally over the line of a slash, on the RS of the garment, with its raw edge level with the edge of the underarm seam allowance. Pin and baste.

Stage 3 Set the machine to a short stitch, and beginning at the edge 6 mm ($\frac{1}{4}$ in.) to one side of the slash line, stitch to the end of the slash. Turn, taking one or two stitches across the point, and return along the other side of the line, ending 6 mm ($\frac{1}{4}$ in.) from it. Shorten the stitch to 1·5 mm (18 stitches per inch) for 2 cm ($\frac{3}{4}$ in.) on each side of the point.

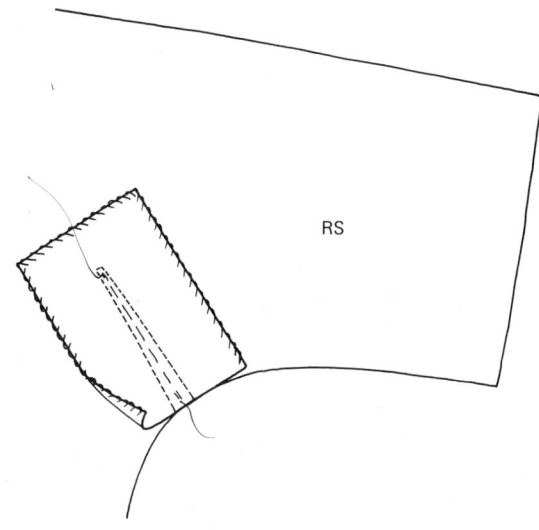

Stage 4 Cut along the slash line to the point, press the facing over the stitching line, and turn it through to the WS. Press again and baste, rolling the seam line slightly to the WS.

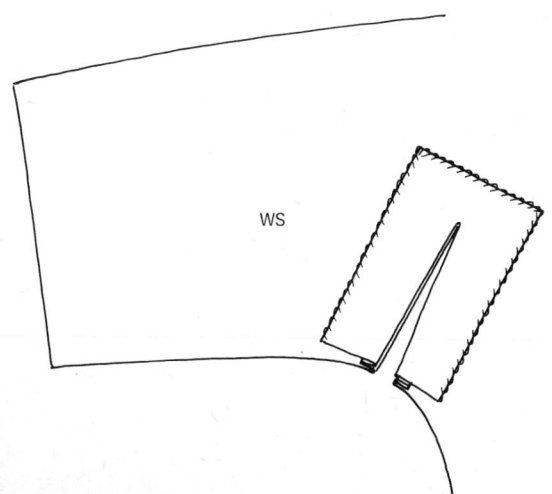

Stage 5 Cross-pin, baste and stitch the underarm and side seams, matching the edges of the slashed sections carefully, and leaving the gusset space as a diamond-shaped opening at the under arm. Press the seams open, clipping where necessary.

Stage 6 Carefully position the gusset piece in the space, with the RS of its seam allowance against the slash facing. Cross-pin and baste. Working from the RS, edge-stitch the sides of the slashes to the gusset. Remove the basting and press.

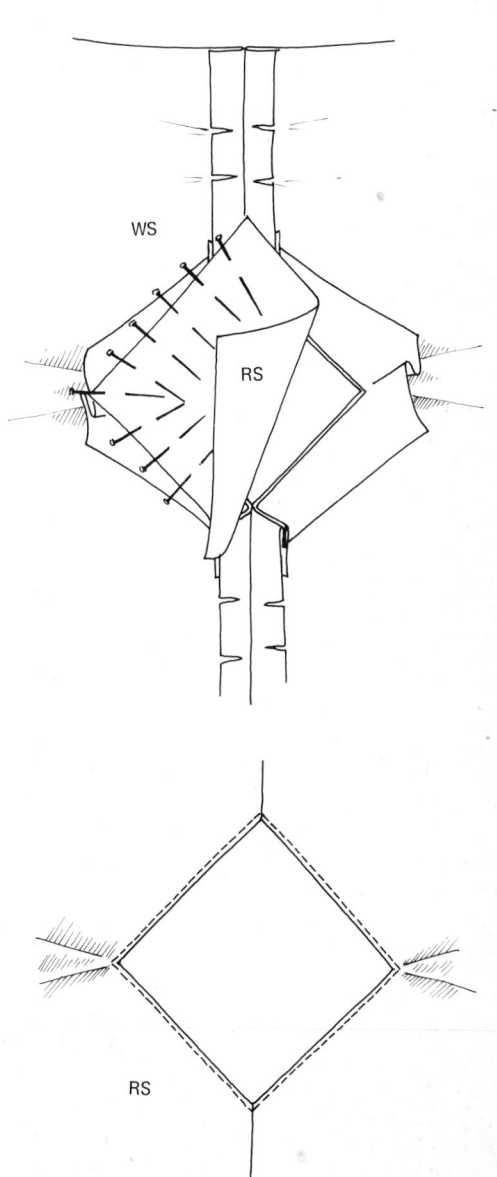

145

Inserting a two-piece gusset

Face the slash, following the instructions for inserting a one-piece gusset to stage 4.

Stage 5   Position a gusset piece in a slash with the RS of its seam allowances against the slash facing. The long edge of the triangle should be in line with the raw edge of the underarm seam allowance. Cross-pin and baste.

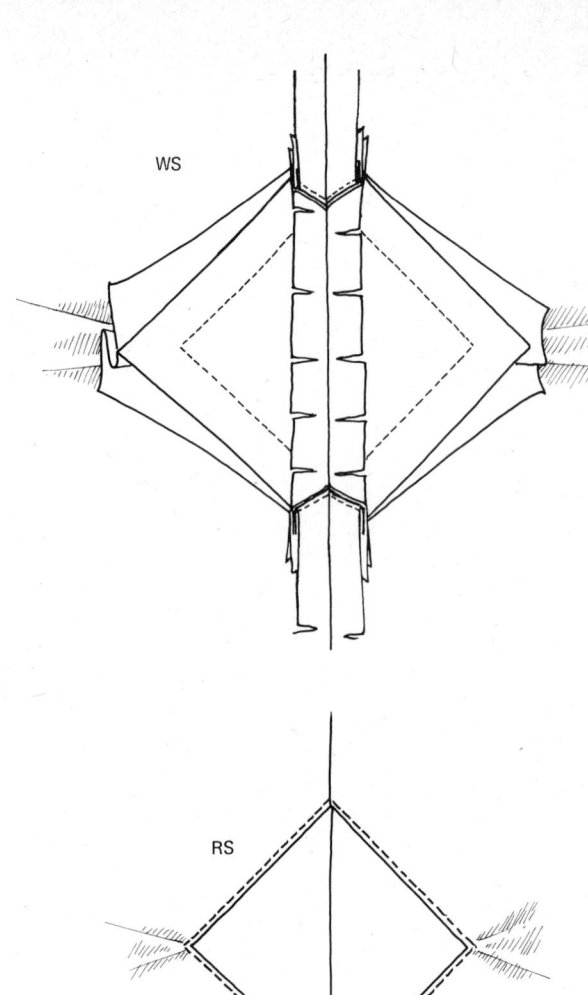

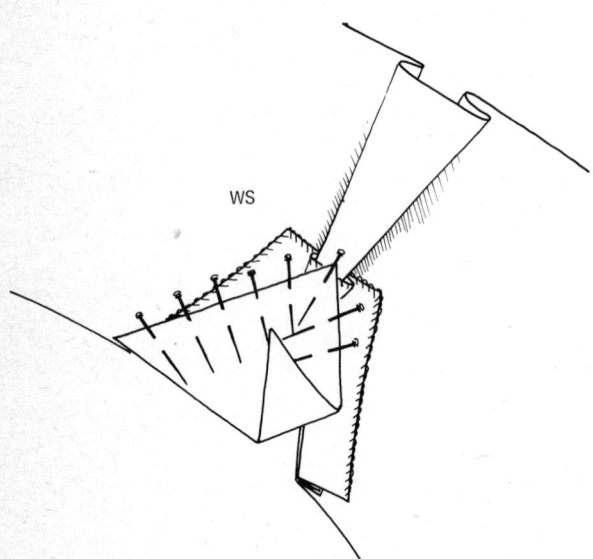

Stage 6   Edge-stitch the sides of the slash to the gusset piece. Remove the basting.

Stage 7   When all the gusset pieces have been inserted, cross-pin and baste the RS of the garment together, being careful to match the edges of the slashes. Stitch the underarm seam, gusset, and side seam in one continuous run. Clip the seam allowances and press them open.

11 Pockets

Pockets may be decorative, functional or both; but whether they are applied, or whether their position is betrayed only by a flap or slit, accurate workmanship is essential, because a pocket is often intended to be an eye-catching detail. After making any major adjustment in length to a pattern, remember to check the pocket position, because it may, as a result of the alteration, come inconveniently close to a hem, or the relationship of the placement marks may have been altered. When planning to add a functional pocket to a garment, make sure that it will be conveniently placed, and that its opening will be wide enough to admit a hand.

Patch pockets may be any shape the designer wishes. They may be attached by hand or machine, finished with top stitching, saddle stitching, or decorated in a variety of ways, but there are only two basic methods of making them: single with a facing, or lined. Both types are most conveniently attached before the back and front of the garment are joined. When making up strongly patterned fabrics, care should be taken either to match the pocket to the part of the pattern on which it will be placed, or to arrange a deliberate contrast (eg in a dress where the stripes run vertically, the stripes on the pocket might be arranged to run horizontally). When adding a patch pocket to a garment, cut a pattern the same size and shape as the finished pocket, and try this on the garment to find the most satisfactory position.

A patch pocket and its facing can always be cut in one piece if the pocket has a straight top edge. If the top edge is shaped, it is simpler to make a lined pocket than to cut a separate part facing.

Stage 1   Cut out the pocket, allowing 1·5 cm ($\frac{5}{8}$ in.) for seam allowances at the bottom and sides, and 5 cm (2 in.) at the top for the facing.

Stage 2   Finish the edge of the facing which will remain free.

Stage 3   Fold the facing to the RS of the pocket and baste it into place.

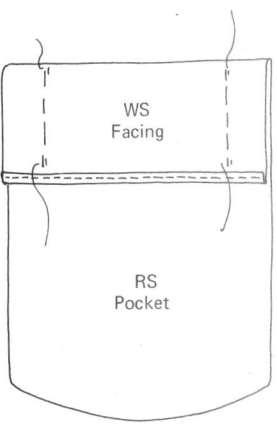

Stage 4   Stitch around the pocket exactly 1·5 cm ($\frac{5}{8}$ in.) from the raw edge, beginning and ending at the top edge fold. Finish off the thread ends.

Stage 5   Clip or notch the seam allowance where necessary, and trim off the corners. Turn the facing to the WS and press it, bringing each stitching line to its fold.

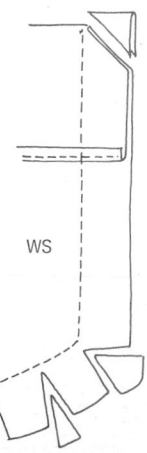

Stage 6   Turn the pocket seam allowances to the WS so that the guide line of stitching is just on the WS of the pocket. Baste the seam allowances into place and press lightly.

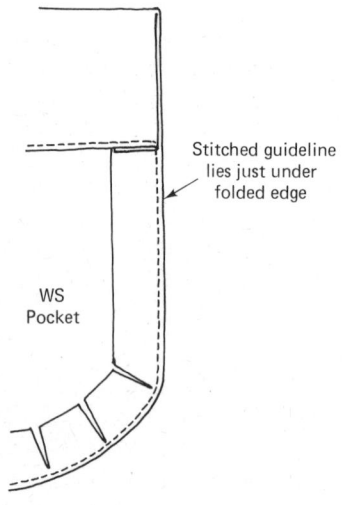

Stitched guideline lies just under folded edge

WS Pocket

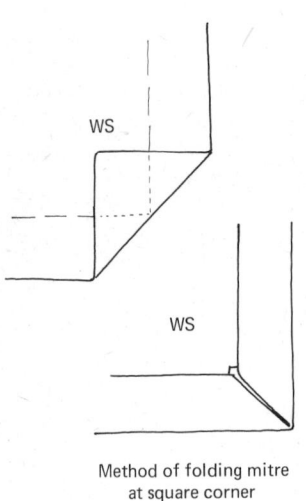

Method of folding mitre at square corner

A lined patch pocket is made from two pieces, which may both be garment fabric, or, if this is too bulky, the inner layer may be cut from lining.

Stage 1   Cut out the pocket and lining pieces allowing normal seam allowances all round. Baste interfacing to the WS of the pocket piece, and stitch it to the seam allowance 1 mm ($\frac{1}{16}$ in.) from the seam line. Trim off the interfacing seam allowance.

Stage 2   Place the pocket and its lining piece with their RS together. Cross pin and baste.

Stage 3   Stitch the pieces together, but leave a 5 cm (2 in.) gap in the stitching in an inconspicuous place, bearing in mind that it will be easier to close this gap neatly in a straight, or slightly curved edge than in a sharply curved one. Finish off the thread ends.

Stage 4   Grade, clip and notch the seam allowance where necessary, and turn the pocket right side out through the gap. Work the seam line to the edge of the pocket. Baste through all layers to hold the pocket in shape, and press lightly. Close the gap in the edge with slip stitching.

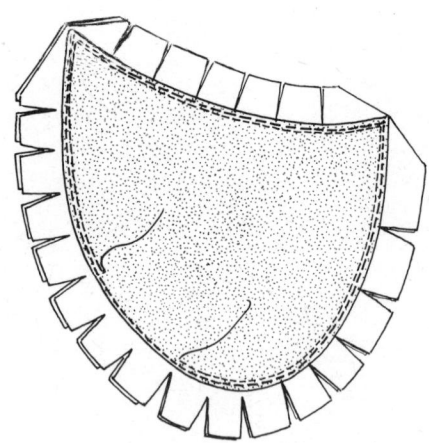

Pocket prepared for turning

Attaching patch pockets

If the opening edge is to be top stitched, this must be done before the pocket is attached. Baste the pocket firmly into place so that it cannot get out of position when permanently stitching it to the garment.

Functional pockets may be edge- or top-stitched into position, or they may be backstitched from the WS of the garment. When a pocket is attached by machine it is usually strengthened by stitching a small triangle or rectangle at each top corner, and these corners may be further reinforced by basting small squares of material to the WS of the garment fabric before stitching.

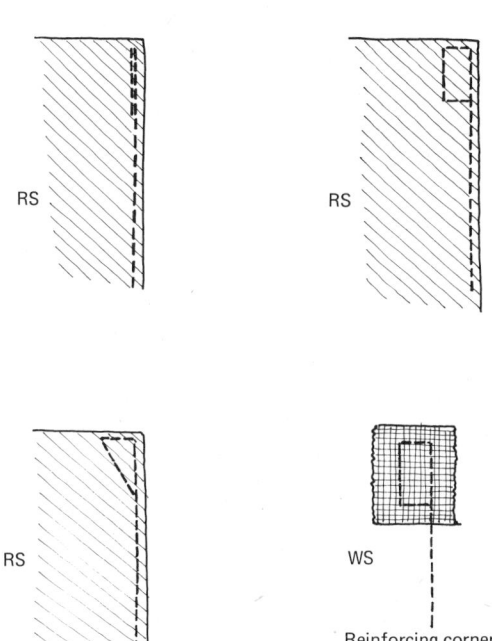

RS

RS

RS

WS

Reinforcing corner with a fabric patch

Pockets intended purely for decoration may be attached with small, firm slip stitches. When using this method to attach a faced pocket, pick up the machine stitches which were used to form a guide for the shape. When attaching a lined pocket by hand, sew through the facing just under the edge of the pocket. Place the garment piece pocket side downwards on a flat surface, and fold the

garment fabric out of the way to expose the edge of the pocket. Stitch alternately into the pocket and the garment, being careful that the slip stitches do not come through to the RS.

Pockets in a seam occur in the side or side front of a garment. The pocket pieces; which should be cut from thin, strong material, both to improve the wearing properties of the pocket and to reduce bulk; should be attached before the garment seams are joined. As a pocket opening is hardly ever on the straight grain, it should be stayed to prevent it from stretching. Make sure, when only a single pocket is being fitted, that it is attached to the correct seam; because the tailor tacks marking the pocket position on pieces which have been cut place-on-fold, or double, will appear on both right and left sides of the garment. This type of pocket may be stitched directly to the seam allowances of the garment. A better method is to extend the seam allowances for the length of the pocket opening. The extensions are called facings, and they ensure that the junction between the pocket and garment piece occurs inside the pocket.

A seam pocket with a facing

Stage 1   Cut a piece of stay tape (if this cannot be obtained, narrow seam binding may be used), 2·5 cm (1 in.) longer than the pocket opening. Using small running stitches, sew it to the WS of the garment piece which forms the front of the pocket opening, positioning it so that it is on the line of the seam, and so that an equal amount of tape overlaps on to the seam line at each end.

Stage 2   Place the RS of each pocket piece and its facing together. Cross-pin, baste and stitch. Remove the basting, grade the seam allowances and finish them if necessary. Press the pocket pieces over their seam allowances.

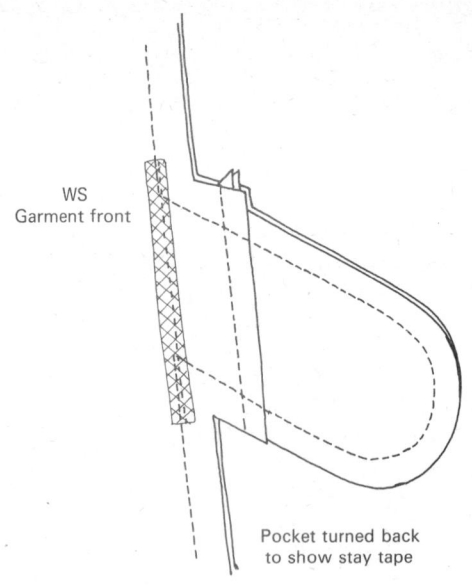

WS Garment front

Pocket turned back to show stay tape

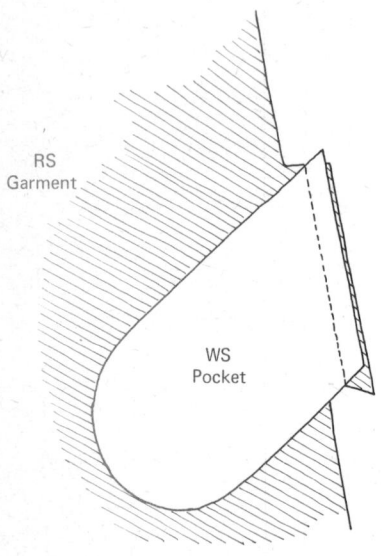

RS Garment

WS Pocket

Stage 3   Pin and baste the garment pieces with their RS together above and below the opening, and pin and baste the seam around the pocket. With the front piece of the garment uppermost, stitch along the garment seam, pivot, stitch around the bag of the pocket, and continue along the remainder of the garment seam. Shorten the machine stitch for the corners, and make sure that the stay tape is kept flat and caught in the seam.

Stage 4   Remove the basting stitches and finish the raw edges of the pocket seam allowances. If the garment seam allowances are to be pressed open, snip the seam allowance of the piece nearest to the CB above and below the pocket. Overcast the cut edges of the snip to finish them.

Stage 5   Turn the pocket towards the CF, and press the roll line of the opening lightly.

A seam pocket without a facing is used if the decision to add a pocket to the garment is made after the garment has been cut out. Make a pattern for the pocket, and use it to cut the pocket pieces. Mark the points on the garment pieces where the pocket will be attached.

Stage 1   Cut a piece of stay tape (if this cannot be obtained, narrow seam binding may be used) 2·5 cm (1 in.) longer than the pocket opening. Use small running stitches to sew it to the WS of the garment piece which forms the front of the opening. Position it on the seam line and so that an equal amount of tape extends beyond each end of the pocket opening.

Stage 2   Place the RS of each pocket and garment piece together, with their raw edges level. Cross-pin and baste. Stitch them together 1 cm ($\frac{3}{8}$ in.) from their raw edges.

Remove the basting, grade the seam allowances and finish the edges if necessary. Press the pocket pieces over their seam allowances.

To complete the pocket, follow stages 3, 4 and 5 of the previous instructions.

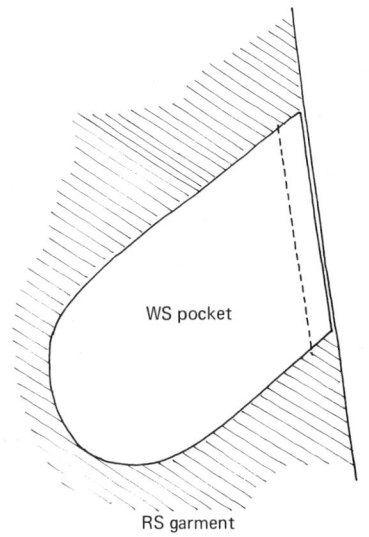

WS pocket

RS garment

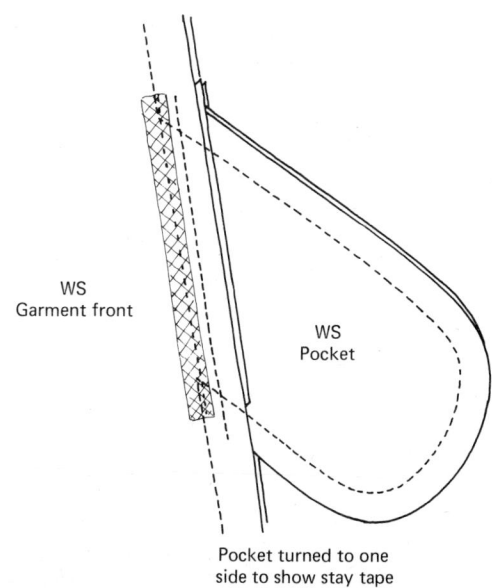

WS
Garment front

WS
Pocket

Pocket turned to one
side to show stay tape

A pocket flap with a roll line may be used to cover the opening of a patch pocket, or be applied to give the appearance of a pocket where none exists.

Stage 1   Cut out the flap and its facing (they may be cut in one piece if the edge of the flap is to be straight). Make each piece the size of the finished flap plus one seam allowance on each edge. Interface the WS of the flap, and baste mark its roll line. Cross-pin the pieces with their RS together, easing the flap on to its facing across the roll line, and baste.

Stage 2   Stitch the ends of the flap (and the lower edge if the flap is separate), beginning and ending 6 mm ($\frac{1}{4}$ in.) from the edge of the flap facing. Change the angle of the stitching just on the seam allowance side of the roll line, as shown in the diagram, to ensure that the seam allowances will not show when the flap is attached.

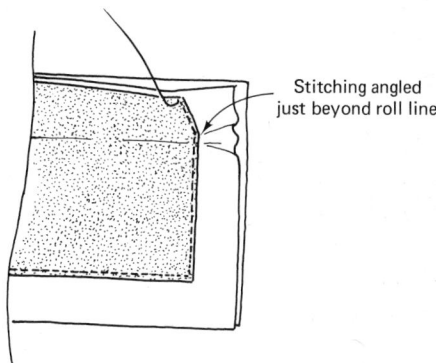

Stitching angled
just beyond roll line

Stage 3   Trim the interfacing seam allowance, and clip the corners. Grade the flap seam allowances and notch them at the roll line. Turn the flap RS out, and press the edge bringing the seam line to the fold. Fold the flap along the roll line, and press lightly.

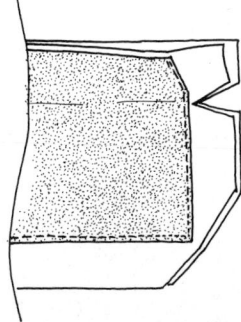

Stage 4   Baste the seam allowances together, just beyond the roll line, adjusting them to allow more length for the roll if necessary. Place the flap flat on the garment, with their RS together, and with the flap pointing towards the top of the garment. Baste it firmly to the garment along the previous line of basting, and stitch it 1 mm ($\frac{1}{16}$ in.) on the roll line side of the basting.

Stage 5   Trim the interfacing, and also the seam allowance which is next to the garment, to 6 mm ($\frac{1}{4}$ in.). Finish by turning in the edge of the untrimmed seam allowance and edge-stitching it to the garment. If the fabric is bulky, use a flatter method.

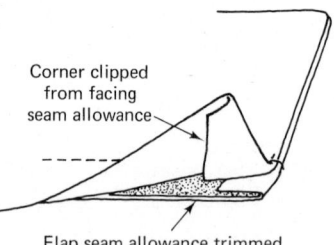

Corner clipped from facing seam allowance

Flap seam allowance trimmed

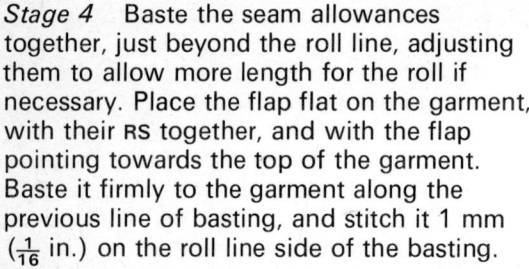

Facing seam allowance will project further than flap seam allowance

RS
Flap facing

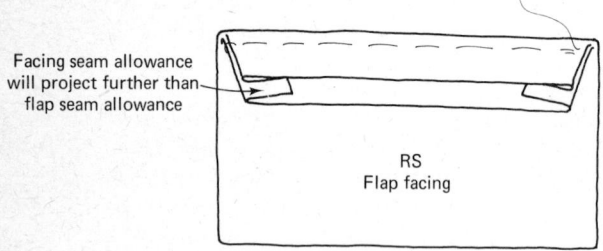

RS
Flap facing

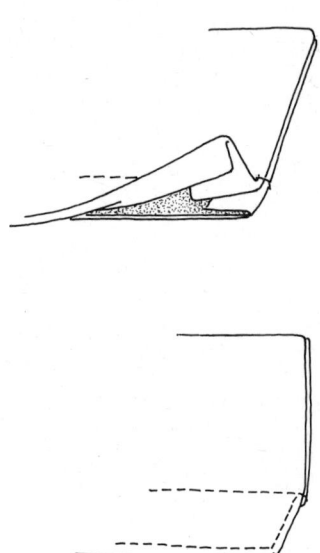

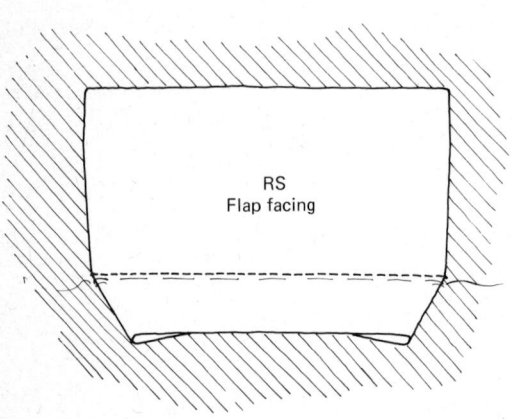

Stage 6   Lightly press the flap downwards, and if it is only decorative, secure it in position with small catch stitches placed about 1 cm ($\frac{3}{8}$ in.) inside the free corners.

Bound pockets, welt pockets and pockets with flaps may be accented by using a fabric which contrasts with that of the garment, and when using checked material, by cutting it on the bias. The opening of these types of pockets is usually made on the straight grain, but it can be set in a slanting position. When adding this type of pocket to a jacket or short coat, make sure that the raw edges of the pocket bottom fall short of the garment hem.

Before starting to make a pocket, the depth of each bound edge or the depth of the welt must be decided upon. The scale of these, and other details, should depend upon the thickness of the material and the size of the pocket. When working in medium-weight or thicker fabric, it is advisable to cut the pocket lining pieces from thin, firm material and to seam them to the pieces used for the binding. When working in light-weight, firmly woven fabric, the whole pocket may be cut from the garment fabric. If, however, the binding for the edge of a pocket is cut on the bias, the lining must be made from fabric cut on the straight grain and seamed on, whatever the weight of the garment fabric.

A bound pocket is in many respects similar to a bound buttonhole. Before starting work on a pocket, decide what depth to make its bound edges because this measurement is required when cutting the pocket pieces. Interface the WS of the pocket opening using a piece large enough to extend beyond the opening in every direction by the width of a seam allowance.

Stage 1   Mark the line of the pocket opening with machine basting.

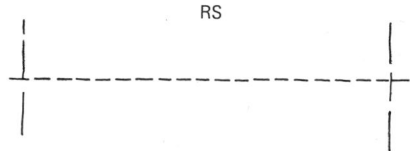

RS

Stage 2   Cut the pocket piece, making its width the same as that of the pocket opening plus two seam allowances. Its length must be twice the depth of the finished pocket, plus six times the depth of a bound edge, plus two seam allowances.

Stage 3   Fold the pocket piece in half crosswise, and mark its centre line. Measure the depth of a bound edge from this line, and machine-baste a second line parallel to the first. Remove the first set of markings.

Stage 4   Place the RS of the pocket and garment together with the marked lines exactly matching. The pocket piece should overlap the marked opening by an equal amount at each end, and the longer half of the pocket piece must be at the top. Pin and baste the pocket piece to the garment around the marked line and 1 cm ($\frac{3}{8}$ in.) from it.

Stage 5   Set the machine to a 1·5 mm stitch (18 stitches per inch), and with the garment WS up, begin stitching round the pocket opening on one of its long sides. Pivot at each corner and overlap the stitching by about 1 cm ($\frac{3}{8}$ in.). The stitching on each long side should be the width of the binding from the centre line, and should cross each end at the point where the opening will finish.

Stage 6   Cut along the centre line of the opening, stopping 6 to 8 mm ($\frac{1}{4}$ to $\frac{3}{8}$ in.) from each end. From these points snip into the corners. Do not cut through the stitching.

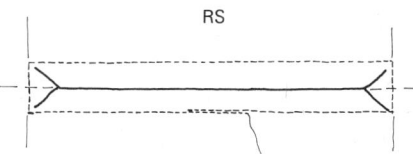

RS

Stage 7   Turn the pocket piece through the slit, and press the seams on the long edges of the pocket open. Pull the pocket fabric at the ends of the opening gently but firmly to make it turn completely to the WS. Press lightly if this is necessary.

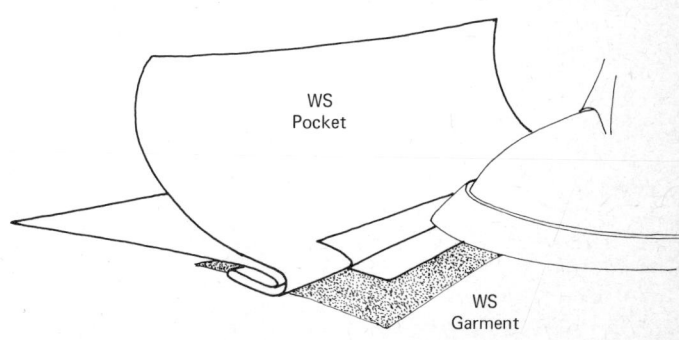

WS
Pocket

WS
Garment

Stage 8 The two lips of the pocket now have to be formed. They must be the same depth as each other, and the opening must be just filled by them. Smooth the pocket piece over the seam allowances which have been pressed towards the opening. Working from the RS, stab-stitch the pocket piece into place along both long sides, sinking the stitches into the seam line to conceal them. Press the pocket opening, but not the ends.

Stage 9 Catch-stitch the lips of the pocket together to keep the opening in shape.

Stage 10 Turn the work WS up. The pocket fabric at the ends of the opening will have been partly formed into inverted pleats. Gently pull these in line with the pocket opening to remove any tendency for the binding to pucker at the corners of the opening. Oversew the pleat folds together from the ends of the opening to the edge of the pocket fabric.

Stage 11 Press the upper half of the pocket downwards. Pin and baste the halves of the pocket together. Fold the garment fabric back at one end of the pocket, to expose the WS of the inverted pleat and the triangle of garment fabric on it. Stitch again on top of the stitching at the end of the pocket slot through the triangle and the pleat. Continue around the pocket to the triangle at the other end of the opening. Trim and finish the raw edges of the pocket seam allowances.

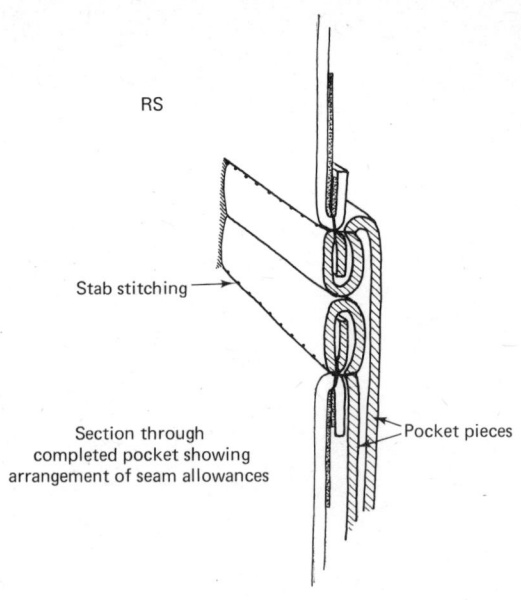

RS

Stab stitching

Pocket pieces

Section through completed pocket showing arrangement of seam allowances

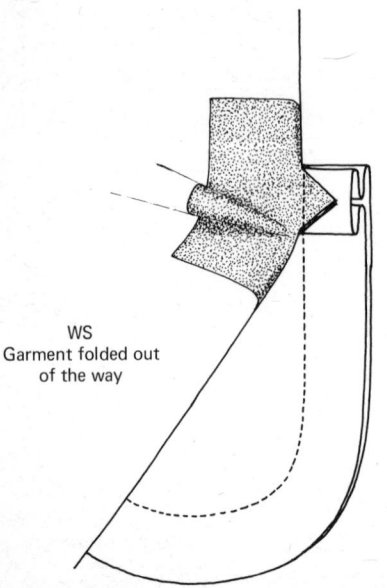

WS
Garment folded out of the way

A separate lining should be used when the binding is cut on the bias, and also when the garment material is not suitable for a pocket lining. The pocket lining is substituted for garment fabric at the ends of the pocket piece. When cutting the pocket piece remember that a minimum of four times the width of the binding, plus two seam allowances must be left on each side of its true centre line. The lining pieces should be placed RS together with the pocket piece and stitched. The seam allowances should be pressed towards the lining, graded and their raw edges finished. The pocket is then completed in the same way as a bound pocket in one piece, following stages 3 to 11. When cutting the pocket piece, if an extra seam allowance is added to the end which will form the back of the pocket, the joins between the lining pieces and the pocket piece will be staggered.

A bound pocket with a flap

Before beginning to make the pocket, decide what depth to make its bound edge, because this measurement is required when cutting the front pocket piece. Baste interfacing to the WS of the pocket opening using a piece large enough to extend beyond the opening in every direction by the width of a seam allowance. It is important that the pocket flap should be made exactly the same width as the opening because otherwise the ends of the pocket opening will not be covered.

Stage 1   Mark the line of the pocket opening with machine basting.

Stage 2   Cut out the front pocket piece making it the width of the opening plus two seam allowances. Its length should be that of the finished pocket plus three times the width of one bound edge plus two seam allowances. The back pocket piece should be the same width as the front one. Make its length that of the finished pocket plus the width of one bound edge plus two seam allowances.

Stage 3   Machine-baste a line across the upper end of the front pocket piece making its distance from this edge equal to the width of the binding plus one seam allowance.

Stage 4   Cut out the flap and its facing and interface the flap. Place the flap and its facing with their RS together, cross-pin, baste and stitch. Trim off the interfacing close to the stitching line, grade the seam allowances, trim the corners and turn the flap RS out. Press.

Stage 5   Trim the seam allowances of the raw edge of the flap to 6 mm ($\frac{1}{4}$ in.). Place the RS of the flap against the RS of the garment, above the opening and with its raw edge against the marked line. Hold it in place by basting it close to the line.

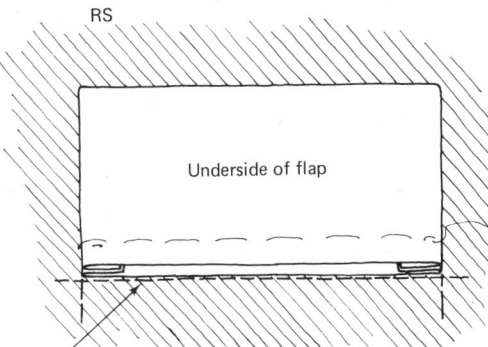

Stage 6   Place the RS of the front pocket piece and garment together, with the main part of the pocket below the opening. Match the slash lines exactly. Baste the layers into place by stitching around the slash line.

Stage 7   Set the machine to a 1·5 mm stitch (18 stitches per inch), and with the garment WS up, begin stitching the pocket opening on one of its long sides, pivot at each corner, and overlap the stitching by about 1 cm ($\frac{3}{8}$ in.). The stitching on each long side should be the width of the binding from the centre line, and should cross each end at the point where the opening will finish.

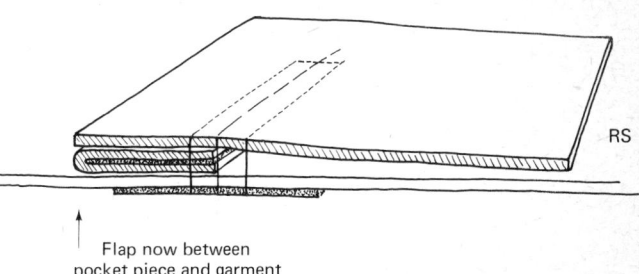

Flap now between
pocket piece and garment

Stage 8   Cut along the centre line of the opening, stopping 6 to 8 mm ($\frac{1}{4}$ to $\frac{3}{8}$ in.) from each end. From these points snip into the corners. Do not cut through the stitching.

Stage 9   Remove the basting, and working around the opening, press the top part of the pocket piece down, then the bottom piece up, and finally the sides in, so that they will turn through easily.

Stage 10   Turn the pocket piece through the slit, and pull the corners gently to flatten out the pieces. Press open the seam along the lower edge of the pocket opening. Press the flap downwards.

Stage 11   To finish the lower edge of the opening, smooth the pocket fabric over its seam allowance forming a band of even width, and working from the RS stab-stitch the pocket piece into place sinking the stitches into the seam line to conceal them.

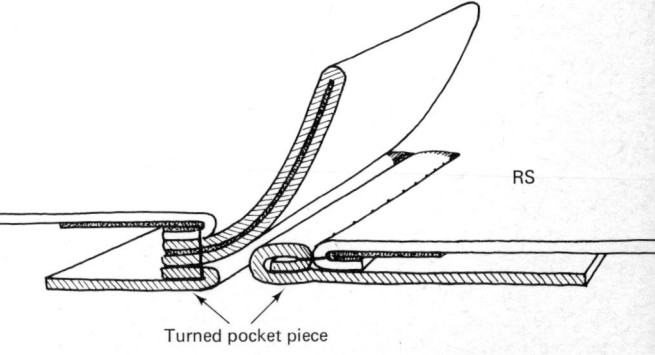

Turned pocket piece

155

Stage 12   Hem the pleat folds which form in the pocket piece at the ends of the opening to hold them firmly and press.

Stage 13   Pin and baste the back pocket piece to the front one with their RS together. Fold the garment fabric back at one end of the pocket opening to expose the WS of the pleat and the triangle of garment fabric. Beginning on top of the stitching at the end of the pocket, stitch through the triangle, pleat and back pocket piece. Continue stitching round the pocket, including the piece which projects above the top of the opening. Trim the pocket seam allowances, finish their edges and press.

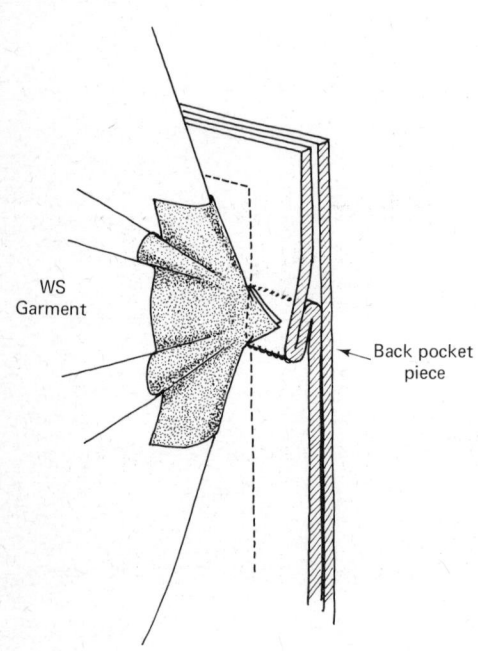

WS
Garment

← Back pocket
piece

A welt pocket

Mark the position of the pocket opening with a line of machine basting. If desired baste interfacing to the WS of the pocket opening, using a piece large enough to extend beyond the top corners of the finished welt. It is important that the finished welt should be made exactly the same in width as the opening, and not less than 2 cm ($\frac{3}{4}$ in.) deep, because it must hide the back pocket seam. The back pocket piece may be cut entirely from garment fabric if this is suitable, or if it is necessary to save bulk, the top part only should be cut from garment fabric, and the remainder from lining.

Stage 1   Cut out the welt piece making it the same in width as the pocket opening plus two seam allowances, by twice the depth of the finished welt plus two seam allowances.

Stage 2   Interface one half of the welt piece. Fold the piece in half lengthwise with its RS together, and stitch across the ends. Trim off the interfacing seam allowances close to the stitching, trim the corners and grade the seam allowances. Turn the welt RS out and press.

Stage 3   Trim the seam allowances at the open edge of the welt piece to 6 mm ($\frac{1}{4}$ in.). Place it, interfaced side down, on the RS of the garment so that the trimmed edge is against the marked line, and the welt piece is below the opening. Baste it to the garment, close to the stitching line.

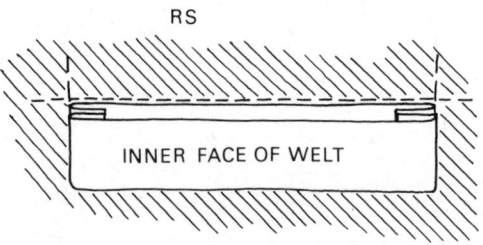

RS

INNER FACE OF WELT

Stage 4   Cut out the front pocket piece from lining fabric. Make its length the same as the depth of the finished pocket plus one seam allowance. Its width should be equal to the length of the slash plus two seam allowances. Make the back pocket piece the same width and its length one seam allowance greater than the front one.

Stage 5   Place the RS of the front pocket piece on the RS of the garment below the opening, and with its raw edge against the marked line. Pin. Similarly pin the back pocket piece above the opening. Each piece should overlap the ends of the line of the opening by an equal amount. Baste them firmly to the garment.

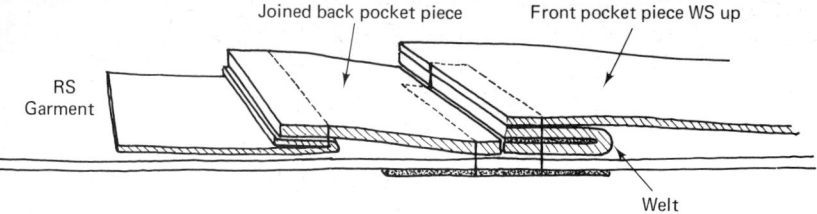

Joined back pocket piece   Front pocket piece WS up

RS
Garment

Welt

Stage 6 Working from the WS, begin stitching the pocket opening on one of its long sides. Pivot at each corner, and overlap the stitching by about 1 cm ($\frac{3}{8}$ in.). Make the stitching 6 mm ($\frac{1}{4}$ in.) from the centre line on each long side, and cross each end exactly at the end of the line.

Stage 7 Cut along the line stopping 6 mm ($\frac{1}{4}$ in.) from each end. Clip into the corners, being careful not to cut the stitching. Turn the back pocket piece through to the WS and press its seam open.

Stage 8 Turn the work RS up, and arrange the front pocket piece and the welt to lie over the opening with their seam allowances pointing down inside the pocket. Press. Turn the front pocket piece through the opening and press it downwards. Pull its edge in line with the opening to make it set.

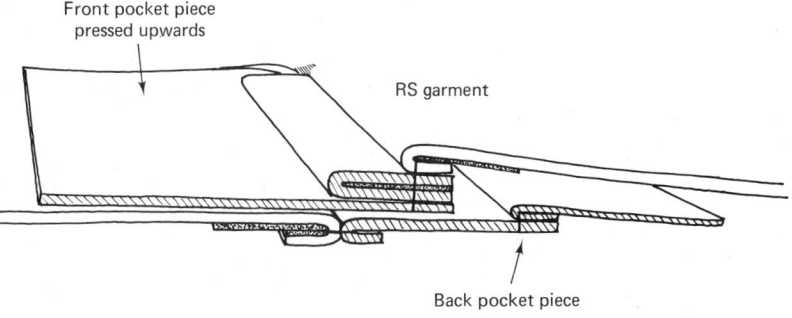

Front pocket piece
pressed upwards

RS garment

Back pocket piece

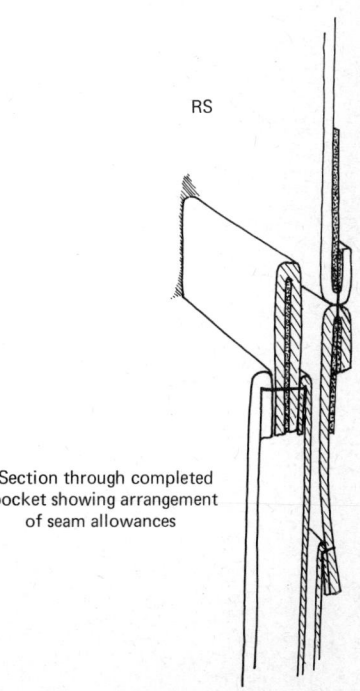

RS

Section through completed
pocket showing arrangement
of seam allowances

Stage 9 Pin and baste the two pocket pieces together. Fold the garment out of the way to expose the triangle and pocket seam allowances at one end of the slash. Stitch, beginning on top of the previous stitching at the end of the opening, continue round the pocket, and finish at the other end of the opening.

Stage 10 From the RS, slip-stitch the ends of the welt piece to the garment with small, firm stitches. Trim and finish the seam allowances of the pocket. Press.

12 The waistline

Waist seams

When joining the bodice to the skirt, turn the
skirt inside out and slip the bodice, which
should be RS out, inside it. Match and cross-
pin together the corresponding vertical seams
and darts, and examine them from both bodice
and skirt side to see that they are perfectly in
line. Assuming that the garment has been
made up accurately, that no adjustments have
been forgotten and that neither part is
gathered, the waist seam lines will be equal in
length, and they also may be cross pinned.
When the waist seam does include a
gathered or eased section, the gathering
threads must be put in before the two halves
of the garment are joined. Match the balance
marks at each end of the gathered sections
when pinning the bodice and skirt together,
and pull the threads up to make the seam
lines the same length.

Baste along the seam line. Try the garment
on to check that the seam is at the correct
height, and that it is level all the way round.
Adjust if necessary. Baste seam binding or
stay tape along the waistline seam to prevent
it from stretching. If either bodice or skirt is
gathered, baste the tape to the gathered side
of the seam. Stitch the waist seam and remove
the basting. Finish the raw edges of the seam
allowances, and press them away from the
gathered half, or, if neither half is gathered,
press them open.

The waistband is attached when the skirt
has been completed except for the hem. The
waistband of a fitted skirt should be about
2·5 cm (1 in.) shorter than the skirt edge to
which it will be attached. This extra length
must be eased on to the band. Self-fabric
waistbands should be cut on the warp grain
and are usually interfaced. The overlap end of
the waistband should finish level with the
edge of the opening: the underlap end
extends across the top of the opening, behind
the overlap. The fastening usually takes the
form of one or two hooks at the end of the
overlap, and a snap fastener at the end of the
underlap to keep its top edge in line with the
edge of the waistband.

To make a plain waistband, cut a piece on
the straight grain, making it the finished
length plus 7 cm ($2\frac{3}{4}$ in.) to allow for the
overlap and seam allowances. Its width
should be twice that of the finished band plus
two seam allowances. Alternatively, to save
the bulk of a second fold on the inside of the
band, place the stitching line of the inner half
of the band against a selvage, and make the
band twice the finished width plus one seam
allowance. When using this method be
careful, if one end of the band is pointed and
the fabric single sided, to cut out the band the
right way round.

Stage 1   Baste the interfacing to the WS of
the show half of the band, and catch-stitch
it to the fold.

Stage 2   Fold the band lengthwise with its
RS together, and stitch across the overlap end
stopping at the seam line. Stitch across the
underlap end from the fold to the waist seam
line, pivot, and stitch along the waist seam
line as far as the tailor tack which marks the
end of the underlap. Snip the waistline seam
allowances at this point to allow them to
project after the waistband is turned RS out.

Stage 3   Sew in the thread ends. Trim off the
interfacing seam allowances close to the
stitching. Grade the seam allowances of the
ends and trim the corners. Turn the band RS
out and press.

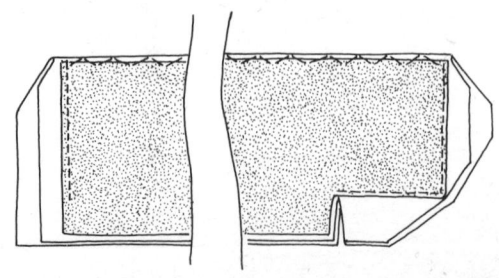

Stage 4   Place the show side of the band to the RS of the garment, with the overlap end of the band level with the corresponding edge of the opening. The projecting seam allowances at the underlap end should be level with the underlap edge of the opening. Cross-pin and baste the show half of the band to the garment.

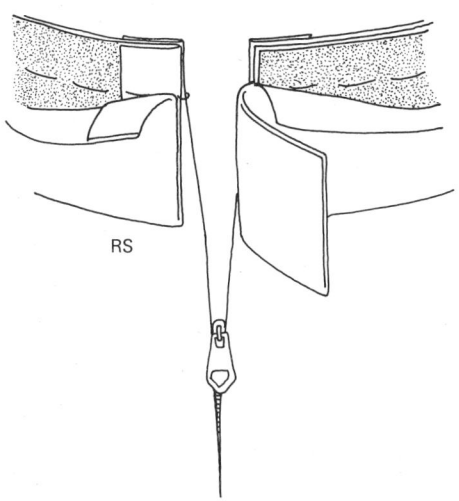

RS

Stage 5   Try the skirt on to check that it fits smoothly, and that it does not drag or wrinkle.
Stage 6   Stitch the show half of the band to the garment. Trim off the interfacing seam allowance, grade the seam allowances and press the band upwards from the RS so that it lies over the waist seam.
Stage 7   Fold in the seam allowance of the free edge of the band and hem it to the line of stitching on the WS, or, if this edge is a selvage, hem this to the machine stitches.

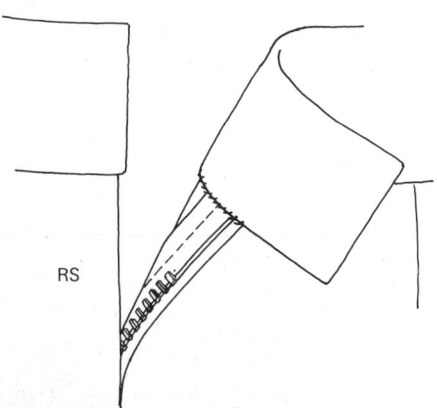

RS

A band finished with top stitching is in many respects prepared and attached similarly to a normal waistband, but the selvage method cannot be used. The interfacing should be cut out with seam allowances only at the ends. It should be basted to the WS of the show half of the band, and its long edges should be catch stitched into place. At stage 4 it is the RS of the non-interfaced half of the band which must be placed to the WS of the garment. The band is turned to the RS and the free edge folded in. It is held in place with top stitching which is continued around the edge of the band.

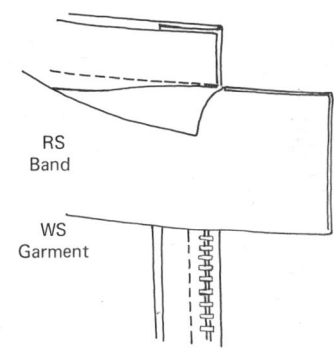

RS
Band

WS
Garment

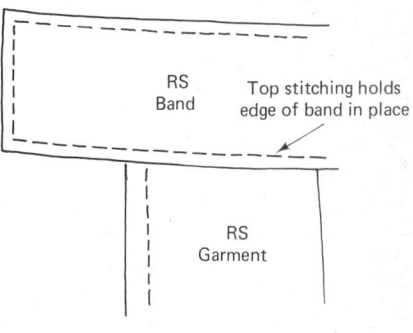

RS
Band

Top stitching holds
edge of band in place

RS
Garment

A petersham band is a neat, flat method of finishing and supporting the top edge of a fitted skirt. Where petersham cannot be obtained, grosgrain ribbon may be substituted but it is not as satisfactory. Curved petersham, or petersham which has been stretched along one edge, should be used by people with a well-defined waistline. The petersham band for a fitted skirt should be about 2·5 cm (1 in.) shorter than the skirt edge. This extra length is eased onto the band.

Stage 1   Mark the waist seam line on the RS of the garment.

Stage 2   To reduce bulk in the fold, trim the seam allowances of seams and darts which run into the waistline as shown in the diagram. Trim the waistline seam allowance to 1 cm ($\frac{3}{8}$ in.), and finish its raw edge if this is necessary.

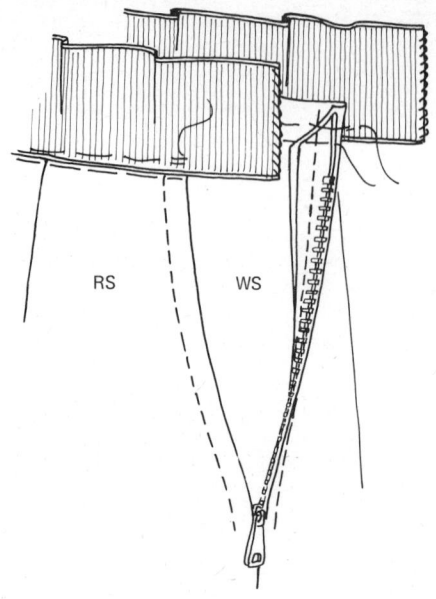

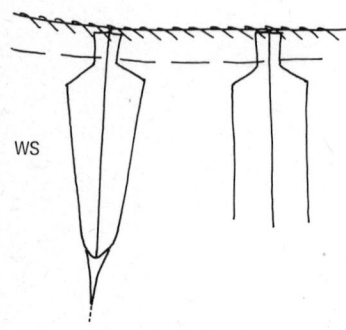

Stage 3   Cut a piece of petersham, making it the finished length plus two seam allowances, and overcast the cut ends. Place the petersham on the RS of the waist seam allowance with its (concave) edge against the marked line. Pin the ends first, leaving 1·5 cm ($\frac{5}{8}$ in.) of petersham projecting beyond each edge of the opening. Ease the skirt waistline evenly on to the petersham.

Stage 4   Baste the petersham into place and try the skirt on to check its fit.

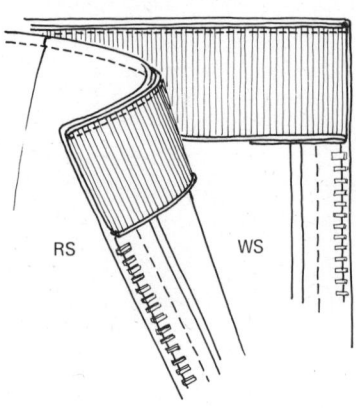

Stage 5   Fold the ends of the petersham to the WS, and turn the band down inside the skirt. With the petersham side uppermost, baste, and then edge-stitch along the top of the skirt through all three layers, being careful to arrange the fold at the upper edge of the skirt so that it just projects above the petersham.

Stage 6   Sew hooks and eyes to the skirt side of the folded ends of the petersham, to fasten it edge-to-edge.

This alternative method of attaching petersham has the advantage of ensuring that its edge cannot show in wear, but it may be used only with light- and medium-weight fabrics. The line of the waist seam must be marked on the WS, instead of the RS of the skirt. Lap the petersham to the WS of the waist seam allowance with its edge against the seam line. Edge-stitch it to the skirt. Trim the seam allowance to 1 cm ($\frac{3}{8}$ in.), and place a piece of seam binding on it so that it covers the raw edge, and so that one of its edges is against the line of stitching. Fold its ends over the ends of the petersham, and stitch along both of its edges. Turn the ends of the petersham to the WS, and hem them to the back of the band. Fold the band down inside the skirt.

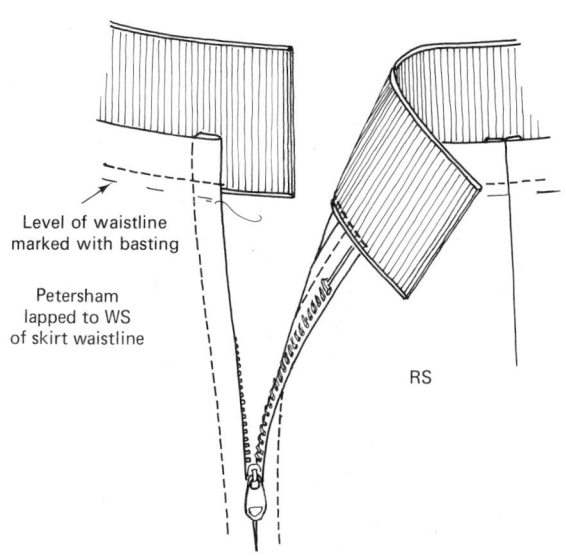

Level of waistline marked with basting

Petersham lapped to WS of skirt waistline

RS

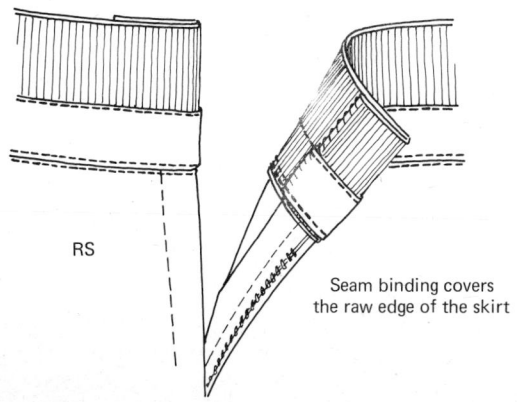

RS

Seam binding covers the raw edge of the skirt

Belts

Unstiffened belts frequently tie, and are usually cut on the straight grain, often along a selvage. In addition to the waist circumference, sufficient length must be allowed for the knot or bow, and for two seam allowances. The width must be twice the finished width of the belt plus two seam allowances.

Stage 1   Place the RS of the long edges of the strip together. Pin, baste and stitch along the seam line, leaving a 5 cm (2 in.) gap in the stitching half way along the edge, through which the belt will be turned.

Stage 2   Remove the basting and finish off the thread ends. Press the seam allowances open over a sleeve roll to avoid creasing the belt elsewhere.

Stage 3   The belt seam may be arranged to lie either centrally on the inner surface or along one edge. Position the seam, and stitch across the ends of the belt to close them. Trim the corners.

Stage 4   The belt may be turned by pushing the closed ends through the gap in the middle with a ruler or yardstick, or with the unsharpened end of a pencil. Do not use an object which might pierce or cut the fabric.

Stage 5   Press the belt, and close the gap with slip stitching.

If the belt is very narrow, place the RS of the strip together. Fold the seam allowances of the ends to the WS, and stitch them in this position when stitching the long seam. Turn the belt RS out through one end. Close the ends with slip stitches.

Stiffened belts have a tailored appearance
and are sometimes shaped along their length.
They are usually fastened with a buckle,
occasionally with hooks. Because the exact
width of the belt is determined by the length
of the bar of the buckle, it is advisable to
choose the buckle before making the belt.
The type of stiffening used should relate to
the weight of the fabric and to the character
of the garment; it may vary from a light-
weight interfacing to stiff, commercial belting.

A one-piece interfaced belt
Stage 1   Cut out the belt on the warp grain
of the fabric allowing twice the width of the
belt plus two seam allowances. The length
should be that of the waist measurement, plus
two seam allowances, plus 15 cm (6 in.) for
overlap and fastening around the bar of the
buckle.
Stage 2   Cut out the interfacing. If it is the
iron-on type, make it exactly the same size as
the finished belt will be before the buckle is
attached. With other types of interfacing
allow seam allowances at both ends only.
Stage 3   Baste-mark the central lengthwise
fold of the belt. This will lie along the top
edge of the belt when it is finished.
Stage 4   Place the interfacing on the WS of
the show half of the belt, with its edge against
the centre line. Remember that the buckle
must come at the right hand end of the belt
when it is worn, and that the seam should be
at the lower edge. Baste or iron the interfacing
to the belt. Catch-stitch non-iron interfacing
to the fold.

Stage 5   Turn the seam allowance of the
long edge over the interfacing and baste it.
Fold 2 mm ($\frac{1}{16}$ in.) more than the seam
allowance to the WS along the opposite edge
and baste.

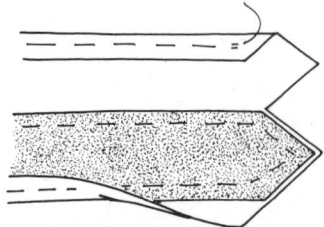

Stage 6   Fold the belt lengthwise with its RS
together along the centre line, pin and baste
across both ends. Using a 1·5 mm stitch (18
stitches per inch), stitch across the full width
of the ends, and sew the threads in. Trim
away the interfacing seam allowances and
clip the seam allowances of the belt at the
corners.

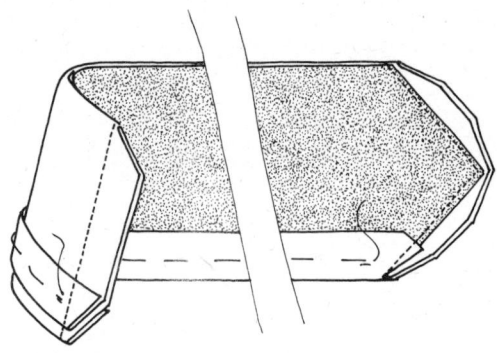

Stage 7   Turn the belt RS out bringing the
stitching at the ends right to the fold. Press.
Stage 8   Slip stitch the fold at the lower edge
of the belt, remove the basting and press. The
belt may be top stitched if desired.

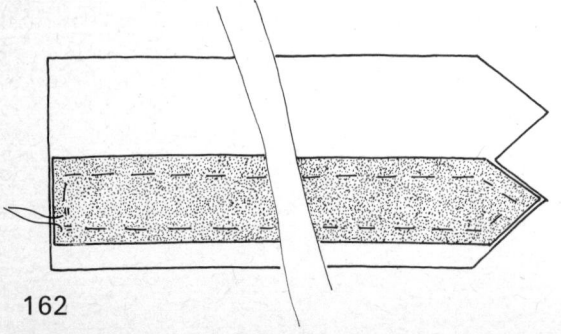

Stage 9 Punch and embroider a small oval eyelet hole for the prong of the buckle about 3 cm (1⅛ in.) from the square end. The buckle should be attached as shown in the diagram.

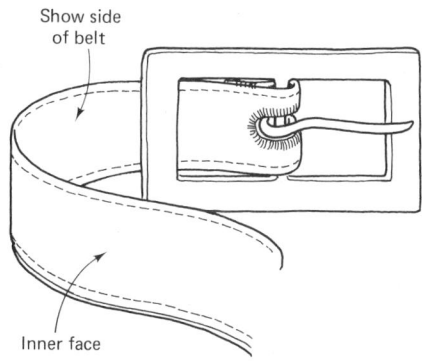

Show side of belt

Inner face

Stage 10 Hem the end to the inner surface of the belt, and to keep the buckle in position, oversew the edges of the belt together with small firm stitches at a point just behind the bar of the buckle.

Stage 11 Make the eyelet holes in the pointed end of the belt (see page 164).

If commercial belting is used, it is cut to the exact size of the finished belt and basted to the WS of the show side. The belt is then made up exactly as described above. If the belt will be top stitched, do not use this stiffening because it has reinforced edges which are very tough and they are liable to break the machine needle.

A shaped belt may be made from two pieces of garment fabric cut on the warp grain, or from one piece of garment fabric and one of thinner matching material. Seam allowances should be given on both long edges. The belt is stitched across both ends, and along the upper long edge, but in other respects the method of making it is the same as that given for a straight belt.

A belt carrier can be made either in the same way as a rouleau loop, or similarly to an embroidered bar, from buttonhole twist. If the distance between the points of attachment is made 5 mm (³⁄₁₆ in.) greater than the width of the belt, the amount of clearance will be sufficient. Belt carriers made from rouleaux may be stitched into place when the side seams are joined if the dress has no waist seam. Alternatively their ends may be turned in and neatly hemmed to the RS of the garment at the side seams. Thread loops have the advantage that they do not have to be attached at a seam, and therefore are convenient if the belt requires support elsewhere.

A sliding belt carrier is used to hold the free end of a belt.

Stage 1 Cut a strip of material on the straight grain, twice the width of the belt plus two seam allowances plus 1 cm (³⁄₈ in.) for clearance. The width should be three times that of the finished carrier.

Stage 2 Each seam allowance should be made equal to half the width of the finished carrier (one sixth of the total width of the strip). Turn the seam allowances to the WS along both edges, and crease them with an iron.

Stage 3 Place the RS of the two ends together, opening the creased seam allowances out flat, and stitch. Press the seam open, trim the seam allowances to 5 mm (³⁄₁₆ in.) and clip the corners.

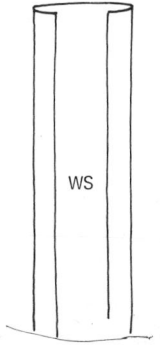

WS

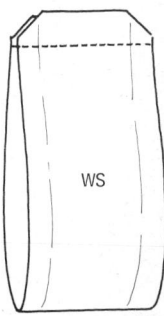

WS

Stage 4 Turn in the seam allowances of the long edges. Bring the folded edges together and slip-stitch them. Turn, and press the carrier so that the seam lies centrally along the inner surface.

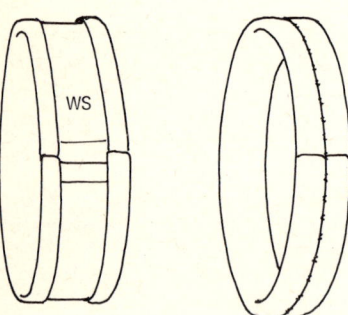

Eyelet holes may be bored with a stiletto or cut with a punch. In medium- or light-weight fabrics, the hole should be bored and embroidered. Holes made in thicker fabrics, and in garment pieces which include interfacing between the layers, should be punched, and may be finished either by hand stitching or with metal eyelets. Eyelet holes can be embroidered using overcasting or loop stitch. A decorative variation can be made by setting the knots of the stitches at the outer edge of the circle. The hand embroidered eyelet made to admit the prong at the buckle end of a belt must be slightly oval to allow the prong to move up and down. This can be cut by punching two or more overlapping holes.

When punching holes for metal eyelets, the hole should be only just large enough for the tube of the eyelet to pass through. There must be sufficient thickness of fabric for the eyelet to grip firmly (extra interfacing may be used if necessary). Where metal eyelets are to be used in the tongue of a belt, they should be large enough to allow the prong to lie flat.

Index